Wallace L. Chafe

meaning and the structure of language

The University of Chicago Press
Chicago and London

D0607001

International Standard Book Number: 0–226–10055–3
Library of Congress Catalog Card Number: 79–114855
The University of Chicago Press, Chicago 60637
The University of Chicago Press, Ltd., London
© 1970 by The University of Chicago
All rights reserved
Published 1970
Printed in the United States of America

Contents

Preface

Anyone who attempts to write a book of this sort owes an
inexpressible debt to his original teachers, to his colleagues, to
his students over the years, and to the authors of uncounted books
and papers he has read. I would like to acknowledge a diffuse debt
of gratitude to the many individuals who belong in these
categories for me. I think, however, that I should mention a
special debt to my present colleagues and students at Berkeley,
as well as to my former students Joseph L. Malone and Michael S.
Flier, whose detailed and perceptive criticisms of earlier versions
of this work were especially helpful and whose encouragement was
a major factor in enabling me to overcome my own periodic
discouragement. I am grateful to Judith Kujawa and Susan
Schwartz for their help in typing the manuscript.

The first draft of this work was written in 1966 and the final
version sent to the publisher in the summer of 1969. Inevitably,
there are various points that I would in the meantime treat
somewhat differently. I have in mind both the characterizations of
certain meanings and some details of semantic and "postsemantic"
formulations. The most important change I would make now
would be to implement the suggestion in Chapter 20 that a set of
well-formedness conditions should replace the rules given here for
the generation of semantic structures. Statements of such
conditions, however, will contain much of the same information
that is in the present rules. In subsequent publications I hope to
elaborate on this and other topics growing out of this book.

Berkeley, California   W.   L.   C.
July 1970

Special Symbols

The following notational conventions employed in the statement of rules will be clarified when they are first introduced in the text, but they are listed together here for convenience.

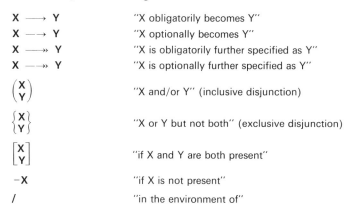

X ⟶ **Y**	"X obligatorily becomes Y"
X —→ **Y**	"X optionally becomes Y"
X ⟶» **Y**	"X is obligatorily further specified as Y"
X —»→ **Y**	"X is optionally further specified as Y"
$\begin{pmatrix} \mathbf{X} \\ \mathbf{Y} \end{pmatrix}$	"X and/or Y" (inclusive disjunction)
$\begin{Bmatrix} \mathbf{X} \\ \mathbf{Y} \end{Bmatrix}$	"X or Y but not both" (exclusive disjunction)
$\begin{bmatrix} \mathbf{X} \\ \mathbf{Y} \end{bmatrix}$	"if X and Y are both present"
−**X**	"if X is not present"
/	"in the environment of"

1

Introduction

1.1   The work to which this chapter forms a preface arises out of a deep and prolonged dissatisfaction which the author has felt with both past and present theories of the structure of language. This dissatisfaction may be understood more readily, and the suggestions which make up the body of this work may appear in clearer perspective, if I begin with a few remarks of an autobiographical nature. The intrinsic importance of these remarks is minimal, but they may provide a useful background for what follows.

1.2   Unquestionably my thinking about language has been influenced by the fact that I was first educated in linguistics at Yale in the mid-1950s. Yale had been, and under the leadership of Bernard Bloch still was at that time, one of the major centers of what has often been called the *structuralist* school. Four years of exposure to that school (including the time spent in writing a dissertation on the structuralist model) left me with what I think was a good understanding of its assumptions and methods, which for a time I did not question seriously. By a fateful coincidence I last attended a graduate course in the spring of 1957, the year in which Noam Chomsky's *Syntactic Structures* began to shake the foundations of structuralism. At the time I was in no particular sympathy with the new development, whose revolutionary effect I would not have predicted. Perhaps it was due to the effectiveness of the teaching at Yale that I felt no pressing need to replace my views on language overnight. The willingness—

even eagerness—of more and more linguists to accept the new doc-
trine surprised me, and at first I was inclined to attribute it to some
defect in their education which prevented them from fully understanding the structuralist view. In no small way, too, I found myself
repelled by the arrogance with which these other ideas were
propounded. One opinion that has remained with me from then
until now is that the complexities of the universe, linguistic or otherwise, are so vast that one cannot help but be awed and humbled
by them, and that arrogance in a linguist betrays at least a lack of
perspective on the problems which confront him. In a more specific
vein, it seemed to me that the criticisms of "phrase structure
grammar" then being presented missed a crucial point in the so-
called immediate constituent model which had been set forth by
Bloch and especially by Rulon Wells.[1] To put it as briefly as possible,
Bloch, Wells, and Leonard Bloomfield before them had posited the
existence of *constructional meanings* or "episememes" whose effect
was to make the meaning of a syntactic construction more than the
sum of the meanings of its constituents alone. Thus, to use Chomsky's
own example, the immediate constituents of *the shooting of the
hunters* could be regarded as joined in two altogether different
constructions, each with its own constructional meaning. In one of
the constructions this meaning could be described as *action-actor*
(the shooting is done by the hunters). In the other, it could be
characterized as *action-goal* (the shooting is done to the hunters).
At the time I thought that this apparatus, which was missing from
Chomsky's phrase structure model (it was not simply a matter of
labeling the nodes in a phrase structure tree, as was sometimes
alleged),[2] was adequate to explain the ambiguity of phrases like the
one just mentioned, and at first I saw no need for the device of
transformations. Chomsky's notion of phrase structure seemed
to me at best to be a caricature of the immediate constituent model
as I understood it.

1.3   I don't believe, however, that I thought very deeply about these
matters until I began to teach courses in linguistics, at first only part-
time at Georgetown and Catholic universities in 1960 and 1961, later
full-time when I came to Berkeley in 1962. In order to teach I
found that I needed some coherent model of language structure to

---

[1] Wells 1947, Bloch 1953.
[2] E.g. Postal 1964:21–22.

present to students, and it was then that I began to realize with ever-increasing clarity that my own education had left a great deal unaccounted for. Although in consequence I found myself more and more at sea, somehow it never occurred to me to look for a reliable mooring among the Chomsky group, whose style and assumptions I still found unattractive. Instead I felt compelled to put together a coherent picture of my own, although for some time I continued to rely heavily on the structuralist ideas that were most familiar to me. It seemed to me from the outset, I remember, that any model of language had to account first and foremost for the link between sound and meaning that language provides. At first I saw this link as a more straightforward thing than I did later on. It became apparent to me fairly early that the "morphemes" which had been a central concern of the structuralist school were really units that were oriented wholly in the semantic direction. To take an example that is both simple and unequivocal, I had been taught that the English *plural* morpheme was a class of "morphs," each with its own particular phonemic shape: *s*, *z*, *en* (as in *oxen*), and the rest. These morphs were essentially phonetic. But there was nothing of a phonetic nature that justified pulling them all together; the only thing that was present consistently was the meaning *plural*, and that, I concluded, was what the morpheme was all about. All the criteria such as the "noncontrastive distribution" of morphs which had been talked about in connection with the discovery of morphemes were indirect and not always conclusive ways of trying to locate constants of meaning. An aphorism which I coined for myself at the beginning of the 1960s, and which seemed to me a useful starting point for further attempts at understanding language structure, was "morphemes are to meaning as phonemes are to sound."[3] Looking back, I think now that the principal idea contained in this aphorism was correct, but that the terms *morpheme* and *phoneme* glossed over some grievous complexities that I was then only dimly aware of.

1.4 I was also influenced at that time by a close professional association with ethnologists, brought about through work with American Indian languages and particularly by a period of employment in the Bureau of American Ethnology. The concern which ethnologists had with "componential analysis" was already familiar to me through, especially, the work of Floyd Lounsbury at Yale, and it was

[3] I intended this to be the point of Chafe 1962.

natural that the thoughts I had concerning semantic structure were influenced by the componential model.[4] What especially pleased me was the realization that both morphemes, on the semantic side, and phonemes, on the phonetic side, had *components*. Bloch had already given me the idea that phonemes were not the smallest units of phonology, but that they were actually bundles of simultaneously occurring units like *labial, voiceless, nasal*, and so forth. The picture I had of phonemic structure was of a linear sequence of such bundles —a picture that was not unlike the current model which envisages a matrix of distinctive feature specifications, the sequentially arranged columns (or "segments") being roughly comparable to what I thought of then as phonemes. But at the same time I had learned from Lounsbury to regard a morpheme like *father* as actually a bundle of simultaneously occurring semantic units such as *male, noncollateral*, and *first ascending generation*. Components were evidently present not only in lexical items like *father*, but also, for example, in pronominal morphemes, which could be visualized as bundles of components such as *first person, singular, subjective*, and the like. The apparent fact that morphemes were simultaneous bundles of semantic units just as phonemes were simultaneous bundles of phonetic units seemed to me to support in a rather nice way the parallelism between morphemes and phonemes mentioned at the end of the last paragraph.[5]

1.5   I realized that one had to look not only for the substructure of morphemes and phonemes but also for the ways in which morphemes combined with morphemes and phonemes with phonemes to produce larger structures. On the phonemic side the situation was reasonably clear, and has already been mentioned: phonemes simply followed one another in linear sequence. Of course there might be higher levels of organization such as clusters, syllables, and breath groups which placed constraints on these linear sequences, and I saw in such phenomena an analogy to the "constructions" made up of "immediate constituents" which I thought played a parallel role on the morphemic side. It will be sufficient here, however, to emphasize the nature of phonetic structure as a linear concatenation of bundles of phonetic components along a dimension which was ultimately the dimension of time. In my pursuit of

[4] See, for example, Lounsbury 1956.
[5] This and related topics formed the basis of Chafe 1965.

phonetic-semantic parallels, sooner or later I came up with the
following idea. It was obvious that\morphemes (I was still using
this term for units of semantic structure) were not arranged, as
phonemes were, along a single linear dimension. It was inconceiv-
able that there was one dimension in the semantic area analogous
to the phonetic dimension of time. While sound was inescapably
tied to such linearity, meaning certainly was not. Might there not
be, however, certain conceptual dimensions—not one, but several
—whose semantic roles were in significant ways like the phonetic
role of the temporal dimension? My candidates for such dimensions
were the same phenomena which earlier I had been taught to
identify as constructional meanings. I began to think of these
phenomena in terms of what I called semantic *axes*: the *actor-
action* axis, the *action-goal* axis, the *possessor-possessed* axis, the
coordination axis, and others. Most, though not all, of these axes
I saw as polarized, unlike their phonetic analog. That is, the actor-
action axis was restricted to two terms, an actor and an action,
whereas the temporal phonetic axis had no such restriction. Aside
from this difference, however, and the plurality of semantic axes,
there existed important parallels. The phonetic picture was one of
elemental components combined into simultaneous bundles, phonemes, which were then strung out along the temporal axis. The
semantic picture seemed to be one of elemental components
combined into simultaneous bundles, morphemes, which then might
be placed at one pole or the other of one of the several available
semantic axes. Perhaps the diagram of the sentence *My father
laughed* which is given in (1) will help to clarify this picture. I thought

(1)

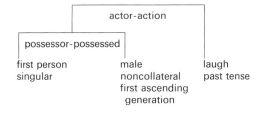

of such a diagram as more like a mobile than a tree, with the
possessor-possessed axis oriented in one dimension in semantic
space, the actor-action axis in a different one.[6] The possessor-

---

[6] This metaphor was invented and has been developed in a somewhat different way
by my colleague, William S-Y. Wang.

possessed axis then had at its possessor pole a morpheme which was a simultaneous bundle of the components *first person* and *singular*, at its possessed pole a bundle made up of *male, noncollateral,* and *first ascending generation.* The entire possessor-possessed construction then formed the actor pole of the actor-action axis, whose action pole was occupied by a morpheme made up of *laugh* and *past tense.* I thought of each morpheme as a simultaneous bundle of semantic components, but simultaneity was defined, of course, with reference to the semantic axes, not with reference to time.

1.6   At the same time that this sort of picture was taking shape, I was becoming aware belatedly of a number of virtues in the Chomskyan approach, which by then had skyrocketed to ascendancy. For example, although I retained a nostalgic attachment to structuralist "discovery procedures" until at least 1963, around that time it became clear to me that it was futile to look for some recipe that could be applied to phonetic data (with perhaps a light seasoning of semantic data thrown in) to produce the grammar of a language. The extent to which the search for such a recipe was the main preoccupation of the structuralist period is hard to imagine today. Once I had abandoned it, I felt a new and productive sense of freedom. Not unrelated was the question of the nature and extent of language universals. Again I found it refreshing to abandon the assumption "that languages could differ from each other without limit and in unpredictable ways,"[7] and to begin to focus attention on the numerous and far-reaching ways in which languages were alike. The theoretical acceptance of extensive likenesses among languages seemed to me to be increasingly confirmed by whatever facts I came across, while the differences between languages began to seem more and more superficial.

1.7   But the Chomskyan insight which influenced my conception of language structure in the most specific way was the recognition of transformations or, better put, of a disparity between *deep structure* and *surface structure.* This disparity, I believed, was not to be considered in isolation from the parallel distinction which had been recognized between so-called systematic phonemic and systematic phonetic representations on the phonological side. This latter distinction was not as radical a departure from the practices of the

[7] Joos 1966:96.

structuralist period. It, or something like it, had always lurked in the background in the guise of "morphophonemics." The exaggerated empiricism of the structuralists, however, had been responsible for a natural distrust of any but the most transparent abstractions. Although there had been many instances in practice where it was virtually impossible to operate without a unit like the morphophoneme, the guilt which had accompanied the use of such units had been only partly assuaged by characterizing morphophonemes as "artifacts of analysis or conveniences for description, not elements in a language."[8] This structuralist schizophrenia appears now to have been a classic example of the way a philosophical bias may hinder the recognition of a theoretical concept whose efficacy would otherwise be unquestioned. Since I had worked extensively on a language that cried out for description in terms of abstract phonological elements and processes, I was well aware of the impossible difficulties a linguist created for himself by refusing to stray more than a phoneme's length away from phonetic data. As soon as I was able to accept the freedom offered by Chomskyan theory in this regard, I realized that I was already in possession of numerous examples that demonstrated the value of that freedom. Some years before I had treated essentially the same material within a historical framework; specifically, with the methodology of internal reconstruction in mind.[9] Doubtless because of that background, I could not help but see underlying forms and phonological processes as closely paralleling historical forms and phonetic changes. It seemed to me quite plausible to hypothesize that the speaker of a language behaves, in learning the language, as a sort of internal reconstruction machine which recapitulates part of the history of his language, albeit in an incomplete, simplified, and often distorted way.

1.8 As usual I began to look for parallels on the semantic side of language. They were not hard to find. In fact, in the form of the already mentioned deep structure vs. surface structure distinction, they seemed impossible to overlook. To make clear the manner in which I now sought to integrate that distinction (along with the notion of transformations) into my own thinking, I must recapitulate the model of language which I had devised up to that time. I have said

[8] Hockett 1961:42.
[9] Chafe 1959.

that I thought of language in terms of semantic units, structured in a certain way, being linked to phonetic units. The precise nature of the link was something which I did not pay too much attention to for a while. I thought of language in terms of an H-shaped figure in which the left vertical line represented semantic structure and the right vertical line phonetic structure. The horizontal line which connected the two I called, quite misleadingly, "morphophonemics," simply because I thought of it as connecting semantic morphemes with phonetic phonemes. The recognition, just discussed, that phonetic structure can be explained satisfactorily only by positing underlying, more abstract phonological representations had now shed light on what the right side of the crossbar of the H might contain, as suggested in (2). It was the distinction between deep and

(2)

semantic structure . . . . underlying phonology $\longrightarrow$ phonetic structure

surface structure which now illuminated the nature of the left side of the crossbar as well, the portion which is indicated in (2) by the series of dots. For a long time I had been concerned with the place of idioms in language structure. I found them of special interest because they seemed to be clear instances of morpheme arrangements in which the morphemes themselves could not be looked upon as semantic units. If I say that *Henry is dragging his feet*, for example, it is likely that neither the meaning of *drag* nor the meaning of *feet* is present, but rather some other meaning much closer to that of *procrastinate, delay,* or *temporize*. I saw that it was this latter meaning which functioned in semantic structure in the way in which I had thought of morphemes as usually functioning. It became obvious from such examples that at least some semantic units had to be turned into configurations of other units before they could enter the phonological area; that the unitary meaning similar to that of *temporize*, for example, had to be turned into the *postsemantic* configuration *drag one's feet* before anything further could be done in the way of eventually converting it into sound. I began to think in terms of a discrepancy between many semantic units and their *literalizations*, a discrepancy which clearly had something to do with that recognized by Chomskyan linguists as existing between deep and surface structure. I did not, however, nor do I now, see any reason for identifying deep structure with anything other than semantic structure. The discrepancy I have mentioned seemed to me nothing but a difference between those linguistic units and arrangements which are most closely related to meaning and those which are immediately subject to conversion into units of phonological relevance. Furthermore, as on the phonological side, I saw language change as responsible for the discrepancy. This time it was not phonetic change that was responsible, but a kind of change that could be labeled *idiomaticization*. Presumably at an earlier stage of English *to drag one's feet* had only the literal meaning. At some point in the history of English a change occurred which amounted to the creation of a new semantic unit with the meaning alluded to above. The conversion of this new meaning into sound, however, made use of material already in the language, material such as *drag* and *feet* which might otherwise have semantic relevance but which in this case played only a postsemantic role. Thus, again, the situation on the semantic side seemed much like that on the phonetic. Language change, it was possible to say, was responsible for extensive modifications in the too simple picture where morphemes were represented or, as I have more recently said, *symbolized* by phonemes. On the one hand phonetic change was responsible for pushing apart the underlying phonology from the configurations that were directly phonetic. On the other hand semantic change, in particular idiomaticization, was responsible for pushing apart surface and semantic structures. The incomplete picture diagramed in (2) could thus be rounded out in the manner shown in (3).[10]

(3)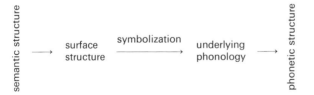

1.9   Thus it became clear that semantic structures were often very different from their corresponding surface structures. It was no longer necessary to feel narrowly confined by surface considerations

[10] A model of this kind was sketched in Chafe 1967.

in the investigation of semantic phenomena. My subsequent thinking about the nature of semantic structure was significantly influenced by two additional factors. One was a change in my conception of what I had originally conceived of as constructional meanings and later thought of in terms of semantic axes. I now began to see this aspect of semantic structure in terms of a small set of relations borne by a noun to its verb: relations such as *agent*, *patient*, *beneficiary*, and the like. I came to see semantic structure as built around a central verb, which was then accompanied by nouns related to it in these several ways. More was involved than simply a change in terminology from *constructional meaning* to *semantic axis* and then to *noun-verb relation*. For one thing, I became more conscious of the central role of the verb in determining what these relations would be. For another thing, stimulated particularly by the work of Charles Fillmore,[11] I began to look more carefully for relations which were of truly semantic significance—which were not necessarily tied to particular surface constructions. Thus, while I might earlier have thought of *Peter laughed* and *Peter fell* as exhibiting the same semantic axis, I now became aware that the semantic relation of the noun to the verb in these two sentences was clearly different. The second factor which recently came to assume a crucial role in my thinking about language was a realization that there is a fundamental distinction—essentially semantic but with postsemantic consequences—between those elements in a sentence which convey new information and those which convey old information. The ramifications of this distinction now seem broad indeed, and I see it as one of the most promising areas for further study (see chapter 15).

1.10   In the foregoing I have roughly sketched a progression of ideas which has led to the formulation presented in the chapters following. A constant theme has been the view of language as a system linking meaning with sound. A second theme has been the attempt to identify certain noun-verb relations (as I now call them) as forming the backbone of semantic structure. Many of the ideas involved, however, have undergone considerable change, much of it centered around an increasing appreciation of the broad gap which separates meaning from sound, and especially semantic structure from surface structure. It may well be wondered why I take the trouble to set

[11] Especially Fillmore 1968.

down these ideas at this time, since past experience would indicate that they will continue to change and be replaced by others. I feel, however, somewhat more content with this formulation than with any I might have presented earlier. Furthermore, I am convinced that linguistics at the present time needs some new alternatives. The shortcomings of the theory which dominated the field during the 1960s have become increasingly apparent, but alternatives which are significantly different are not present in conspicuous quantity. This work, therefore, is offered in the belief that at least a few of its ideas may help to provide a different and productive direction in which further investigations of language structure can proceed.

1.11   The over-all organization of the work is as follows. Chapters 2 through 6 build up an increasingly complex picture of language structure, the presentation following a hypothetical sequence of changes that plausibly may have taken place during language evolution. Chapter 7 summarizes the picture of language that results. Basic to this picture is the finding that at the heart of an adequate theory of language must be an adequate theory of semantic structure. Chapter 8 discusses some general considerations with regard to semantic structure, and leads into the more specific discussions which follow. Most of the remainder of the book is an attempt, necessarily provisional and exploratory, to formalize various aspects of semantic structure with particular reference to English. Chapters 9 through 15, as well as 18 and 19, make use of English examples exclusively, and attempt to establish a formal description for selected aspects of the semantic structure of English. Chapter 16 looks at a few of the postsemantic rules in English which are relevant to the conversion of a semantic structure into a surface structure. Chapter 17 provides an illustration of both semantic structure and postsemantic processes in a language of a different type, but it is seen that the significant differences lie more in the postsemantic than in the semantic area.

1.12   This book, particularly its later chapters, will not be easy reading. Often the reader will be called upon to test its assertions through difficult and perhaps prolonged cogitation. The observation of semantic facts is impossible without an expenditure of cerebral energy. Often, too, the reader can expect to find himself in disagreement with the author. Semantic observation seems to lead inevitably to controversy on particular points. I do not take such controversy to mean that semantic facts do not exist, or that they are not "hard" facts, but only that they are often frustratingly hard to ferret out. I shall be content if some of my readers some of the time agree with the observations I describe. Lack of agreement will mean that I am wrong, that the reader is wrong, perhaps that both of us are wrong, or that our individual semantic structures simply differ (although I believe that that is the case less often than is commonly assumed). It will not mean, however, that semantic questions are undecidable. That, at least, is the assumption on which this work rests.

part one

In general

2

Symbolization

2.1   Language is a system which mediates, in a highly complex way, between the universe of meaning and the universe of sound. On the one hand we have "things to say," on the other hand we make noises which, under ordinary circumstances, convey these things to a listener or listeners. Language enables a speaker to transform configurations of ideas into configurations of sounds, and it enables a listener within his own mind to transform these sounds back into a reasonable facsimile of the ideas with which the speaker began. This basic view of language has been held by the best-known linguists of recent times. Ferdinand de Saussure, for example, asserted that "the linguistic sign unites . . . a concept and a sound-image."[1] Edward Sapir wrote that "the essence of language consists in the assigning of conventional, voluntarily articulated sounds, or of their equivalents, to the diverse elements of experience."[2] Leonard Bloomfield, too, noted that "in human speech, different sounds have different meanings. To study this co-ordination of certain sounds with certain meanings is to study language."[3] The same recognition is found in the writings of Noam Chomsky in such statements as, "A generative grammar . . . is a system of rules

[1] Saussure 1959:66.
[2] Sapir 1921:11.
[3] Bloomfield 1933:27.

15

that relate signals to semantic interpretations of these signals."[4] If we look at language in the broadest perspective, then, there seems no need to debate its nature as a link between meanings and sounds.

2.2   The conversion of meanings into sounds allows human beings to transfer ideas from one to another. Ideas, I assume, have some kind of electro-chemical existence in the nervous systems of individuals. Whatever their representations there may be, they cannot pass from one person to another in that form, for there is no direct neural connection between two separate organisms, no pathway over which ideas can travel in their original state. Language, like other communicative devices, provides a means of bridging this gap by converting ideas into a medium which does have the capacity to pass between one nervous system and another. John Locke made the same point a good many years ago:

> Man, though he have a great variety of thoughts, and such from which others as well as himself might receive profit and delight; yet they are all within his own breast, invisible and hidden from others, nor can of themselves be made to appear. The comfort and advantage of society not being to be had without communication of thoughts, it was necessary that man should find out some external sensible signs, whereof those invisible ideas, which his thoughts are made up of, might be made known to others. For this purpose nothing was so fit, either for plenty or quickness, as those articulate sounds, which with so much ease and variety he found himself able to make.[5]

2.3   A communication medium must fulfil at least two requirements: it must be manipulable by the organism within which the message to be communicated originates, and it must be perceptible to the receiving organism through one or more of the latter's sense modalities. The channels used in various types of animal communication, whether human or nonhuman, include all of the sensorily perceptible media: sound, sight, smell, and so on. One may speculate on why the medium used by language should be sound. Initially, it would seem, the organs of ingestion and respiration in prehuman animals provided a basis for the evolution of an apparatus with which sound could be subtly manipulated. An auditory apparatus appropriate to the reception of these sounds was also available. From a practical point of view, it is obvious that sound, unlike

[4]Chomsky 1966b:4–5.
[5]Locke 1894:8.

sight, permits communication regardless of whether the sender and receiver are visible to each other. Unlike smell and taste, it permits rapid and finely graded variation essential to a communication system of a high degree of complexity. Unlike touch and some common uses of sight, it leaves the hands free to do other things while communication is going on. Through the direction-finding ability of the ears, it allows the receiver to identify (to a degree) where the sender is located. In addition, and perhaps as something which evolved in concert with the evolution of language, human beings have a special ability to retain sound within their minds for a short time after it has been heard. The reader can easily test this ability by noting how something that is said to him remains accessible for several seconds, while something that is seen is gone as soon as the stimulus is removed. This remarkable ability and its significance for language has been given little or no attention, so far as I know, but clearly it enables us to retain linguistic utterances long enough to process them as wholes, not necessarily "from left to right." The chief drawback of sound, its impermanence beyond the brief retention period just mentioned, has been overcome during the last few millenia through the development of writing systems, supplementing sound with the medium of sight. Thus I am able to communicate with you now, although you may be far in both time and space from the range of my voice. Writing, nevertheless, is handicapped by its inability to provide the quick interchange between the roles of sender and receiver which is another positive feature of sound-channeled language.[6]

2.4   In its broadest outline, language involves the following process. A configuration of concepts arises within the nervous system of a human being, who, for some reason, often but not necessarily associated with purposeful communication, is led to convert these concepts into sound. The sound travels to whatever other person or persons are within hearing distance, and is normally reconverted within their nervous systems into some facsimile of the original concepts. The facsimile is usually imperfect for a variety of reasons: the inevitable differences between the conceptual repertoires of different individuals, for example, and the lack of complete congruence between their linguistic systems. Even so, language does

[6] For further discussion of some of the points mentioned in this paragraph see Hockett 1960.

permit the transfer of concepts in remarkably subtle and effective ways.

2.5 The path which leads from meaning to sound is not direct but often remarkably devious. A brief look at the sentence *It is raining* may serve to illustrate this point. The reader should consider what this sentence means in relation to the way it sounds. We shall give more attention to the details of semantic structure later, but there are aspects of the meaning here which should be readily apparent. A concept which has to do with water falling from the sky is surely present, and it is evidently linked to the sound which we spell *rain*. If all of language showed an equally direct tie between meaning and sound, linguists would have much less to occupy them than they do. Aside from the sound *rain,* however, the other sounds in *It is raining* reflect either indirectly or not at all the other concepts which are present in the sentence. One of the other concepts, apparently, is that which has been associated with such labels as *progressive aspect*: a concept that the event is currently in progress but at the same time limited in duration. This concept seems to be linked to the sound spelled *is* together with that spelled *ing*. Its representation is not only discontinuous but peculiar in another way: whatever other meanings this *is* and this *ing* may serve to reflect, the meaning here seems altogether unrelated. The rest of the sound in this sentence—spelled *it*—apparently has nothing to do with the sentence's meaning at all. In other sentences of superficially similar makeup, *it* reflects the conceptual presence of some nonhuman object, as in *It's falling* or *It's eating*. In *It's raining,* no such meaning is present, and the sound *it* is wholly unmotivated so far as the meaning of the sentence is concerned. Conversely, there may be other elements of meaning in this sentence which have no reflection at all in its sound.

2.6 The kinds of discrepancies which one finds between the meaning of a sentence and its sound are varied and have various explanations. Rather than discuss them all at once, I shall attempt in this chapter and some of those which follow to introduce the most important of them gradually, and thus to build up by stages a picture of the total complexity which exists. In part, the discussion will provide a basis for speculation about the evolution of language. My primary aim, however, is to arrive at an understanding of the variety of factors which enter into the design of language as it exists today. Except possibly for some aspects of Chapter 5, the separate pieces of this discussion are not new, but it seems to me that the way in which they

are assembled here may cast some new light on what language is
and on why it should be that way.

2.7 The simplest conceivable communication system is one in which
only a single idea can be transmitted. Imagine, for example, a town
whistle that is sounded every day at noon, and only then. The sender
is the town clock, together with its associated sound-producing
mechanism. The concept *It is noon* is transformed into a whistle
blast that passes through the air and strikes the ears of people in
the town, who reconvert the sound into a cognizance of noon.
Suppose we let A represent the idea *It is noon* and X represent the
whistle blast. The conversion of the message into the sound can then
be pictured as follows:

A $\longrightarrow$ X

(I shall use a single-headed arrow like this one to signify "becomes,"
"is converted into," or the like.) The process which is pictured here
can be referred to as one of *symbolization*. We can say that X
symbolizes A, that A is symbolized by X. Symbolization in this
context is the conversion of something from the universe of ideas or
concepts into something capable of bridging the gap between sender
and receiver—in this case, something from the realm of sound. The
idea *It is noon* is symbolized by the sound *whistle blast*.

2.8 A communication system that goes beyond the extreme simplicity
of this example must allow for the transmission of more than a
single concept. There must then be some kind of differentiation
within the area of possible concepts. The conceptual universe cannot
be simply an undifferentiated whole—as in the case of *It is noon* as
described above—but must contain some internal structure. And if
conceptual differences are to be communicated, there must also be
some differentiation within the universe of possible sounds. Two
general kinds of structuring appear to be present in nature: continuous and discrete. The conceptual universe, according to the
first possibility, may be differentiated continuously along some
particular dimension or dimensions, in which case there must be a
corresponding continuous differentiation along some associated
dimension in the area of symbols:

A   X

| $\longrightarrow$ |

B   Y

In this diagram the arrow representing symbolization may link any point between A and B with some associated point between X and Y. A and B need not be opposite poles, but may join to form a circle, as X and Y may then do also. A celebrated example of a natural communication system of this kind is the so-called language of the bees.[7] Here the conceptual dimensions include, among others, the direction from a hive to a source of nectar. The directions which are possible vary continuously over a 360-degree circle. To symbolize this continuous range of concepts, there is a "dance" which discoverers of the nectar perform on the surface of the hive. The possible orientations of this dance also vary continuously over 360 degrees, each point on the circle symbolizing a point on the circle of concepts. In analogous fashion, the continuously variable rapidity of the dance is used to symbolize the distance from the hive to the nectar, also a continuum. It is not only bees that have continuously structured communication systems; they are prevalent enough among primates, including man, where they seem to be used especially for the communication of emotional states. A significant property of emotions is their variability over a range of intensity; thus, it is appropriate that continuous structuring should be employed in a system used to communicate them. The range of emotional intensity, for example, may be associated symbolically with a range of intensity in sound or gesture. A frightened woman may scream louder, longer, and with higher pitch in relation to her degree of fright.

2.9   On the other hand the conceptual universe, and then necessarily also the universe of symbols, may be discretely structured; there may be a number of separate concepts, each linked to its own symbol:

A ⟶ X
B ⟶ Y
C ⟶ Z

Here the arrow representing symbolization links A with X, B with Y, and C with Z. The particular bee dance which, by its rapidity,

[7] See, for example, Frisch 1955. The findings of Frisch and his collaborators recently have been brought into question, however, by Adrian M. Wenner, Patrick H. Wells, and Dennis L. Johnson, who have found that bees rely on smell rather than dancing for their information, as reported in the University of California Bulletin of May 19, 1969. At the moment I cannot evaluate the significance of this most recent work.

symbolizes the distance from a hive to a source of nectar is used only when the source is approximately 100 meters or more away. It has been called a *wagging dance*. When the source is closer than 100 meters, another kind of dance, called a *round dance*, is performed. In the round dance speed and orientation are not significant. So far as the communication system is concerned, the round dance is a symbol which carries the single message, "There is a source of nectar closer than 100 meters from the hive." The bees who receive this message fly off in all directions and search for the source close to the hive. This communication system of bees, then, contains these two discretely different concepts (as well as others), each symbolized by one of two discretely different symbols. One of the pairings of concept with symbol, however, allows continuous differentiation within itself:

$$
\begin{array}{l}
A \longrightarrow X \\
B \qquad Y \\
\Big| \longrightarrow \Big| \\
C \qquad Z
\end{array}
$$

The symbolization arrow connects A ("nectar close by") with X (round dance), or it connects some point in the range B–C (distance from the hive) with the corresponding point in the range Y–Z (rapidity of the wagging dance). We shall be interested henceforth in discrete structuring. It is worth remembering, nevertheless, that humans also have a number of continuously varying ranges super-imposed on various discretely different units. Thus screaming, within which continuous variation is possible, is discretely different from sobbing or laughing, just as the respective concepts—fright, sadness, or amusement—allow within themselves continuous variation but are discretely different from each other. Continuous variation is imposed in various ways on language also, and is manifested in sound by voice loudness, pitch level, the expansion of pitch intervals, and so on.

2.10 The simplest kind of discrete communication system consists of a certain number of conceptual units and symbols, each of the former linked to one of the latter. Each message consists of a single conceptual unit; that is, only one such unit is communicated at a time. Observation of communicative behavior among nonhuman primates suggests that such animals have systems of this kind, which I shall refer to as *primitive symbolization systems*. Different species seem to have from half a dozen to perhaps three dozen discrete conceptual units in their repertoires.[8] The following partial list of conceptual units and their symbolizations is taken from a tentative list of thirty-six described for the vervet monkey.[9] The sounds are accompanied typically by postures, facial expressions, and gestures:

aggressive threat	$\longrightarrow$	bark
nonaggression	$\longrightarrow$	lip-smacking
approach and/or proximity of foreign group	$\longrightarrow$	long aarr/short aarr
high intensity warning of proximity and/or approach of major avian predator	$\longrightarrow$	rraup

2.11   Do primitive symbolization systems like this have anything to do with language? It is popular nowadays to assert that they do not: "Modern studies of animal communication so far offer no counterevidence to the Cartesian assumption that human language is based on an entirely distinct principle . . . Human and animal communication fall together only at a level of generality that includes almost all other behavior as well."[10] Now, it is plausible to assume that our remote ancestors, long before they possessed any ability very closely resembling language, did possess the ability to communicate through the kind of primitive symbolization just described. That is to say, they made noises which transmitted certain messages from one nervous system to another. This is a plausible inference from the fact that all nonhuman primates, as well as other animals, possess such systems today. Modern man even communicates in this way himself, in addition to making use of language. Two of the things which we know about language are (1) that it contains a vastly greater number of conceptual units than any other natural communication system and (2) that it changes. In the chapters which follow, I shall suggest ways in which the growth of the human conceptual universe, coupled with the factor of change, might be expected to act on a primitive symbolization system to transform it into language as we know it. Why the conceptual universe of our early ancestors should have expanded so remarkably is another question, one on which I shall not attempt to speculate. Given this growth, however, and given the factor of change, it seems to me that

[8] Marler 1965:558.
[9] Struhsaker 1967.
[10] Chomsky 1966a:78. See also Lenneberg 1967, chap. 6.

the evolution of language is not the mystery it so often has been thought to be. Here, however, I am less concerned with that question than with the light which the following chapters throw on the nature of language today.

3

Duality

3.1   The messages communicated by nonhuman primates are narrowly circumscribed: "The information transmitted to the receiver refers primarily to the current emotional disposition of the signaler. The consequences of effective reception are largely modifications of the emotional dispositions of the receivers."[1] If there is any extension beyond purely emotional messages, it remains within the area related to gross biological survival, as with messages relevant to eating and reproduction. Regardless of how or why, it is apparent that the evolution of man has included as one of its most significant components an extraordinary broadening of the conceptual universe. Inextricably interwoven with that development has been a vast increase in the number and variety of ideas which man can communicate. The nature of language as a system reflects an evolutionary history of accommodations to this increase. Not only has there been a growth in the number and complexity of ideas which can be communicated, there has also been a change in kind. Through language man communicates not only the emotions and messages essential to his survival, but also an endless array of states, relations, objects, and events both internal and external to himself. Most remarkably, perhaps, it has become possible for man to communicate regarding matters totally foreign to his immediate environment—the Civil

---

[1] Bastian 1965:598.

War, yesterday's news, tomorrow's weather—and even matters which have never had any external reality at all, like griffins, unicorns, and Valhalla.

3.2   Given certain practical limitations of the human organism and of the nature of communication, the primitive symbolization system described at the end of Chapter 2 is simply inadequate to handle the transmission of such a large number of distinct concepts. In that system each separate conceptual unit was symbolized by its own individual symbolic unit, and only one concept was transmitted at a time. With the expansion of the conceptual universe, neither characteristic of the primitive system was viable. In the first place, if the primitive system was to be maintained while the inventory of conceptual units continued to grow, it was necessary for the inventory of symbolic units to keep pace. The conceptual universe developed the capacity for a vast degree of differentiation; its boundaries became elastic. The same was by no means true of the universe of symbols. On the contrary, even with the likelihood that some minor expansion in the inventory of symbols did occur through changes in the larynx, tongue, and auditory apparatus, the number of different sounds available for the transmission of messages remained extremely small. The existence of such a limitation is confirmed by the paucity of elementary sounds which are found distributed among the world's languages today. Being on the order of a few dozen, perhaps, it is in striking contrast to the thousands of conceptual units which any language has at its disposal. We may speculate that as the number of conceptual units in the primitive symbolization system of our remote ancestors began to increase, the number of distinct units of sound needed to symbolize them soon approached the practical articulatory and perceptual limits of the sound universe: "The available articulatory-acoustic space became more and more densely packed; some [sounds] became so similar to others that keeping them apart, either in production or in detection, was too great a challenge for hominid mouths, ears, and brains. Something had to happen, or the system would collapse of its own weight."[2] Undoubtedly another factor was the requirement that the system function in spite of various kinds of "noise" in the communication channel: both literal and figurative noise, including remoteness of the receiver from the

[2] Hockett and Ascher 1964:144.

sender, impreciseness of articulation on the part of the latter, and inattentiveness on the part of the former. Thus the communicative function of the system would have tended to break down in many settings where communication was desirable even before the limits of articulatory and perceptual discrimination were approached.

3.3   It is useful to consider the international Morse code. This is a communication system in which the things symbolized are about fifty in number, including the twenty-six letters of the alphabet, the ten digits, and various punctuation marks. The symbolic resources available to it include monotone buzzes whose length is variable, and variable periods of silence between the buzzes. Could these resources be used to symbolize the fifty odd messages just described, if a primitive symbolization system of the kind discussed in Chapter 2 were to be maintained? In such a system each of the units to be symbolized would have to be linked to its own unitary symbol. Fifty distinct buzzes of fifty different lengths are conceivable. But the human organisms which utilize the Morse code are simply unable to produce or to receive buzzes of fifty different lengths with the degree of facility and accuracy that would make possible effective communication. Imagine having to associate a buzz of two centiseconds with A, of four centiseconds with B, of six centiseconds with C . . . Instead, of course, the symbolic units of the system are held to only two easily distinguishable lengths of buzz (plus periods of silence, longer than those which otherwise intervene between buzzes, to symbolize letter and word boundaries). Most importantly, *there is no direct link* between a *dit* (short buzz) or a *dah* (long buzz) and the units to be symbolized. Each letter of the alphabet, digit, or punctuation mark is symbolized by some arbitrary combination of dits and dahs. The letter A is symbolized *ditdah*, the letter B *dahditditdit*, the digit 4 *ditditditditdah*, the question mark *ditditdahdahditdit* . . . In this way an inventory of two symbols is used to symbolize a considerably larger inventory of things to be symbolized.

3.4   In language the difficulty presented by the coupling of an expanding conceptual inventory to a severely limited symbolic inventory was solved in an analogous way. In any language today we find a small number of symbolic units such as (for example) *voiceless, nasal,* and the like, entering into combinations which arbitrarily symbolize items from a very large conceptual inventory. Instead of the simple linkage of concept to symbol pictured at the beginning of 2.9, language exhibits symbolization of the following kind, where XYZ, WX, and TWYX are meant to suggest various arbitrary combinations of repeatedly occurring symbolic units:

A ⟶ XYZ
B ⟶ WX
C ⟶ TWYX

Hockett has referred to this kind of symbolization system as one which possesses *duality*; Martinet has used the term *double articulation* for the same phenomenon.[3]

3.5   Neither in the Morse code nor in language, of course, do the things to be symbolized occur in isolation, one at a time. Like the symbolic units, they too combine together, and probably no act of communication through language contains only one unitary concept. If, in the Morse code, the following symbolizations are established:

C ⟶ dahditdahdit
A ⟶ ditdah
T ⟶ dah

the letters C, A, and T may be found in a sequence like CAT, whose symbolization is then straightforward:

CAT ⟶ dahditdahdit ditdah dah

We can now take note of a significant way in which the Morse code differs from language. In both systems the symbolic medium is sound. A prime characteristic of sound is that it flows through time in a linear fashion. Symbols in this medium are distributed necessarily along the temporal dimension, and must occur either sequentially or simultaneously with respect to each other. On paper, of course, we have the convention of representing this temporal dimension of sound by the horizontal dimension of the page, so that progression from left to right (in our culture) represents the flow of sound through time. In the Morse code the units to be symbolized are also arranged along a single linear dimension: the left-to-right sequence of letters in our writing system. (This left-to-right linearity of writing ultimately reflects the linearity of sound too.) It is therefore possible for the Morse code to link the linearity of what is symbolized directly to the linearity of the symbols, as illustrated in the CAT example above.

[3] Hockett 1960, Hockett and Ascher 1964, Martinet 1962:23–25 and elsewhere.

3.6   Concepts, however, are not arranged like letters along a single linear dimension. As a very simple example, the concepts *cat* and *plural* when they are combined to form *cats* are not in any apparent linear relation. There is no apparent justification for saying that *cat* precedes *plural* along some conceptual dimension, or that *plural* precedes *cat*. We might represent this absence of sequential ordering by placing *cat* and *plural* in vertical rather than horizontal relation to each other on the page:

cat
plural

If, now, the conventions of symbolization in English yield the following:

cat $\longrightarrow$ kæt
plural $\longrightarrow$ s

we have no way of knowing, based on the nonsequential arrangement of the concepts, how the symbols *kæt* and *s* are to be sequentially ordered. The concepts, it would seem, must undergo some process of *linearization* before symbolization can take place. The simultaneous arrangement of *cat* and *plural* must be transformed into a linear arrangement first:

cat   ┌──────┐
        $\longrightarrow$ cat   plural
plural

The necessity for such processes along the path from meaning to sound follows naturally from the recognition that conceptual units in language combine into larger configurations, that such configurations are not linear, and that sound symbols *are* linear because of the unavoidable linearity of sound. The process of linearization involves more complexities than have been suggested by this example, but here it is enough to notice that processes of this kind are essential if configurations of ideas are to be converted into configurations of sounds.

3.7   The characteristics of the kind of system that has been described so far can be summarized as follows. To begin with, there are concepts, as well as ways of combining them into a broad range of varied configurations. Henceforth I shall use the term *semantic structure* for this area. Language provides ways for particular semantic structures to be converted into sound. One step in this conversion is the process of linearization, by which semantic structures are re-shuffled so that they are laid out on a single dimension. It will do little violence to the accepted use of the term to call the result a surface structure. A subsequent step is symbolization, by which each linearized conceptual unit is converted into an arbitrary configura-tion of symbolic units, a result which can be termed a *phonetic structure*. The conversion of the concepts *cat* and *plural* into the phonetic *kæts* can be pictured, according to this system, as follows:

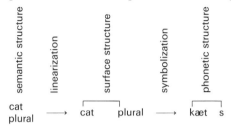

4

The Effect of Phonetic Change

4.1   It is possible that language would resemble closely the system described at the end of Chapter 3, were it not for the influence of language change. Change through time is the inexorable fate of the entire natural world, and language is not exempt. Change in language can be identified on three different levels. First, there is the broad, evolutionary kind of change which eventually turned a primitive communication system into language. It is at least roughly comparable to phylogenetic change in biology. Second, there is the narrow, ontogenetic change which takes place during the acquisition of language by a single individual. Its study promises eventually to throw additional light on language as a system, and even on language evolution to the extent that it provides a partial reflection of the latter. The kind of change whose effect will be our concern now, however, is more like genetic drift. It is the kind of change which makes particular languages different from one another. The term language change has, in fact, nearly always been used to refer to this third type, the traditional province of historical linguistics. Our concern will be with the ways in which it modifies the system described at the end of Chapter 3.

4.2   I do not mean to imply that this kind of change was not operative even on the primitive symbolization system described in Chapter 2. What I do want to suggest is that change can have a more radical effect when it operates on a system with duality; that it can have an effect which actually modifies the nature of the system itself. With primitive symbolization we find a small inventory of semantic units, each linked directly to some phonetic unit. The physical nature of the sounds may change; one grunt may replace another or the like. The nature of the concepts may change as well. And items may be added to or subtracted from the semantic inventory, normally with the concomitant addition or subtraction of phonetic units. It is even possible that particular conventions of symbolization will be modified. A, previously symbolized by X, might come to be symbolized by Y. The important point, however, is that such changes do not affect at all the nature of the system itself, which remains one in which each semantic unit is directly linked to some unitary symbol.

4.3   The advent of duality removed the necessity for a change on the semantic side to be linked to a change on the phonetic side, and vice versa. The addition of a new semantic unit, for example, no longer required the addition of a new phonetic unit but only of some new convention of symbolization by an arbitrary configuration assembled from the already existing stock of phonetic units. Conversely, the addition or subtraction of a phonetic unit no longer needed to be tied to any change whatsoever on the semantic side. Duality freed concept and symbol from each other to the extent that change could now modify either one without affecting the other. Such independent change, whether of concept or symbol, introduced crucial new complications into the conversion of meaning into sound. The general nature of these complications will occupy us now.

4.4   The details of phonetic change have been the main preoccupation of historical linguistics, and we have more knowledge available to us here than when we turn to analogous phenomena on the semantic side, although there is much about phonetic change too which is still problematic. The general point which I wish to make here can be illustrated with an example that will be unfamiliar to nearly all readers, but which will allow me to focus on nothing more than the issue at hand. In Onondaga, an Iroquois language spoken on a reservation adjacent to Syracuse, New York, and on the Six Nations Reserve in Canada, the semantic configurations *big house* and *big box* in some bygone day probably were converted into sound in roughly the manner shown in (1).[1]

[1] See Chafe 1970.

(1)

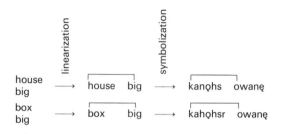

Much more could be said about the conceptual configurations on the left, but the oversimplified representations given here will suffice for now. I have indicated that *house* was symbolized by *kanǫhs* and *box* by *kahǫhsr*, but, as the reader might guess, *ka* actually symbolizes a prefix which is present in both instances. The sounds *kanǫhs-owanę* and *kahǫhsrowanę*, in any case, conveyed the meanings *big house* and *big box* respectively (ǫ and ę were nasalized vowels). Imagine now that a change took place in the language by which back vowels (including ǫ) become front vowels (including ę, corresponding to ǫ) if the original back vowel was preceded by *r*. The semantic configuration *big box* was now symbolized by the phonetic structure *kahǫhsrewanę*, with an *e* in the third syllable. Presumably this change came about because the tongue position required for the pronunciation of *r* was not relinquished completely during the pronunciation of the following vowel, thus drawing that vowel toward the front of the mouth. Any linguist is familiar with many similar changes in other languages. To be emphasized here, however, is the fact that this change had nothing whatsoever to do with the semantic side of this language. The phonetic configurations affected by it were not just those linked to *box* and *big*, but any in which *r* was followed by a back vowel. As time passed, another change took place in the phonetic area of this language: *r* was lost. (The sound *r*, whether because of its articulatory or because of its acoustic properties, seems particularly prone to loss in a number of languages, and this change, too, is not an unusual one.) The *r* was not lost completely but left behind a trace in a compensatory lengthening of the following vowel. Thus, the meaning *big box* was now converted into the sound *kahǫhse·wanę*, where the raised dot indicates a lengthened vowel. At some time, also (whether before or after the changes just mentioned), another relevant change took place: penultimate vowels became accented and, when in an open syllable as here, became lengthened as well. With this change the sounds linked to the meanings *big house* and *big box* became *kanǫhsowá·nę* and *kahǫhse·wá·nę* respectively. These, essentially, are the phonetic structures associated with these two semantic structures in Onondaga today.

4.5   But because of these phonetic changes (and many others like them) the system by which meaning is converted into sound in Onondaga could no longer be of the type described at the end of Chapter 3. As that type was described, each semantic unit was linked to one, and only one, configuration of phonetic units. After the changes just mentioned, the system could be viewed in two distinctly different ways, each of which has had its advocates. I shall speak of the *allomorph* view and the *process* view. The allomorph view would say that the phonetic changes mentioned resulted in changes in the conventions of symbolization, so that *box*, for example, which was earlier symbolized *kahǫhsr*, came to be symbolized *kahǫhs* as a result of the loss of *r*. Such a change in itself would be of minor consequence. More significant is the fact that these phonetic changes brought about a modification in the nature of symbolization itself, for now it would be necessary to say that *big* is symbolized *owá·nę* in one instance but *e·wá·nę* in the other. Furthermore, when the *a* of this symbolization is not penultimate (as is possible), we find the symbolizations *owanę* and *e·wanę* as well, and there are in fact others. These variant symbolizations have been called *allomorphs*, for reasons which belong to the history of twentieth-century linguistics. The process view, on the other hand, would say that even after the changes, *big* remained symbolized by the one single configuration *owanę* as before, and *box* by *kahǫhsr* (or, if not precisely by *kahǫhsr*, in any case by something different in its final portion from *kanǫhs*, the symbolization of *house*). In order to explain the varying phonetic representations of *big* and the fact that *box* is phonetically indistinguishable from *house* in its final portion (*kahǫhs* and *kanǫhs* respectively), the process view would assert that symbolization does not lead directly to a phonetic structure. Rather, it leads to what may be termed an *underlying phonological structure,* on which various phonological processes operate to produce a phonetic structure in much the same way as it was produced by the relevant historical changes in the language (though not necessarily in just the same way). Thus, the allomorph view can be pictured as in (2), in the case of *big*, while the process view can be pictured roughly as in (3).

(2)

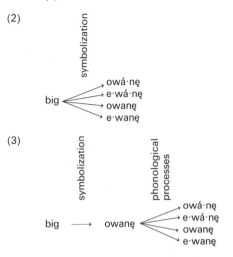

(3)

4.6   Are there general grounds for preferring one or the other of these two views? The arguments for and against each, I think, can be divided into two categories: arguments in terms of *descriptive convenience* and arguments in terms of *psychological reality*. As far as descriptive convenience is concerned, the argument would be that, given only data of the kind presented above (that the semantic structure *big box* is converted into the phonetic structure *kahǫhse·wá·nę*, etc.), one or the other of the two views allows us to describe the situation more effectively, more simply, or more elegantly. On such grounds the process view is decidedly preferable. It is preferable above all because the processes which it hypothesizes are in many instances general processes. The particular processes described above, for example, do not apply solely to the symbolizations of *big house* and *big box* but to all relevant symbolizations in the language. Thus, the fronting of back vowels after *r* takes place whenever the conventions of symbolization lead to underlying forms in which *r* is followed by a back vowel. The allomorph view gives us no effective way to explain when the symbolization of *big* is *owá·nę*, when it is *e·wá·nę*, and so on. The best that can be done is to say that it is *owá·ne* after the symbolizations of some items, including *house*, but *e·wá·nę* after the symbolizations of others, including *box*. But such statements are not only clumsy but inadequate, for they do not account for the countless other cases where *o* "alternates with" *e* (or *e·*), *ǫ* with *ę*, *a* with *æ* . . . We are discussing complications in the conversion of meaning into sound which arose as a result of historical processes. It is not surprising that the results of such processes can be described effectively only in terms of processes too.

4.7   The argument based on psychological reality would say that the conversion of semantic structures into phonetic structures takes place within the human brain, that linguistics is thus concerned with mental phenomena. The description of a language cannot be divorced from considerations of what is "in people's heads." Since we cannot look into people's heads directly, we can only hypothesize what goes on there on the basis of indirect evidence. It is interesting to note that, unless we have other evidence to the contrary, the argument in favor of the process view in terms of descriptive convenience is also an argument which is relevant to psychological reality. That is, given the fact that we do not have direct mental evidence, the best mental hypothesis has to be formed on the basis of evidence which we do have, and that evidence recommends the process view as the simplest way to explain the facts. The allomorph approach was popular during a period when linguistic thinking was dominated by behaviorist assumptions in psychology. If I were to take the liberty of restating the assumptions of that period in my own terms, so far as they relate to the problem at hand, I would say that the human brain was thought to be capable of symbolization, but only of symbolization which led more or less directly to a phonetic output. I say "more or less" because it was the practice to posit a not-quite-phonetic entity, the *phoneme,* whose psychological validity, though disputed by some linguists,[2] was probably assumed by most. In any event, the mind was not thought to be capable of operating in terms of anything very far removed from physical sound, and specifically not in terms of underlying forms and processes of the sort described above. This assumed psychological limitation, if it were valid, would be the only defensible reason for wholehearted adherence to the allomorph view, so far as I can see. If we do not accept this limitation on the way the human mind can work, there appear to be several additional justifications for attributing psychological validity to the initially simpler process view. One stems from the kind of evidence cited by Sapir, to the effect

[2] E.g. Twaddell 1935:56–60.

that speakers of a language show, in one way or another, a covert awareness of nonphonetic entities. One of several incidents which Sapir reported involved a Southern Paiute speaker who was asked to syllabify a word whose meaning *at the water* was linked to the phonetic output *pa·βaʻ*. "To my astonishment," wrote Sapir,

Tony then syllabified: *pa·*, pause, *paʻ*. I say "astonishment" because I at once recognized the paradox that Tony was not "hearing" in terms of the actual sounds (the voiced bilabial was objectively very different from the initial stop) but in terms of an etymological reconstruction: *pa·*: "water" plus postposition **-paʻ* "at". The slight pause which intervened after the stem was enough to divert Tony from the phonetically proper form of the postposition to a theoretically real but actually nonexistent form.[3]

When Sapir said "nonexistent" he of course meant that this form was not directly related to observable sound; *paʻ* was an underlying, not a phonetic form. Another possible kind of evidence favoring the psychological validity of underlying forms comes from languages of the so-called polysynthetic type. To take an example from Caddo, an American Indian language originally spoken in northern Louisiana and adjacent areas, we might say that the semantic configuration *after-plural-eat-nominalization-end-causative-past* (that is, *after they had eaten*) has the underlying symbolization *nat-wa-ʔáh-t-yúk-iʔn-ah*, where each of the linearized semantic units is set off by hyphens.[4] After phonological processes by which *tw* becomes *pp, ty* becomes *c,* the vowel *i* (being in a certain weak position) is dropped, and the resulting syllable-final *k* becomes *h,* the phonetic output can be represented as *nappaʔáhcúhʔnah*. Now it seems very likely that the speakers of such languages sometimes construct words which they have never before uttered, for words in those languages often correspond to entire clauses or sentences in languages like English. If so, they must make use of underlying forms and processes similar to those just described, for otherwise they would be unable to arrive at the proper phonetic structures. In other words, if one has not heard and memorized a phonetic structure like *nappaʔáhcúhʔnah* from previous experience, one cannot invent it directly. It can be arrived at only through recourse to phonological processes like those described above. Not only would

[3] Sapir 1951:48–49.
[4] Some discussion of phonological processes in this language is included in Chafe 1968d. A more complete description is in preparation.

it be remarkably inefficient for the mind to operate without any recourse to such processes—to memorize the direct phonetic symbolization of each utterance as a whole—but in many instances it would be impossible; in those instances, that is, where the utterance has never been available for memorization. Actually, this argument does not apply to polysynthetic languages alone, but probably to all languages, for there seem always to be some processes which apply within the domain of the *sentence* in the way that the processes just described apply within the domain of the Caddo *word*. There is no doubt that one often constructs sentences whose phonetic output has not been memorized, and it would seem impossible to do even this without resort to underlying forms and phonological processes. One more kind of evidence supporting the psychological reality argument comes from the finding that certain kinds of language change cannot be explained as phonetic change but must be explained as a change in underlying forms or, most interestingly, as a change in a phonological process itself. In this last category belong not only modifications of the specific nature of a particular process, but also such phenomena as the reordering of processes. Significant investigations are being conducted in this area at the present time.[5] Suffice it to say that if change in the nature or ordering of processes themselves is a true kind of language change, then processes have an obvious reality that cannot be ignored.

4.8   The point of view that will be accepted here, then, is that phonetic change creates complexities of symbolization with which speakers of a language can cope only if these speakers operate as if they were, in a certain sense, internal reconstruction devices which reconstruct nonphonetic underlying forms and the processes which lead from such forms to an eventual phonetic output. Several reservations must be clearly understood. First of all, it is not necessary to assume that the "reconstructions" made subconsciously by the speaker of a language are identical with those that a historical linguist would make, or that there is an exact coincidence between the processes internalized by the speaker of a language and the historical processes which led to the language he now speaks. The speaker's "internal reconstruction" may differ in many ways from the historical facts, being in general, we might guess, considerably simpler. It is not necessary, either, to assume that the speaker

[5] For example Kiparsky 1968.

operates always and only in terms of underlying forms and processes. As a matter of fact, he undoubtedly memorizes directly the phonetic structure of specific words and sentences a good deal of the time. In so doing, it is significant to note, he is actually achieving one kind of economy while bypassing another. He is not taking advantage of the generalizations which underlying forms and processes afford, but he *is* making things simpler in individual instances by ignoring that whole abstract apparatus in favor of a more direct jump from meaning to sound. It is only in terms of the language as a whole, not in terms of individual, frequently used items, that the device of underlying forms and processes represents a greater economy. I suspect, in fact, that the speaker of a language achieves some kind of balance, in a way that is not at present understood, between direct phonetic symbolization and symbolization mediated through processes of the sort described above. I suspect also that different speakers may achieve different balances between these two opposite kinds of economy. It may even be that such differences between speakers constitute one of the principal causes of further language change itself, so that the interaction between language change and the complexities of symbolization perpetuates itself through a momentum of its own. If it is true that at present we cannot draw a dividing line between processes which are psychologically real and those which are not, and if it is even likely that different speakers of a language draw the line differently, what can a linguist do when he wishes to describe a language? Perhaps the best he can do at the present time is to describe the language as it would be if a speaker were to take maximum advantage of all the generalizations which could be made, if the speaker's mind were a maximally efficient process-using device. Thus, many underlying forms and many processes which the linguist may posit may have no psychological validity for any speakers, while others may have validity for some speakers and not for others. Furthermore, certain underlying items like the *r* described for Onondaga above may be too specific as descriptions of what a speaker actually knows. Can a speaker of Onondaga operate subconsciously with an underlying *r*, when there is no phonetic *r* in the language at all, or does he distinguish between *kahǫhsr* and *kanǫhs* in some other, more abstract way? Questions like these are open to various speculative answers at the moment, but chiefly they show that there is a great deal which we do not yet understand.

4.9   In any case, it is undeniable that phonetic change makes it impossible for the system described in Chapter 3 to be viable in just that form. Instead, I shall assume here, symbolization is separated from phonetic structure by underlying phonological structures and intervening phonological processes. Whereas symbolization in the system of Chapter 3 leads to phonetic structure directly, phonetic change pushes the two apart, making symbolization itself more abstract in the sense that it is no longer directly related to sound, as

(4)

symbolization	underlying phonological structure	phonological process 1	intermediate phonological structure	phonological process 2	final phonological process	phonetic structure
⟶	XXX ⟶		YYY ⟶		. . . ⟶	ZZZ

shown in (4). As an example, the conversion of the semantic structure *big box* into a phonetic structure in Onondaga might be diagramed as in (5).

(5)

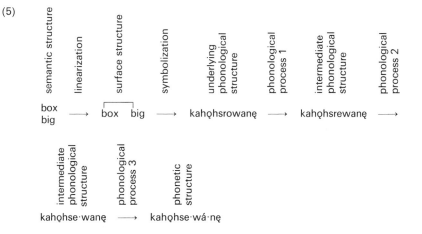

5

The Effect of
Idiomaticization

5.1   In Chapter 4 we saw how phonetic change creates a discrepancy
between symbolization and phonetic output, how it leads to situations in which the linearized units of surface structure are not
symbolized by phonetic configurations directly but only through a
series of prephonetic stages connected by phonological processes.
Just on a priori grounds we might expect that semantic change
would have an analogous effect on the other side of the symbolization link. It was already true in the system described at the end of
Chapter 3 that semantic structure was not symbolized immediately,
since at least linearization had to be applied before conversion into
phonetic configurations was feasible. In the description of that
hypothetical system, however, it was assumed that linearization
involved nothing more than the linear redistribution of units which
still retained their semantic character. The question now is whether
semantic change creates a difference between semantic structure
and surface representations which is over and above the linearity
difference, so that the elements of surface representations are no
longer semantic elements but *postsemantic* ones, analogous to
underlying elements on the phonological side. We shall find that
semantic change does indeed have this effect. We can say, therefore,
that semantic and phonetic change respectively serve to push
semantic structure and phonetic representation away from the
process of symbolization, both thereby increasing the ultimate

distance between a semantic structure and its eventual phonetic output. This effect which language history has on language is suggested in (1).

(1)

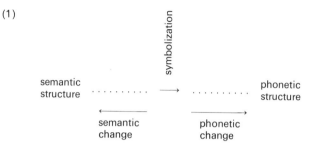

5.2   But what kind of semantic change is it that creates this gap between semantic structure and symbolization? In large part, I believe, it is the growth of new semantic units. I asserted earlier that an increase in the size of the semantic inventory was one of the principal factors in the evolution of language, and in Chapter 3 we saw how such an increase provides an explanation for the duality of language. In this chapter we shall see how this same expansion of the semantic inventory can lead to one of the most important kinds of discrepancy between semantic structure and symbolization. The crucial consideration here is that new semantic units need some way of being converted into sound. They need not, however, acquire a sound which is distinctively their own but may avail themselves of the fact that there are other semantic units which already have established symbolizations. There are several historical paths through which a new meaning can be provided with a sound, but the question of which is followed in a particular case cannot be disassociated from the question of how the new semantic unit itself came into being. Often, for example, a new concept is acquired from a people speaking another language—as was the case with our assimilation of *sauerkraut*—and the symbolization given to this concept may be an imitation of the symbolization which was given to it in the other language. We are interested now, however, in cases where no new symbolization is acquired from an outside source. How, in such cases, is a conversion into sound provided for? What happens almost invariably, I think, aside from those rare instances where a new symbolization is consciously invented (like *Kodak* or *gas*), is that the symbolization resources of already existing semantic units are appropriated. In brief, the new semantic unit is converted postsemantically into another semantic unit or configuration of semantic units, and the latter then go on to be symbolized as usual.

5.3   One kind of semantic change is the sprouting of a new meaning from an old one in some particular context.[1] Such a new meaning will be vigorous and independent in that context but will not exist elsewhere. A historical development of this kind, for example, must be responsible for the meaning usually carried by the sound *red* in the context of *hair*. *Red hair* is usually thought to mean hair that is of a color which would not otherwise be called red, something actually closer to orange, perhaps. Suppose we call the old meaning red_1 and the new one red_2. When a new meaning like red_2 develops in some context, it does not completely eclipse the old one in that context, although the new one is much more likely than the old one to occur there. Hence the sound *red hair* is ambiguous; either red_1 or red_2 may be present in the semantic structure, though the latter is more to be expected. Outside of the context of hair, however, only red_1 is found (if we ignore the several other meanings which the sound *red* may carry). This example shows for one thing that the new meaning is a discretely different semantic unit from the old one. *Charley has red hair* surely has the two meanings described and they are clearly distinct, not intergraded "shades of meaning." Either Charley has red hair in the common sense with red_2, or someone may have spilled paint on his head to make it the color of red_1. What is most significant to our present purpose, however, is that this example shows how a new meaning like red_2 is converted into sound: it receives the same symbolization as the old meaning red_1. That is to say, a new meaning which sprouts from an old meaning remains linked to the same phonetic representation as the old one. In moving from meaning to sound, therefore, we can say that the meaning red_2 is first converted into red_1, which then goes on to receive the symbolization which it has always received. In this case red_1 can be termed *postsemantic* rather than semantic. It is not present in the semantic structure—it has no meaning in this case—but it must be introduced postsemantically to explain the eventual phonetic output. The process can be pictured as in (2). The ambiguity

---

[1] The ideas on which the remainder of this chapter is based were foreshadowed in Chafe 1965:33–36 and were elaborated in Chafe 1967 and especially Chafe 1968c.

of *red hair* is explained by the fact that red_1 can be semantic as well as postsemantic, that the situation pictured in (3) exists alongside that pictured in (2).

(2)

semantic unit | postsemantic process | postsemantic unit | symbolization | phonetic structure

$red_2 \longrightarrow red_1 \longrightarrow red$

(3)

semantic unit | symbolization | phonetic structure

$red_1 \longrightarrow red$

5.4   The reader may wonder why it is necessary to hypothesize that red_2 is converted into red_1 before symbolization takes place. Could we not say equally well that red_2 is directly symbolized *red*? Several arguments for the view represented in (2) can be mentioned. In the first place, the historical development is from red_1 to red_2. On the analogy of phonology, where phonological processes tend to mirror processes of phonetic change, we might expect that postsemantic processes would mirror semantic changes. (It is interesting to note, however, that they do so in a reverse direction. While historically red_1 was the source of red_2, the language copes with the resulting situation by converting red_2 back into red_1. In phonology, on the other hand, the direction of phonological processes is identical with the direction of phonetic change. The reason for this difference is perhaps made clear in (1), where the two kinds of change are seen to push semantic structure and phonetic structure away from symbolization in opposite directions. Conversion from meaning to sound, however, takes place in one direction from beginning to end, thus producing, with relation to historical processes, the upstream-downstream phenomenon just mentioned.) There is, secondly, an imbalance between red_1 and red_2, in which the former carries more weight than the latter. Red_1 is, for these purposes, contextually unrestricted, while red_2 is severely limited in occurrence. Speakers of English "know," I think, that red_2 is a special or peculiar offshoot of red_1; no one would say that the meanings are of equal status.

This imbalance is captured in part by hypothesizing a system in which only *red₁* is given a symbolization, and *red₂* is symbolized only indirectly through the mediation of *red₁*. But perhaps the most convincing evidence is of a kind that is not directly available in this example. Let us turn to a semantic unit in English which we can label *make₁*, having to do with acts of putting something together: *Chris makes radios*. There is another, contextually very limited unit *make₂* which, when applied to a bed, means something like *restore to a properly neat condition*. Thus, *make a bed* is ambiguous in the same way as *red hair*. Now, a peculiarity of *make₁* is that when it occurs together with the semantic unit *past*, the combination of the two is not symbolized in the regular way (which, if it existed, we would spell *maked*), but rather in the idiosyncratic way which we spell *made*. The point which is of interest is that *make₂* when combined with *past* also leads to the sound *made*. This irregularity of symbolization is something special which happens to *make₁*. There is no need to posit the same irregularity again for *make₂*; a simpler system in which it applies only to *make₁* is achieved if we say that *make₂* is first converted into the other, which then goes on to be symbolized with *past* in its own peculiar way.

5.5   A semantic unit like *red₂* or *make₂*—one which does not have a direct symbolization of its own but which trades on the symbolization of another (or others)—can be called an *idiom*. Actually, the idioms which have been illustrated are of a special kind, characterized by their limitation to very narrow contexts (the contexts of hair and beds in these examples). We might distinguish them by calling them *restricted idioms*.[2] The postsemantic units into which they are converted (like *red₁* and *make₁*) may be called the *literalizations* of these idioms. It is characteristic of the literalizations of restricted idioms that they are units of the same kind as the idioms themselves. Thus, both the idiom *red₂* and its literalization *red₁* are single lexical units of the same specific kind. There is, however, another kind of idiom which may be called *unrestricted*, since it is not limited contextually in the way that restricted idioms are. An unrestricted idiom, furthermore, is characterized by the fact that its literalization is not a semantic unit of the same kind as the idiom itself but a more complex postsemantic configuration. We might take *off base* as an initial example. The historical development here

---

[2] In Chafe 1965 and 1967 I called them *metaphors*.

seems transparent. At one point not too long ago in the history of American English the surface structure configuration *off base* reflected unambiguously a semantic configuration relevant to the game of baseball. We need not concern ourselves with the details of this configuration or how it arose historically itself, but certainly it included a concept *base*, of the baseball type, and a concept of being *off* or not in contact with the base. Now, for a person to be off base in a game is for him to be, in a sense, not where he ought to be, and this more abstract component of the originally concrete baseball meaning became at some point a new semantic unit, with the special twist of *egregiously wrong*. This new unit in American English is a unitary concept not completely identical with any other. In order to discuss it here I shall give it the label *off-base*, with the hyphen indicating that it is a single unit and not composed of parts like *off* and *base*. Historically, then, the semantic configuration *off base* underwent a process of shrinkage or abstraction to yield the new semantic unit *off-base*. As before, this idiomaticization process did not eclipse the earlier meaning; hence the phonetic representation *Mike is off base* is ambiguous, carrying both the concrete baseball meaning and the abstract meaning *off-base* that is something like *egregiously wrong*. And as before we can see that *off-base* is not converted into sound directly but must first be transformed into its historical source, the configuration *off-base*,

(4)

semantic unit	postsemantic process	postsemantic structure	symbolization	phonetic structure
off-base	$\longrightarrow$	off base	$\longrightarrow$	off base

as in (4). The ambiguity of *Mike is off base* is explained by the fact that *off base* may be a semantic as well as a postsemantic configuration, as indicated in (5). We see then that *off-base* is a semantic unit

(5)

semantic configuration	symbolization	phonetic structure
off base	$\longrightarrow$	off base

like *red*$_2$, insofar as it has no symbolization of its own and must be given a literalization before symbolization can take place. Hence both *off-base* and *red*$_2$ come under the heading of idioms. But *off-base* differs from *red*$_2$ in having a literalization which is, as it were, larger than itself—not a single unit, but a more complex configuration. In addition, *off-base* is not severely limited in its occurrence in the way that *red*$_2$ is, and for that reason the label *unrestricted idiom* seems appropriate.

5.6   We might take the perhaps ambiguous phonetic representation *Dick flew off the handle* as an example to illustrate another point, already made in 5.4 with respect to the restricted idiom *make*$_2$. Present in the most likely semantic structure which has this phonetic output is an idiom having to do with becoming angry, converted postsemantically into *fly off the handle*. Why should we posit the conversion of the idiom into this postsemantic configuration rather than the direct symbolization of the idiom by the underlying phonological structure of *fly off the handle*? There are, first of all, the general arguments that the idiom developed from the more complex configuration historically, so that we might expect its conversion into sound to retrace (in reverse) the change which created it, and also that speakers of English "know" that the idiom is derived from the other, so that a description of the language somehow ought to reflect this knowledge. Again, however, there is the more specific argument that the combination of the semantic units *fly* and *past* is symbolized irregularly as *flew*, just as *make*$_1$ and *past* are peculiarly symbolized as *made*. In this case too it is preferable to be able to state the irregularity only once, and not to have to state it independently for the idiom. The evidence is even stronger in the present case, for there is no apparent way to explain the symbolization *flew* at all if the idiom and *past* are regarded as symbolized directly; we might rather expect something like *fly off the handled*. Other factors, such as the assignment of stress within *fly off the handle*, also serve to confirm the view that it is the symbolization of a composite postsemantic configuration and not of a single semantic unit.

5.7   There is another important kind of evidence in support of the view of idioms which has been presented. Let us this time take *George is on the wagon* as an example. There are two semantic structures which lead to this one surface structure. One of them contains an idiom involving abstinence from alcoholic drinks. This idiom is literalized into a postsemantic configuration which, for our present purpose, we can say contains the postsemantic units *on* and *wagon*, with the latter further specified as *definite* and *singular*. When the idiom is present, these other units are not present semantically but only postsemantically. They are not available therefore, to the various kinds of semantic manipulation which can be applied to units in semantic structure. The unit *wagon*, for example, is not available to be made semantically *indefinite* or *plural*. Hence phonetic representations like *George is on a wagon* or *George and Harry are on the wagons* cannot result from semantic structures containing the idiom. As another example, *Helen spilled the beans* may reflect a semantic structure containing an idiom which involves the indiscreet disclosure of information. Its literalization is a postsemantic configuration *spill the beans* which includes units like *spill* and *bean*, the latter further specified as *definite* and *plural*. Since these units are not present in the semantic structure containing the idiom, they cannot be manipulated semantically. Hence a surface structure like *Helen spilled some beans* cannot reflect a semantic structure in which the idiom is present. It is interesting, furthermore, that this idiom has the semantic properties of an "intransitive verb" and that like all such verbs it cannot be made "passive" (see chap. 15). Thus, *The beans were spilled by Helen* also cannot be a phonetic representation of a semantic structure with the idiom. We can compare this idiom with the one that is present in *Helen pulled George's leg*. The meaning of this idiom is roughly *tease*. Unlike *spill-the-beans*, it functions as a transitive verb and as a consequence it can be "passivized." Thus, *George's leg was pulled (by Helen)* is quite possible as a surface structure based on a semantic structure in which the idiom is present.

5.8   The historical reasons for the development of a particular idiom are by no means always clear. It seems easier to see why *off base* became the source for its idiom than why *spill the beans* developed in the way it did, but the development of *fly off the handle* is perhaps even less transparent. The historical details of idiomaticization need not concern us here, although we might take passing note of the fact that the overwhelming tendency is for semantic units and configurations involving concrete, tangible meanings to yield idiomatic units involving more abstract and intangible meanings. This is true of the examples given above, and of other typical idioms:

The judge threw the book at me, Mary broke the ice, or *This issue is a red herring.* This fact means that concrete semantic units tend to be symbolized directly, while a great many abstract semantic units must be given a postsemantic literalization before they are symbolized. It does not seem out of line to speculate that this situation, which I suspect exists in all languages, indicates that the more recent growth of the human conceptual inventory in large part has been a matter of adding concepts that are more abstract to a basic inventory of concrete concepts. It must also be pointed out that an idiom, when it first comes into being, has a literalization whose units are still semantic as well as postsemantic, but that these units *as semantic units* may very well drop from the language later on. They may still be kept in their postsemantic function, however, so that sentences containing them are no longer ambiguous, having only the idiomatic meaning. Phonetic representations like *spic-and-span* or *come a cropper* carry only idiomatic meanings so far as I am concerned. These idioms must still be converted into postsemantic configurations, but one or more of the units in such a configuration is no longer a semantic unit, so that the postsemantic configuration cannot alternatively be a semantic one. Sometimes such obsolete units are reinterpreted as if they *were* semantic units still in the language, as has happened in the case of *eat humble pie.* The concept *umbles* (earlier symbolized *numbles*), the inferior parts of a deer, having dropped from the semantic inventory of at least most speakers of English, was retained as a postsemantic unit in the literalization of the idiom but then eventually replaced there by *humble,* which was still a semantic unit in the language. (Undoubtedly this replacement had something to do with the fortuitous closeness of meaning between *humble* and the idiom.) Still other idioms have literalizations which, while all the units they contain are possible semantic units, do not form possible semantic configurations. An example is the idiom whose phonetic output is *trip the light fantastic.* An idiom like this one seems typically to arise as a truncated quotation from some well-known story, poem, or song—in this case from "The Sidewalks of New York," with apologies to John Milton ("L'Allegro"). The discussion in the latter part of this paragraph has been intended to bring out the fact that an idiom need not have a literal counterpart; that is, some idioms have postsemantic literalizations which are not at the same time possible semantic structures.

5.9 Idioms are semantic units, and we shall see as we proceed that semantic units fall into a number of different categories. A particular idiom may belong to one or another of these categories; thus, *off-base* and *on-the-wagon* are in traditional terms "adjectives," *spill-the-beans* and *trip-the-light-fantastic* are "verbs," while *red-herring* and *lily-of-the-valley* are "nouns." Semantic units like these all belong to a type which I shall later call *lexical*, characterized by a relatively high degree of information content, relative infrequency in use, and various features of semantic distribution. Other semantic units may be called at this point *nonlexical*. It will be enough for the reader to associate them with traditional "inflections"; they are meanings such as are typically represented by "affixes" and the like, meanings which in a sense are satellite to the lexical units. Such units can also be idioms. We might take as examples the so-called progressive aspect and perfective aspect in English. Clearly they are semantic units; they "have meanings" (see chap. 13). How are these meanings converted into sound? It is quite evident that they are not symbolized directly. In surface structures such as *Steve is eating* and *Steve has eaten* we find symbolizations, on the one hand of the appropriate form of *be* followed at a distance by *ing*, on the other hand of *have* followed at a distance by *en*. The semantic unit *progressive* is thus an idiom whose literalization consists of *be* and *ing*, while *perfective* is an idiom with *have* and *en* in its literalization. Both lexical and nonlexical semantic units can thus be idioms, subject to conversion into other units before they can be symbolized. These other units may or may not be units which can themselves be semantic as well as postsemantic.

5.10 The purpose of this chapter has been to show how the historical phenomenon of idiomaticization, by creating semantic units that

(6)

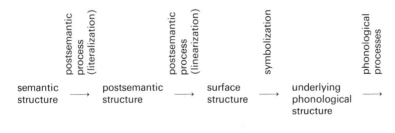

semantic structure $\longrightarrow$ postsemantic structure $\longrightarrow$ surface structure $\longrightarrow$ underlying phonological structure $\longrightarrow$

postsemantic process (literalization) postsemantic process (linearization) symbolization phonological processes

phonetic structure

do not have a direct symbolization of their own, has the effect of separating semantic structure from the symbolization process. We have ignored the processes of linearization and phonological modification that were discussed in Chapters 3 and 4, but let us now combine all these processes in (6), a summary of the kind of system at which we have now arrived.

6

Other Postsemantic Processes

6.1 So far we have seen two general ways in which the semantic structure of a language differs from its surface structure. Many semantic units do not appear themselves in surface structure but are subject to *literalization* processes in which they are replaced by other, postsemantic units which may or may not under other circumstances be semantic units in their own right. In addition, it is impossible for semantic configurations to be converted into phonological configurations directly because of the linear nature of sound. There must be, therefore, *linearization* processes which apply before symbolization can take effect. Besides these two kinds of differences, however, there are other ways in which semantic structures and surface representations differ, and our picture would be incomplete unless we gave at least passing recognition to them in this brief chapter.

6.2 Instead of being replaced by another unit, or a configuration of other units, a semantic unit is often simply repositioned. Thus, a surface structure may show units in different positions than those they occupied in the underlying semantic structure or in a literalization that has already taken effect. Sometimes the unit is not deleted from its original position but is merely copied into other positions, thereby occurring more than once within the surface representation. The processes responsible for such redistribution are typically those that are called *agreement* (or *concord*). In some languages it may be said that a verb "agrees with" the number of its subject. This is to say that a number unit which is present semantically in a "noun" (again, we need not concern ourselves at the moment with the semantic significance of terms like this) is redistributed so that it appears postsemantically in the "verb," perhaps remaining in the noun as well, perhaps not. In German we find *Das Kind singt* but *Die Kinder singen*. Semantically, singularity and plurality are specifications of the noun *Kind*. In the surface representations of these sentences, however, the singular-plural distinction appears in three different places: in the noun (*Kind* vs. *Kinder*), in the verb (*singt* vs. *singen*), and in the "article" (*das* vs. *die*). In the English sentences *The child is singing* and *The children are singing*, too, the difference between *is* and *are* reflects a difference which is located semantically in the noun *child* and is retained there (*child* vs. *children*) as well as being copied into the postsemantic verb *be*. It would appear that languages of the "polysynthetic" type, whose surface representations exhibit unusually long and complex "words," are simply languages in which there is a prevalence of postsemantic agreement processes. In an Onondaga Iroquois sentence like *waʔakwanǫhsahninǫnyǫ́ʔ* "we bought the houses," the surface structure verb root (*-hninǫ-*) is not only accompanied by its own semantic specifications as to "past tense" (*waʔ-*) and "punctual aspect" (*-ʔ*) but it has acquired the person (*-ak-*) and number (*-wa-*) of its subject noun; it has also absorbed, postsemantically, its entire object noun (*-nǫhsa-*) together with the plurality of the latter (*-nyǫ-*). In Chapter 17 we shall look more closely at the processes which produce surface representations in languages of this type. The point is that postsemantic processes very commonly shift semantic units (or already postsemantic units) from one place to another, and that the same unit may even be repeated at various points in a postsemantic representation. I shall not try to discuss the historical developments which are responsible for such processes, but it seems evident that language change ultimately does lie behind them.

6.3   Extremely common are processes which delete semantic (and also some postsemantic) units; that is, there are many things present in a semantic structure which do not appear in surface representations. Some semantic units have no relevance at all outside of semantic structure; they are consistently deleted. For example, an important semantic distinction in English is that between so-called mass nouns and count nouns, but neither *mass* nor *count* appears as a surface structure unit. Other semantic units (or already introduced postsemantic units) are optionally deletable. Beginning with the surface structure *Did you go or didn't you go?*, the alternatives *Did you go or didn't you?*, *Did you or didn't you go?*, and *Did you go or not?* show several possible deletions which the speaker may or may not choose to apply. Similarly, the second person subject of an imperative verb may or may not be deleted, though it most commonly is: *You eat!* or *Eat!* It seems evident that in general deletion is an economy measure, enabling the speaker to save his breath by omitting from surface representations, and therefore from the eventual phonetic outputs, parts of semantic structures which he judges it unnecessary to symbolize.

6.4   Very commonly a lexical unit which is deleted leaves behind a trace in the form of certain nonlexical units that were semantically associated with it. One such process is generally called *pronominalization*, since the units it leaves behind form surface structure *pronouns*. Thus, I may ask you *When did you buy it?* if I have reason to believe that you know the lexical unit which I have omitted at the end of this surface representation. In place of that unit I have left only a representation of its "nonhumanness" and singularity, symbolized as *it*. I may assume such knowledge on your part from either the linguistic or the nonlinguistic context. That is, you may have just said *Let me show you my new Volvo*, or I may have met you just as you were climbing out of your obviously new car. One of the factors which is evidently relevant to the determination of which lexical units can be deleted in this way is the linear order of the elements involved. If we disregard other complicating factors, in general an item can be pronominalized after it has appeared once in the linearized postsemantic sequence. Thus we can say *Walter promised that he would come* but not *He promised that Walter would come* if it is the same Walter that is referred to in both cases. It is interesting to note that if linear order is relevant to the determination of what can be pronominalized, then pronominalization must take place after the process of linearization. So far we have thought of the latter as one of the last processes to apply before a surface structure is achieved, but evidently pronominalization must come even later. The literalization of an idiom, on the other hand, must be an earlier process, one that applies shortly after the departure from semantic structure. It is interesting to ask, in that case, why *the wagon* cannot be pronominalized in *George is on the wagon*, or *the beans* in *Helen spilled the beans*, for certainly *George is on it* and *Helen spilled them* do not carry the idiomatic meanings. The answer is apparent from the nature of pronominalization and from what was earlier said about idioms. In order for pronominalization to take place it is necessary that the pronominalized noun be present in the semantic structure, where its identity of reference with another noun is established, or at least where its reference has already been established by the nonlinguistic context. But in the semantic structures underlying *George is on the wagon* and *Helen spilled the beans*, no nouns (*the wagon* or *the beans*) are there. It is impossible for nouns which are not there to have identity of reference with anything. On the other hand, for nouns which are present in semantic structure and which do have a referential tie, it is plain that this tie is an important piece of semantic information which must be retained up to the time pronominalization applies.

6.5   There are, then, a variety of postsemantic processes operative in every language to convert a semantic structure into a surface one. Such processes apparently have their origin in three different areas. First, there is the necessity that nonlinear semantic structures be converted into linear configurations appropriate to further conversion into sound; hence the need for linearization processes. Second, there is a drive toward economy of phonetic outputs and therefore of the surface structures which such outputs represent; hence the need for deletion processes, including pronominalization. Third, there is semantic change (and probably various kinds of postsemantic change as well), leading to the need for literalization processes, agreement processes, and, in general, processes which add and redistribute semantic and postsemantic units.

7

The Resulting Picture

7.1   The preceding chapters have attempted to construct in stages a picture of language as it is, and to suggest some of the reasons why it should be that way. The result we have arrived at is summarized in (1). Starting from the proposition that language is a way of converting meaning into sound, we can hypothesize an initial area of semantic structure where configurations of meanings are assembled. These semantic configurations are then subject to postsemantic processes yielding a series of differing postsemantic representations, the last of which can be termed a surface structure. The latter still contains semantic-like units, some of which, however, will not have been present in the semantic structure. Next there is a process of symbolization by which units of the surface structure are converted into underlying phonological configurations. The first, or "morphophonemic" representation thus arrived at is subject to a series of phonological processes which lead ultimately to a phonetic representation. Three distinctly different kinds of processes are evident in this picture. First, there are processes of "formation" by which a semantic structure is constructed at the outset. Second, there are processes of "transformation" by which a semantic structure is modified to become a surface structure, and by which, as well, an underlying phonological representation is converted into a phonetic one. And, third, there are processes of "symbolization" by which postsemantic units of a surface representation are replaced by underlying phonological configurations.

(1)

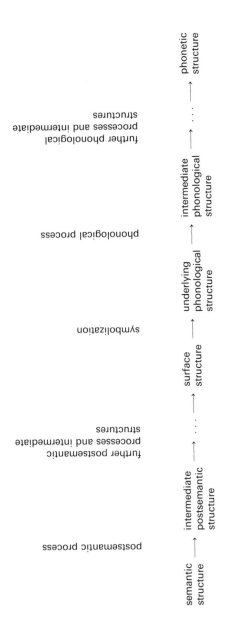

7.2 One obvious and possibly controversial feature of the view of language illustrated in (1) is its directionality. The arrows all point from left to right, indicating processes which move from a semantic structure toward a phonetic structure and not in the other direction. Furthermore, in earlier chapters I have often characterized language as converting meaning into sound, not sound into meaning. The view I have presented conflicts with another possible view, that these processes are bidirectional, allowing passage from meaning to sound and from sound to meaning in a wholly symmetric way. This other view owes much of its plausibility to the observation that people are both speakers and hearers of language. As speakers they convert meaning into sound, but as hearers they convert sound into meaning. Thus the idea has arisen that, as put by Louis Hjelmslev, "expression and content are coordinate and equal entities in every respect," and one can pass between them in either direction with equal facility.[1] I would like to suggest that this idea is mistaken, that the directionality suggested by (1) is a real characteristic of language. First of all, and contrary to Hjelmslev's statement, there is an obvious imbalance between the semantic side of language and the phonetic side (Hjelmslev's "content" and "expression") from the point of view of sheer size and complexity. Much has already been made of the fact that the semantic inventory of language is incomparably larger than the phonetic inventory—the development of this imbalance was seen as one of the chief factors leading to the system of language as we know it. The complexity of semantic configurations is surely also much greater than that of phonetic ones, and postsemantic processes are more numerous and diverse than phonological processes. Symbolization, too, is not a balanced tie between one postsemantic unit and one prephonetic one, but an asymmetric linking of, typically, one postsemantic unit with a prephonetic configuration.

7.3 There are several other considerations which seem to me especially relevant to the question of the directionality of language. One of them I would like to call the *directionality of homonymy*. Homonymy seems to be a characteristic even of primitive symbolization systems. From a pioneering field study of gibbon behavior, for example, it was concluded "that many of the stereotyped vocalizations of primates are *multivalent*, i.e., the same sound patterns have several

[1] Hjelmslev 1961:60.

different stimulus values in different situations. Though the sound patterns remain the same, [their] motivation and biological functions vary, within limits, from one situation to another"—that is, apparently, different semantic units may be symbolized by the same phonetic unit.[2] In language, of course, we find numerous cases of homonymy, as when a winged mammal and an item of baseball gear are both symbolized *bat*, or when a sentence like *Bob enjoys pleasing women and children* can be the output of at least four different semantic structures. There are countless instances in language where different semantic structures are given the same phonetic representation because of a convergence that is accidentally brought about by transformations or symbolizations. The question is whether such convergences are found in the opposite direction—whether one and the same semantic structure can result in two or more different phonetic representations. Is there, in other words, such a thing as *synonymy*? Synonymy of a certain kind does seem to be real: that which results from the application or nonapplication of optional postsemantic and phonological processes. Thus, for example, it may be that the phonetic outputs *What did you see?* (with sustained high pitch throughout) and *You saw what?* (with a rise to a sustained high pitch on the last word) represent the same semantic structure (see 19.35). In the first a postsemantic process has moved *what* to the beginning of the sentence and positioned *you* between *did* and the verb. The process is, however, optional in questions of this type; when it is not applied, the second kind of output results. Such instances remain distinct in nature from instances of homonymy. Homonymy, far from being a matter of the application or non-application of optional processes, arises in what may be called a sporadic, whimsical, and accidental way. Synonymy, if it were parallel, would be of the sort that might be suggested to exist between *violin* and *fiddle* or between *Henry is unmarried* and *Henry is a bachelor*, where a single semantic structure, quite accidentally, has a multiple phonetic representation. I wish to hazard the opinion that the semantic structures are *not* identical in such cases—a fiddle being a violin that is regarded less elegantly, the state of being a bachelor constituting more of a present social status than simply being unmarried. Such semantic differences are often difficult to describe, but that does not make them less real. If they are real, then

[2] Carpenter 1940:179.

there is nothing which parallels the phenomenon of homonymy in the opposite direction.

7.4   The directionality of language appears most convincingly, however, in what may be called the *directionality of well-formedness*. Briefly, it is in semantic structure that the well-formedness of sentences is determined. If a semantic structure is properly put together, in accordance with the rules of semantic formation which a language dictates, then a well-formed phonetic output is usually assured. The processes which are applied to the semantic structure will lead automatically to a phonetic representation. The reverse is clearly not the case. It is impossible to imagine rules of phonetic formation which would produce phonetic structures which in turn, by a reversal of phonological and postsemantic processes, would lead automatically to well-formed semantic structures. Most well-formed phonetic structures would be nonsense, carrying no meaning whatsoever. Earlier it was noted that the existence of both a speaker and a hearer in the act of speech might suggest that language is a bidirectional system. If we look a little closer at the use of language, however, it will be seen to confirm the semantics-to-phonetics directionality that has been posited here. Meaning and sound do not play balanced roles in the act of speech. Meaning is at both the beginning and the end of such an act, whereas sound occupies a position in the middle. The speaker creates a semantic structure and converts it into sound. The hearer does not create a phonetic structure and convert it into meaning. Normally the hearer assumes that the sound which he hears has a meaning underlying it, already produced by the speaker. Presumably the hearer retrieves that meaning by applying the phonological, symbolization, and post-semantic processes of his language in reverse, but he applies them to something which has already been produced by these processes during their original application. It is the speaker who "generates" the semantic structure in the first place, and it is the semantic structure that determines what comes after. The hearer's role is a matter of recovering what the speaker began with, a second-hand role at best.

7.5   It may be useful to compare this view of language with two other views which, in sequence, have dominated thinking about language in the United States since the 1920s. The earlier view, which prevailed until the late 1950s, was that which has often come under the heading of *structuralism*. The view which replaced it to a large extent, and is still dominant, goes under such names as *transformational* or *generative-transformational* theory. I shall refer to it here as *syntacticism*, for reasons that will become apparent. Both of these views were founded on a basic distrust of semantic data, a distrust which led inevitably to an overemphasis on the phonetic side of language. I shall refer, therefore, to the *phonetic bias* which underlies both structuralism and syntacticism. This phonetic bias did not develop only in the twentieth century; its various manifestations throughout the history of linguistics would be interesting to trace, but here we need concern ourselves only with its most recent influences. It seems likely that the posthumous compilation of the ideas expressed by Ferdinand de Saussure at the beginning of this century was important among the factors which imposed this prejudice on modern linguistics. Saussure spoke of the "linguistic sign" as uniting a "concept" and a "sound image." This notion captures, in fact, the essence of the primitive communication system discussed in Chapter 2. At another point Saussure wrestled with the question of what constituted the "basic unit" of language. Unfortunately, as it now seems, he reached the conclusion that the basic unit "is a slice of sound which to the exclusion of everything that precedes and follows it in the spoken chain is the signifier of a certain concept." [3] Why a slice of sound? Why was the concept not chosen as the basic unit, or both the concept and the sound as basic units of two different kinds? The phonetic bias is evident. A concurrent factor—one which has made the phonetic bias particularly strong in this century—has been the influence on linguistics, as on psychology, of the belief that scientific progress can be achieved only if one restricts one's attention to "hard facts," the kind of data that are concretely observable, as are the facts of behavior or of sound production. The observation of meaning depends to a large extent on introspection, and data obtained in such a way have been judged too variable and too subjective for a scientific discipline to take seriously.

7.6   If one believes in the reliability of phonetic data and the unreliability of everything semantic, two different conclusions are possible. The wiser conclusion was reached by Leonard Bloomfield, who wrote that "so long as the analysis of meaning remains outside the

[3] Saussure 1959:104.

powers of science, the analysis and recording of languages will remain an art or a practical skill."[4] In other words, if semantic data belong to language equally as much as phonetic, no adequate understanding of language can be reached when there is a restriction to phonetic data only. The main trend of structuralism, however, ignored this insight of Bloomfield's, proceeding on the assumption that "language is a system of arbitrary vocal symbols," and that a coherent, self-contained, and significant view of language was possible even when it was based largely, if not exclusively, on phonetic data.[5] It was never denied that language had something to do with meaning (how could it be?), but it was believed that linguistics would benefit from avoiding that area as much as possible, and sometimes it was thought that the greatest success of linguistics would be in avoiding meaning altogether.

7.7   The preoccupation with what was concretely observable also led structuralist linguistics to distrust the abstract, and at the same time to eschew any recognition of *processes* in language. Neither an underlying phonological configuration nor the processes which apply to it are very close to what can be directly observed, and such notions therefore were not looked upon with favor. The only kind of abstraction that was tolerated, in fact, was the notion of a class. A class itself cannot be observed directly but its members can be, as can quite often the common property which makes them members of the class. Thus arose the abstract notion of the *phoneme*—in one popular view a class of *phones*. Phones themselves were thought to be observable, and usually the property that united them in a phoneme was observable too. Phonemes were believed to group together in configurations called *morphs,* and morphs in turn to unite in classes called *morphemes*. A morpheme was much like a unit of surface structure in the view of language being advocated here. At one and the same time, however, it was held to be a class of phonemic configurations and to "have meaning." We have seen, and will see again and again in later chapters, that elements of surface structure are only indirectly related to meaning, and that they are related to sound only through symbolization and various phonological processes. From this point of view no such item as a morpheme could possibly exist, for it would combine the incom-

[4] Bloomfield 1933:93.
[5] Bloch and Trager 1942:5.

patible ingredients of meaning on the one hand with the almost-but-not-quite phonetic phonemes on the other. So far as structuralism went beyond the recognition of phonemes and morphemes, it attempted to deal with the arrangement of morphemes into larger configurations within the area now called surface structure. Since morphemes themselves were impossible monstrosities, and since surface structure can only be accounted for as a representation of a deeper semantic structure, it is not surprising that at this point structuralism ran into insuperable difficulties.

7.8   The view of language which to a large extent has replaced the structuralist one is characterized especially by a much less slavish tie to concrete data; that is to say, it is willing and even eager to explain phonetic data with bold abstractions. Thus, it has gone behind, and in many quarters discarded, the notion of the phoneme and has substituted the kind of system of underlying phonological units and processes that is advocated here. On the phonetic side of the symbolization process there is no basic difference between the syntacticist view and the one which I set forth above. There remain many problems in this area, but they are essentially the same problems for both theories and essentially the same considerations are relevant to them. Syntacticism, however, like structuralism, gives no recognition to the symbolization process as such. Underlying phonological units are introduced by "lexical insertion" somewhere in the sequence of what I have been calling postsemantic processes. Such units have already been present for some time before a surface representation is reached, and they are a principal component of the surface structure itself. The clear-cut transition from semantic-like units to phonetic-like units which I have been calling symbolization plays no role. Surface structure already faces in the direction of the phonetic output; it is not seen, as I have seen it, as a final, distorted reflection of semantic structure. This failure to recognize the process of symbolization as an important ingredient of language undoubtedly has something to do with the failure to recognize any common ground between nonlinguistic animal communication and language, as mentioned in 2.11 above, for it is precisely this process which language and these more primitive systems do have in common.

7.9   Early arguments in favor of the syntacticist view of language as opposed to the structuralist view were based on such facts as that sentences like (a) *John admires sincerity* and (b) *Sincerity is admired by John* have much the same meaning, although their surface structures are radically different. Conversely, various surface structures, such as (c) *Flying planes can be dangerous* were seen to have more than one meaning, and meanings often quite different from each other. To account for these facts and others of a similar nature, a theoretical framework was developed in which sentences have not only surface structures but also *deep structures*. Thus sentences (a) and (b) above were said to have nearly identical deep structures, the slight difference between them being responsible for transformations which produce the very different surface structures. On the other hand, sentences like (c) were thought to originate with two very different deep structures which, by chance, are converted by transformations into one and the same surface structure. The general picture became that of a central *syntax*, including both deep structures and their transformations into surface structures, and two *interpretive* components: a *semantic* one leading from deep structures to an interpretation in meaning and a *phonological* one leading from surface structures to an interpretation in sound, as shown in (2). More recently it has been suggested that surface

(2)

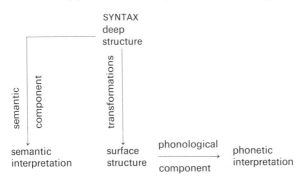

structures also contribute to meaning, if in a subsidiary way; a broken line from surface structure to semantic interpretation might therefore be added.[6] There are linguists for whom this picture is so deeply ingrained that its validity has been said to be "uncontroversial."[7] Figure (2), it is important to observe, yields no one-way route from meaning to sound. We may begin with deep structure

[6] See Chomsky Ms. 30ff.
[7] Chomsky 1966b:9.

and proceed thence to surface structure and on to sound, but the arrow to meaning leads in the opposite direction. The creative aspect of language resides in deep structure, which lies somewhere between semantic and surface structure. Deep structure reaches out toward meaning in a way that the morphemes and morphemic arrangements of structural linguistics did not, but it continues to maintain its footing close to the more solid ground of phonetically oriented surface structure. It remains incapable, therefore, of embracing meaning fully. It was for that reason that the prosthetic semantic component was tacked on as a necessary, if ill-understood, appendage.[8]

7.10 I wish, then, to contrast the views of language pictured in (1) and (2), the semanticist and the syntacticist views as they might be called. Before I state some general arguments in favor of the semanticist view, it may be necessary to cope with the objection that there is really no significant difference between these two views. The suggestion has been made that either view involves nothing more than the mapping of one representation onto another. Customarily it has been said that a deep structure is mapped onto a surface structure, which is in turn mapped onto a phonetic representation, and that a deep structure is also mapped onto a semantic interpretation. But, according to this argument, it could just as well be said that in the same system a semantic interpretation is mapped onto a deep structure, which is mapped onto a surface structure, which is mapped onto a phonetic representation. Or it could be said, within the same system, that a phonetic representation is mapped onto a surface structure, which is mapped onto a deep structure, which is mapped onto a semantic interpretation. In other words, mapping has no direction, and it makes no difference whether we start at one end and work toward the other, whether we start at the opposite end, or whether we start somewhere in the middle and work in both directions, as is the case with syntacticism. One and the same system, then, is involved in (1) and (2), as well as in other possible views which might be dubbed "phoneticist" or "(surface) structuralist." Since the mapping of one representation onto another has no direction, these are distinctions without a difference. This argument has been proposed in respected quarters,[9] and deserves an

[8]See Katz and Fodor 1963.
[9]Chomsky Ms.

answer. The main point to be made in reply is that language is more than a system of mappings. The various objects which are so related in language are highly complex objects, and there arises the question of how these objects are formed in the first place. It might be said that there are processes of *formation* as well as of transformation. The assertion made in this work is that the processes of formation must be located in the semantic area, that a well-formed semantic structure will lead naturally to well-formed surface and phonetic representations. To try to locate processes of formation in the area of phonetic structure would be an absurdity, as was pointed out in 7.4. Structuralist linguistics attempted to locate them in the area of surface structure, and must be said to have failed. The next development was an attempt to locate them in a hypothetical syntactic deep structure, since it was still felt necessary to avoid an outright commitment to semantics, but I believe that this attempt has proved a failure also and am suggesting that a commitment to semantic structure as the place where well-formedness is established is now unavoidable. The difference between the semanticist and syntacticist positions, then, is this very difference as to where the well-formedness of linguistic utterances is determined—whether it is in semantic structure or in a fancied deep structure lying somewhere between semantic structure and surface structure.

7.11   Let us turn now to some arguments of a general nature in favor of the position here adopted. It seems to me that there is an aesthetic argument which should not be disregarded. Certainly the best theories of any subject matter are beautiful theories, and the scientist no less than the artist is one whose career is dedicated to a search for beauty. I would like to suggest that semanticism has more aesthetic merit than syntacticism. The phonetic bias of the latter brings to it an inherent awkwardness. It may be noted in (2) that *all* of syntax—deep structure, surface structure, and the intermediate stages which lie between them—is relevant to the eventual phonetic representation, while it is largely deep structure alone which is relevant to the semantic interpretation. The central component of language thus is oriented predominantly toward phonetics, and the semantic component is left hanging on the side, relegated to peripheral specialists who may take some interest in that sort of thing. The question is whether this awkwardness reflects something basic about the nature of language—whether language itself is awkward in this way—or whether it is only a relic of the phonetic bias which was so influential during the structuralist period and which was inherited by the proponents of syntacticism. The recent history of linguistics, it seems to me, suggests the latter.

7.12   Second, it is obviously much easier to explain language *use* on the basis of the semanticist model. When we use language we start with something that we have to say—with meanings. If we are going to communicate these meanings, they must be structured in a way that conforms to the semantic structure of our language. Language then proceeds to give us a way to convert this semantic structure into sound. It is evident that the syntacticist model has nothing directly to do with language use. For that reason its advocates have been forced to use as a rationalization the distinction between *performance* and *competence,* between what happens when language is used and the underlying system of which use is made. This is all very well—I do not mean to deny the validity of the competence-performance distinction, and I see the model advocated here as equally one of competence. But a theory of competence must bear a relationship to language use, and there is no reason to assume that it is a virtue for this relationship to be as obscure as possible. On the contrary, all other things being equal, a theory of competence which is more closely related to performance is preferable to one which is more distantly related. To search for points of contact between performance and the syntacticist model is a very unsatisfying pursuit.[10]

7.13   Third, as I hope I was able to suggest in earlier chapters, the theory advocated here is significantly more consonant with informed speculation as to why language is the way it is. Advocates of syntacticism have been forced to deny that investigations of nonlinguistic animal communication have any relevance to studies of language. What seems rather to be the case is that such investigations have no relevance to syntacticism. On the other hand, the characteristics of nonlinguistic animal communication can be seen easily as antecedent to characteristics of language in the semanticist framework. For the most part, in fact, the remarkably greater complexity of language can be seen in terms of adjustments within the system to accommodate a tremendous increase in the number and complexity of messages to be communicated, as I have tried to show.[11]

[10] See Katz and Postal 1964:166–72.
[11] See also Chafe 1967.

7.14   Fourth, we might consider the uncertain nature of *deep structure,*
        which plays so central a role in syntacticism: the area of language
        where the generative process is based, the creative heart of language.
        From a semanticist perspective, it is difficult to see why some
        representation intermediate between semantic structure and surface
        structure should be elevated to such a crucial status. It is also
        difficult to see just what are the characteristics of this representation.
        In the early days of syntacticism, deep structure was very much like
        surface structure, except that the specific elements it contained
        might differ in a few ways, and that their linear order was often
        radically different. For example, the deep structure of the English
        verb with its auxiliaries was described as exhibiting the following
        elements in linear concatenation:

Tense (Modal) (have-en) (be-ing) Verb

Various transformations operated on the several different strings of
elements permitted by this formula to produce appropriate surface
structures. Thus, if all the parenthesized options were chosen, we
might have found the following deep structure sequence within
some sentence:

past can have-en be-ing sing

and permutation transformations would then have led to the
following surface arrangement:

can-past have be-en sing-ing

which is directly relatable to the output *could have been singing.*
The deep structure posited for such phrases simplified their description in various ways; for example, it regularized certain aspects of
English negation and interrogation which are obscure from the
point of view of surface structure alone.[12] In the deep structure of
our sample phrase, however, the items *have, en, be,* and *ing* had no
more relation to meaning than they had in the surface structure.
Meanings which might be termed *perfective* and *progressive* are
indirectly represented by these units, but the kind of deep structure
just described brings us no closer to such meanings. Transformations simply rearranged (or in other cases deleted or added) units
which were posited because of their ultimate relation to sound. The

[12] Chomsky 1957:61–65.

history of the deep structure concept over the last decade or so has seen it moving from its original closeness to surface structure to positions approaching more closely to semantic structure. Fairly early the oddity of a sentence like *The house ate a banana* was explained by saying that the verb *eat* must have an *animate* subject, or something of the sort. But it seems quite apparent that an element like *animate* is a semantic element. Subsequent work has multiplied the number of elements like this one which have been attributed to deep structure, and has tended more and more to obscure the boundary between syntax and semantics, a boundary which I am suggesting is nonexistent. In perspective it seems an odd state of affairs, and something of a historical accident, that anyone should be put in the position of arguing against deep structure. The burden of proof ought to be on those who maintain that some stage intermediate between semantic and surface structure does play such a crucial role.

7.15   Not only are there general considerations of the sort mentioned above favoring the semanticist position, there are also many specific facts about language which can be explained in a simple and natural way only on this basis. Many facts of this sort will be mentioned in later chapters. At this point I shall only remind the reader that facts associated with idioms, as discussed in Chapter 5, fall into this category. Consider, for example, the following sentences:

(3)   a. Henry saw the light.
       b. The light was seen by Henry.
       c. Henry saw the lights.
       d. Henry saw a light.
       e. Henry saw some lights.
       f. Henry saw it.
       g. Henry saw the light.

Sentence (3a) is ambiguous, which is to say that there is more than one semantic structure underlying this one phonetic output. One of these semantic structures contains an idiom, roughly paraphrasable as *became suddenly aware of the truth*. Also underlying (3a) are semantic structures without this idiom—we can call them literal structures—which differ from each other in containing different *lights* (one a "mass" noun, the other a "count" noun). This difference is not relevant to the point at issue, which is that sentences (3b) through (3g) reflect only the literal meanings (or one of them) and not the idiomatic meaning. From the semanticist point of view it is easy to see why this should be so. The idiom in (3a) is what we can call an intransitive verb; hence, it cannot be passivized and cannot lead to a surface structure like that of (3b). (A more formal explanation will be given below in 16.20.) The idiom does not contain either *see* or *light*; these units are introduced only in its postsemantic literalization. Hence, *light* cannot be made plural semantically, as is reflected in the surface structure of (3c), or indefinite as reflected in (3d). Clearly it cannot be made both plural and indefinite, as in (3e). Furthermore, it cannot be pronominalized as it has been in (3f), since its absence from semantic structure means that it cannot refer to something already mentioned. Since *see* is not present semantically when the idiom is present, it cannot be emphasized in a contrastive way, as it is in (3g). The possible idiomaticity of (3a) and the impossibility that (3b) through (3g) are idiomatic are thus natural and predictable if one takes the semanticist position. From a syntacticist point of view, on the other hand, these facts seem peculiar and whimsical, and can be explained only on some ad hoc basis.[13]

7.16   Up to this point language has been presented as if it were a sharply compartmentalized system. A clearly bounded semantic structure has been set off from the postsemantic processes which apply to it, the latter have been seen as sharply distinguished from the symbolization processes by which underlying phonological configurations are first introduced, and the subsequent phonological processes have been seen as another separate part of the whole, with the final phonetic representation occupying its own niche at the end. It would be surprising, I think, if any human institution turned out to have such clear-cut outlines, if the human mind operated in so compartmentalized a fashion. In the remainder of this chapter I shall suggest a few of the ways in which the focus of the picture so far given seems to be blurred and in which there seems to be some interpenetration of the several components of language.

7.17   I should point out in passing that the conversion of meaning into sound is itself a gradual process. I have been using the term "symbolization" to refer to the point in that process where surface structure units are replaced by underlying phonological configurations. Symbolization, however, is not an absolute watershed on one side of which everything faces toward meaning and on the other side of

[13] Cf. Katz and Postal 1963, Weinrich 1969.

which everything faces toward sound. The very first step away from a wholly semantic structure, the very first application of a post-semantic process, is a step away from meaning and toward the eventual phonetic representation. Literalizations of idioms, for example, are posited because the phonetic output is based more nearly on them than on the semantic units which they replace. Linearization is a major step toward linear sound and away from meaning. And once the symbolization divide has been crossed, various features from the semantic side will still be relevant. It is not seldom the case that phonological processes are restricted by surface structure properties which have been retained in the phono-logical configurations. As a simple and common example, processes may apply to phonological units which belong to the symbolization of a verb, but not to other phonological units. The fact that certain phonological configurations are related to a surface structure verb therefore must be preserved after symbolization has applied. The passage from meaning to sound, in short, is a gradual process during which semantically oriented features are cumulatively sloughed off and phonetically oriented features are cumulatively acquired.

7.18   It is often possible to observe a kind of semantic leakage in the literalization of an idiom. If I say, for example, *Sam kicked the bucket,* both my hearer and I may have some vague image of him striking a pail with his foot, even though my intention was to say that he died and even though my hearer understands perfectly well what my intention was. If I use the idiom *red herring* my mind may not be entirely free of thoughts of a crimson fish. Again, if I use a restricted idiom like the *big* in *my big sister* the thought that my sister is large may not be wholly absent. The literalization of an idiom was presented in Chapter 5 as altogether postsemantic and therefore not directly related to meaning at all. Examples like those just mentioned suggest that at least a weak bypassing of the idiom often takes place, whereby a postsemantic literalization is, in a secondary way, a kind of ghost semantic structure. An intentional, playful turning on and off of this effect is exhibited in many puns: "Just now he's sitting on a cloud, but it may not support him very long."

7.19   A more integrated kind of bypassing of postsemantic processes sometimes takes place as well. The cases I have in mind are ones in which the formation of a semantic structure can be continued after certain postsemantic processes have already operated. A limited number of postsemantic processes, that is, produce structures which, though they are postsemantic, are treated in a limited way as if they were still semantic in the sense that some further processes of semantic formation can be applied to them. Certain literalization processes applied to idioms fall into this category. We noted earlier that a surface structure like *The beans were spilled* cannot result from a semantic structure which contains the idiom *spill-the-beans* because the idiom functions semantically as an intransitive verb and, for that reason, cannot be passivized. Some idioms, however, evidently allow their literalizations to be treated as if they were semantic rather than postsemantic structures in this particular respect. The idiom *bury the hatchet,* for example, allows its literalization to be treated as a semantic transitive phrase to the extent that semantic elements can be added to it which trigger the passive transformation. Thus, *The hatchet was buried* is a surface structure which can result from the idiom; it *can* carry the idiomatic meaning. Evidently, then, we must include the literalizations of at least a few idioms among postsemantic processes which allow certain semantic formation processes to follow them.

7.20   Apparently, too, it is occasionally awkward or even impossible to put together a particular semantic structure for no other reason than that this semantic structure would lead to unacceptable postsemantic consequences; that is, sometimes postsemantic factors will work backward to inhibit or prevent the formation of a semantic structure that would be perfectly acceptable in semantic terms alone. In English, sentence (4a) is at least awkward, and (4b) seems entirely unnatural:

(4)   a. Bob has been being good.
       b. Bob has been being punished.

Evidently the consequence of producing two surface structure *be's* in succession leads to the avoidance of semantic structures like those underlying these sentences, although semantically there would be nothing unusual about them. Again, in Russian it is evidently impossible to say literally *I entered the post office* because *voiti* (enter) requires the preposition *v* (into) while *počtamt* (post office) requires the preposition *na*.[14] The latter constraint, particu-

[14] This example was suggested to me by James D. McCawley.

larly, seems clearly postsemantic in nature, but it feeds back into the area of semantic structure to prevent the formation of a sentence that would otherwise be natural enough. Phenomena of this sort seem to be relatively uncommon (although they may be more important from a stylistic or aesthetic point of view). Their rarity, in fact, provides a confirmation of the hypothesis that it is semantic constraints, in the overwhelming majority of cases, which determine the well-formedness of sentences. Only now and then, in thinly scattered instances, is some feedback encountered from the postsemantic into the semantic area.[15]

7.21   I have mentioned here just a few examples whose import seems to be that the picture presented earlier in this chapter is, sometimes and in certain respects, blurred. A semantic structure does not always pass through postsemantic processes in a completely direct and straightforward way. Certain postsemantic processes, for example, may apply before a semantic structure is completely formed. Certain postsemantic factors may affect the formation of semantic structures. I am sure that other, similar phenomena will be found if language is investigated more thoroughly from the semanticist point of view. It does not seem to me that such evidence invalidates that point of view. Rather, as I suggested earlier, I think it should be interpreted as showing the sort of exceptions to a rigid compartmentalization which we ought to expect in a human phenomenon like language.

[15] Not all "surface structure constraints" (Perlmutter 1968) have this effect; many influence the application of postsemantic processes only.

8

General Observations on Semantic Structure

8.1   The position set forth in the preceding chapters makes semantic
structure the crucial component of language. Unless we know the
nature of semantic structure, we cannot describe in any adequate
way the postsemantic processes which operate upon it, for we are
ignorant of the input to those processes. To start somewhere in the
middle of the postsemantic area, as modern linguistics has usually
done, is like trying to describe the production of milk while omitting
the cow. Without a knowledge of semantic structure we are ignorant
of the processes which produce well-formed utterances, for these
are the processes of semantic formation. Linguistics thus finds itself
at the present time in an awkward position, for of all the things it
has learned about the various parts of language, it has learned the
least about semantics. It has handled this area with its left hand,
preferring to concentrate its attention on topics supposedly more
amenable to objective treatment. It has left semantics to a very large
extent to philosophers, "behavioral scientists," and others who have
had no scientific paradigm within which knowledge about language
could be systematically integrated. In consequence, we still know
very little about the nature of language in spite of all the intelligent
labor that has gone into its investigation for so long a time.

8.2   The term *semantic unit* will be used frequently in the chapters which
follow. It indicates an acceptance in this work of a particular point
of view toward meaning which has been dubbed elsewhere the

ideational theory.[1] This theory asserts in essence that ideas or concepts are real entities in people's minds, and that through language they are symbolized by sounds so that they can be transmitted from the mind of one individual to that of another. There is a separate question as to whether concepts would exist in people's minds if we did not have language, but we need not consider that question at the moment. It is simply the reality of concepts as mental entities with which we are now concerned. Many students of language, both linguists and philosophers, have rejected this approach to meaning, but I believe that their rejection has been based on several mistaken assumptions. They have sometimes assumed, for example, that the ideational theory implies a one-to-one relation between concepts and elements of surface structure—perhaps *words*. "Take a sentence at random," suggests William Alston,

for example, "When in the course of human events, it becomes necessary for one people to . . . ," and utter it with your mind on what you are saying; then, ask yourself whether there was a distinguishable idea in your mind corresponding to each of the meaningful linguistic units of the sentence. Can you discern an idea of "when," "in," "course," "becomes," etc., swimming into your ken as each word is pronounced?[2]

Alston's question implies that surface structure words are "meaningful linguistic units," but of course they are not. Any serious modern view of language sees the elements of surface structure as only indirectly related to meaning, so that there is not much point in trying to find a concept that can be attached to each such element. Conceptual structure and surface structure are different things.[3] It is certainly also wrong to equate "concept" with "mental image," as is done in the following quotation:

A little introspection should be sufficient to convince the reader that insofar as his use of the word "dog" is accompanied by mental imagery, it is by no means the case that the mental image is the same on each occasion the word is used in the same sense. At one time it may be the image of a collie, on another the image of a beagle, on one occasion the image of a dog sitting, on another the image of a dog standing, and so on.[4]

[1] Alston 1964:22–25.
[2] Alston 1964:24.
[3] Cf. the criticism of Alston's position in Katz 1966:177–85.
[4] Alston 1964: 25.

But a mental image, in the sense of an imagined visual experience — a kind of internal photograph of some arrangement of visually perceptible objects — is not a concept. For the most part one cannot draw pictures of concepts or imagine them as specific objects. I would assert that speakers of English, and speakers of perhaps every other language, have in their minds a piece of knowledge which can be called the concept *dog*. This piece of knowledge is not an image of a particular dog on a particular occasion, but rather an underlying unity of which images of dogs are only particular and accidental manifestations. There are certainly many concepts which are not related to visualizable phenomena even in this way. Those which underlie words like *truth* and *succeed* are random examples.

8.3   This unwillingness to recognize the reality of concepts, as well as the phonetic bias from which so much of linguistics has suffered, are both traceable to the very real problems which are inherent in attempts to approach concepts through observable data. Sound — the other kind of data relevant to language — is accessible to observation in relatively straightforward ways and from a variety of perspectives. Articulatory, acoustic, and auditory phenomena can be recorded directly or with the aid of sophisticated instruments. Observations can be preserved, inspected, and manipulated at our convenience. Many of these data lie available at the periphery of the human body, in the mouth or larynx, or even outside it altogether as sound travels through the air. Concepts, on the other hand, are located deep within the human nervous system. Presumably they have some physical, electro-chemical reality there, but as yet we are unable to make any direct use of it for linguistic purposes. We can make no conceptual spectrograms, X-rays, or tape recordings to peruse at our leisure. Correlations between concepts and overt human behavior are so tenuous and unsystematic as to be of little help. An easy conclusion to come to, therefore, is that the satisfactory observation of meanings is impossible, that the best that can be hoped for is the development of a theory of language with minimum reliance on such observation. This was, in fact, the conclusion reached by structural linguists, and the one which has influenced the main direction of syntacticism. If such a conclusion is inescapable, then language will continue to remain largely a mystery to us.

8.4   I do not believe that it is inescapable. The widespread despair which
has existed over conceptual data has stemmed in large part from a
pervasive skepticism as to the validity of introspection as a method
of scientific observation. If concepts have their locus within our
minds, that is the place to look for them. but to do so was anathema
to the behaviorally oriented scholars of the recent past. Observations
arrived at through introspection have been characterized as worth-
less or impossible: "The linguistic processes of the 'mind' as such
are quite simply unobservable; and introspection about linguistic
processes is notoriously a fire in a wooden stove."[5] Or more
recently, in criticism of Otto Jespersen's insight on this matter:
"Jespersen's answer to the question 'Where do I find "content-
entities?"' was simply: 'In the mind.' This is obviously unsatis-
factory. An empirical science cannot be content to rely on a
procedure of people looking into their minds, each into his own."[6]
One might with some justification ask, "Why not?" The implication
is that each person will find something different, that the minds of
different speakers do not hold significant things in common. If that
were true, how could language possibly accomplish what it obviously
does accomplish? Language enables a speaker to take concepts
which are present in his own mind and to call forth these same
concepts in the mind of his hearer. The sounds which travel from
him to his hearer do not normally engender new conceptual units
in the mind of the latter. They activate concepts already there,
concepts which both the speaker and his hearer have in common.
They may and often do introduce novel configurations of these
familiar concepts—to that extent, the speaker is saying something
new. But it is normally only the configurations which are new, not
the concepts which make them up. Thus, if I tell you, "My house has
seventeen doors," this may be something you did not know before,
but it is only the complex message as a whole that is new. The
constituent concepts such as are reflected in surface structure items
like *house* and *seventeen* are concepts which you and I have always
shared for as long as we have been able to make full use of the
English language. If concepts like these were idiosyncratic, language
would not be able to function. This is not to say that people think in
identical ways; it takes only a little elementary experience with life
to realize that that is far from the case. It is to say that the speakers

[5]Twaddell 1935:57.
[6]Haas 1954:74.

of a particular language—and probably all people—do hold a large store of concepts in common.

8.5   Cases of linguistic ambiguity are instructive, in that they demonstrate that different conceptual structures can be recognized by introspection, even when the differences are not reflected in phonetic structure. By definition, ambiguity means that two or more utterances differ semantically but not phonetically. Thus, given the surface structure *Peter is standing up,* I think every speaker of English who can understand the issue will agree that its underlying meaning may be either that Peter is in a standing position or that he is in the process of assuming a standing position, and that these are two discretely different meanings, not simply a vagueness of possible interpretations. If I say *The bear eats honey* I may be referring to some particular bear—the one in our local zoo perhaps —or to the entire class of bears. Clearly these meanings are distinct, and clearly they are generally recognized by speakers of standard English, not just by me. It is true that when we are confronted by an ambiguous utterance we usually recognize one of its meanings before the other (or others). But, either by cogitation or by having them pointed out to us, we are easily capable of appreciating the others and of assuring ourselves that they are real. Ambiguities *are* objectively observable; they are clearly *not* matters of idiosyncratic interpretation. What is more difficult to achieve is a conscious awareness of specifically what concepts are present in a given semantic structure. We are hampered not only by the difficulty of bringing largely subconscious meanings into consciousness, but also by the fact that we lack adequate means of talking about or representing these meanings. Even if we are able to arrive at some awareness of a concept, more often than not we are unable to describe it in anything but a clumsy paraphrase. If one has not thought or read about the problem, for example, one is not likely to be able to pinpoint effectively the meaning or meanings that set off *I have seen it* from *I saw it.* (There remains, in fact, serious disagreement even among linguists who have given considerable attention to this matter.[7]) But even if one is able to arrive at a valid awareness of what is involved, it is no simple matter to find ways to convey that awareness most accurately. It is worth remembering, however, that the much more accessible area of sound did not yield overnight to

[7] For a variety of opinions see Twaddell 1960, Diver 1963, Joos 1964, Palmer 1965.

satisfactory observation or the development of a satisfactory terminology, and that there remain many problems in that area even now. The observation of meanings and the establishment of an adequate way of representing them cannot help but be more difficult by a considerable margin. To say that concepts exist, then, is not to say we are able to isolate them in our consciousness at a moment's notice or we have satisfactory ways of representing or discussing them. A proper concern for meanings should lead to a situation where, in the training of linguists, practice in the discrimination of concepts will be given at least as much time in the curriculum as practice in the discrimination of sounds. I suspect that individuals have varying abilities in this regard, just as they differ in phonetic ability. It may be that semantics, when and if it achieves its proper role, will attract into linguistics individuals with interests and talents that have been neglected in the field until now.

8.6   If it is difficult to bring the concepts of our own language into conscious awareness, how much more difficult it is for a linguist to work in this area with a language which is not his own. Even if we can develop sophistication in observing what goes on in our own minds, how can we observe what goes on in the minds of the speakers of a strange language? The seriousness of this problem may well lead to the conclusion that a linguist can accomplish little with a language unless he speaks it with close to native competence. The best hope for discovering the structures of a wide variety of languages would then be the raising up of linguists among the speakers of Chukchee, Choctaw, and all the rest. My own experience suggests that it is often possible to find informants who can be trained to a useful degree of articulate awareness of meanings in their language without being made into full-fledged linguists. Although linguists themselves at present are not well practiced in techniques of semantic elicitation, there is no reason in principle why both they and their informants cannot develop more sophistication in this area. The task is made significantly easier by the degree to which concepts in different languages coincide. The question of semantic universals is one to which we shall return shortly, but there is good reason to suspect that they are extensive. If so, then semantic elicitation to a large extent can rely on the overlap between what a linguist already knows and what he may expect an unfamiliar language to contain. Phonetic elicitation, whether admittedly or not, has always relied on a prior knowledge of many universals, and it is equally or more valuable for semantic elicitation to be able to do the same.

8.7 Let us turn now to a somewhat more specific consideration of what semantic units are like. I have already made the point that they are not to be identified with particular mental images; the concept *dog* is not an internal photograph of a certain dog in a certain situation. There does exist, however, a relation between at least some concepts and particular mental images. The concept *dog* certainly has something to do with images of particular dogs, which in turn, of course, bear a direct relation to certain physical objects which bark and chase cats. We might say of such concepts that they are *manifested* in these mental images. Color concepts provide useful examples of the nature of manifestation, since the mental images which manifest them are directly related to physical phenomena that can be manipulated and controlled in a fairly clear-cut way. Various methods of identifying the manifestations of a color concept have been devised.[8] Most often an informant is given a certain concept (by presenting him with its phonetic representation) and asked to draw an outline of all the colors which could conceivably fall under this concept on a two-dimensional array of color chips, laid out to differ from each other by small degrees along the dimensions of hue and brightness. He may also be asked to indicate the best or most typical representative of the concept. Another method is to present the informant with one color chip at a time and to ask what name he would give to each. In that way areas of greater and lesser consensus among informants can be registered. The figure in (1) gives a very rough indication of the kind of results which such investigations produce. Illustrated here are the manifestations of the English concepts *red, orange, yellow, green, blue, purple, brown,* and *pink*. The figure is meant to be suggestive rather than accurate, but several general conclusions can be drawn.[9] Each concept is manifested in a focus and a gradual, perhaps irregular fading away from that focus. Although the peripheral manifestations of different concepts sometimes may overlap, so that, for example, one and the same color may be called *blue* by one person and *purple* by another, or even *blue* and *purple* by the same person on different occasions, the foci are always distinct. There are strikingly large areas of the physical

[8] See, for example, Lenneberg and Roberts 1956, Berlin and Kay 1969.
[9] Cf. Berlin and Kay 1969:22, Lenneberg and Roberts 1956:26.

(1)

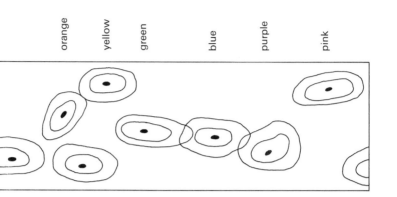

spectrum which are not covered even peripherally by these concepts or, it would seem, by any others held in common by the majority of English speakers. The covered areas are, in fact, a minor portion of the whole. Even unsystematic observation confirms that we are surrounded by many colors for which we have no ready names. It is difficult for us to communicate these colors to others—for example, it would be hard for me to tell you the color of a certain book I see before me now—and it has been suggested that such colors are less "codable."[10] Certainly we are able to perceive and to distinguish colors which do not lie close to any focus, but we have a hard time communicating about them, and we probably also find it harder to identify them on successive occasions. Artists, who are more pre-occupied with colors than the rest of us, do have additional concepts which cover much of the unoccupied or peripheral territory in (1). They are able to identify and communicate about colors in ways that the rest of us are not. To that extent the semantic structures of their languages are different. The main point to be appreciated here is that concepts are typically manifested as "target areas," and that much of the perceptible world is not covered even by the peripheries of these targets. It must be stressed in particular that concepts are not manifested as homogeneous areas which abut on one another so that together they cover all of the perceptible realm. The manifestations of colors have often been represented as in (2), which is surely a distortion.

[10] Brown 1958:235-41.

(2)

red	orange	yellow	green	blue	purple

8.8   I mentioned above that our investigations of semantic structure
may be aided by a matter of great practical as well as theoretical
significance, the fact that the semantic structures of different
languages are much more alike than their surface structures. The
trend of recent linguistic thinking has been away from the exaggerated relativism—the view that there was almost no limit to the
ways in which languages could differ—which stemmed from the
preoccupation of structural linguistics with surface structure. The
surface structures of different languages are indeed radically different,
but more attention to semantic structures, I think, cannot help but
lead to the conclusion that languages differ semantically in relatively
superficial ways. One of the most commonly used illustrations of
semantic relativity used to be the inventory of color concepts in a
language:

> There is a continuous gradation of color from one end [of the spectrum] to
> the other. That is, at any point there is only a small difference in the colors
> immediately adjacent at either side. Yet an American describing it will list
> the hues as *red, orange, yellow, green, blue, purple,* or something of the kind.
> The continuous gradation of color which exists in nature is represented in
> language by a series of discrete categories. This is an instance of structuring
> of content. There is nothing inherent either in the spectrum or the human
> perception of it which would compel its division in this way. The specific
> method of division is part of the structure of English.[11]

More recent investigation, however, has raised the question whether
the structuring of the spectrum by different languages is really as
arbitrary as it used to seem. One study of a representative cross
section of languages has been directed at the manifestations of
"basic" color concepts (those which are not composite concepts
like *bluish* or *salmon-colored,* which are not restricted to a few kinds
of objects like *blond* or *auburn,* etc.). The foci of these basic concepts
turned out to be unexpectedly stable, not only for each language but
from one language to another. The conclusion of this study was that
"although different languages encode in their vocabularies different
numbers of basic color categories, a total universal inventory of
exactly eleven basic color categories exists from which the eleven or

[11] Gleason 1961: 4.

fewer basic color terms of any given language are always drawn."[12]
The best explanation for these findings, if they are valid, is that there
is something in the environment common to all mankind, in the
human genetic endowment, or in both, that leads to cross-language
agreements of this kind. Relevant to the explanation in terms of
environment are facts such as that the focus of the concept *red*
appears to be close to the color of arterial blood, that of *green* to the
color of typical foliage, that of *blue* to the color of the sky on a clear
day, and so on. The genetic explanation, however, seems particularly attractive at the present time, especially in view of the various
arguments which recently have been raised in support of the position that language as a whole is in large part genetically determined.[13] It is no longer implausible to think that many concepts,
colors among them, are somehow built into the human nervous
system. What these concepts are may well go back to factors in the
common human environment, as, for example, *red, green,* and *blue*
may ultimately go back to the salience of blood, leaves, and sky
to humans everywhere. The congruence is so striking, however,
and the acquisition of these concepts by children so rapid and consistent, that biological transmission may well be the most acceptable
explanation.

8.9   The discussion so far has dealt with individual semantic units as if
they were isolated entities. In fact, we never find semantic units
occurring in isolation in language; invariably they are combined
into configurations of greater or lesser complexity. The ways in
which they are combined will concern us in the following chapters,
but it is worth noting here that there are innumerable special constraints which limit the cooccurrence of specific semantic units. To
give a rough and preliminary example, suppose we were to say that
all languages allow semantic units of a type which we may call *nouns*
to stand in the relation of *object* to semantic units of another type
which we may call *verbs*. Let us say that *dog* and *table* are both
nouns, and that *frighten* and *assemble* are verbs. It is natural enough
for *dog* to be found as the object of *frighten,* and *table* as the object
of *assemble*:

(3)   a. I frightened the dog.
         b. I assembled the table.

[12] Berlin and Kay 1969:2.
[13] See Chomsky 1965: chap. 1.

It is not natural to find these objects reversed:

(4)   a. I frightened the table.
        b. I assembled the dog.

Constraints of this kind present linguists with a vexing problem, one which seems crucial to a theory of language grounded in semantic structure. In considering this problem it may be instructive again to look first at the opposite side of language, at constraints on the cooccurrence of sounds. The anatomy and physiology of sound production is such that certain configurations of phonetic units do not occur. The tip of the tongue, while very mobile, is normally able to touch the soft palate only with some difficulty. For that reason, evidently, languages do not exhibit "apico-velar" articulations. Retroflex or "cacuminal" sounds are the practical limit of tongue tip retraction. It is not simply difficult but impossible to hold the vocal chords closed and to vibrate them at the same time; hence, the phonetic unit "voicing" (in the usual sense) does not cooccur simultaneously with a glottal stop. These are restrictions on the simultaneous cooccurrence of phonetic units, but there are also restrictions on what combinations of phonetic units can occur in sequence, also based on the makeup of the vocal apparatus. Because of the nature of voicing with relation to the production of obstruent sequences, for example, we would not expect to find a language with words ending in *sg*. It is not hard thus to invent configurations of phonetic units which are deviant or unnatural because of constraints universally imposed on human beings by the nature of their sound production apparatus. What analog can be found in the realm of meaning? That is, what lies behind universal constraints on the cooccurrence of semantic units? Presumably it is the nature of the knowledge which all human beings share. Is there something deviant about the sentence *My dog has wings*? If so, this deviance must be due to the fact that people know that dogs do not have wings. They know this because the world in which all of them live is so constructed. The configuration of concepts in this sentence is one that conflicts with human knowledge, just as the configuration of sounds in an apico-velar stop is one that conflicts with human anatomy. It is true that a fictional dog can be imagined as having wings, that it is possible to draw a picture of a winged dog or to attach artificial wings to a dog if one is so inclined. But quite evidently these are unnatural situations, and the cooccurring concepts in sentences which describe them are unnatural to just the extent that the situations are unnatural. Now it seems possible that an understanding of universal phonetic constraints, those which limit the cooccurrence of units of sound, is within the grasp of linguists. The number of different phonetic units found in languages around the world is small enough that in all likelihood we will know sooner or later what they are and how they do and do not cooccur. An understanding of universal semantic constraints, on the other hand, those which make a sentence like *My dog has wings* equally unnatural to a speaker of English and a speaker of Japanese, is possible only if we possess an adequate theory of all human knowledge. Such a theory is utopian and not something that linguists can hope to possess in any foreseeable future. In summary, while linguists can hope to achieve a full understanding of the constraints which the vocal apparatus imposes on the cooccurrence of phonetic units, evidently they cannot hope realistically to achieve a full understanding of the constraints which human knowledge imposes on the cooccurrence of semantic units.

8.10 I have argued up to this point that an adequate theory of language needs to be semantically based, that nothing but a superficial understanding of language will ever be possible unless we view semantic structure as the area in which the well-formedness of sentences is determined and the base from which a phonetic representation is ultimately derived. The discussion in the last paragraph, however, indicates that a vast number of constraints on the cooccurrence of semantic units are beyond the reach of linguists, since these constraints depend on nothing less than a systematization of all human knowledge. Must we conclude that the linguist's task is hopeless, that he can do no better than sit in the corner playing with his deep structures, surface structures, and phonologies, awaiting that vague future time when other sciences may have accounted for human knowledge to the extent that he can finally turn his attention to the semantic heart of language? An informed answer to this question requires us to look at other aspects of the situation.

8.11 To the extent that semantic structures similar to them are available in all languages, human beings everywhere doubtless would find the following sentences unnatural, and for the same reasons:

(5) a. My cat is barking.
b. I'm going to eat the rock.

It is part of universal human knowledge that cats do not bark and that rocks are not eaten. This knowledge, however, is tied idio-syncratically to the semantic units *bark* and *eat*. What people know is that only certain animals bark and only certain kinds of things are eaten. The list of animals that bark includes the dog, the coyote, and other members of the genus *Canis*, but also the seal and the muntjac, a small deer of Southeast Asia. Probably the only reason why these particular animals would ever be classed together is the fact that they bark; no other property would define such a class. (Presumably not everyone knows about the barking of the muntjac or even of the seal or the coyote, but that may be simply a matter of lack of familiarity with these animals.) Constraints like those which limit the "subjects" of *bark* are thus idiosyncratic constraints, associated with nothing except these particular lexical items. It would seem that a linguist cannot hope to deal with the myriad constraints of this sort which must exist.

8.12 Consider, however, these sentences:

(6)   a. The noise frightened my chair.
      b. He was tall every night.

Again, these sentences are unnatural because of constraints on the way semantic units can be put together. Again, as in (5), these constraints can be attributed to universal human knowledge. We might say regarding (6a) that chairs are not among the things which are frightened, regarding (6b) that being tall is not something that is normally repeated at intervals. When, however, we consider the class of things that cannot be frightened, we find that it is not a class which is definable on that basis alone, as the class consisting of dogs, coyotes, seals, and muntjacs was definable only with relation to *bark*, but that it is a class which would be posited on other grounds as well. For example, the things which are not frightened are also the things which are not surprised or angered, which do not eat, which do not like things, and so on. In short, they constitute the class of things that are *inanimate*. The fact that *chair* is inanimate is instrumental in explaining the unnaturalness of (6a), since evidently *frighten* requires an "object" which is *animate*, but it also helps to explain the unnaturalness of many other conceivable configurations, such as:

(7)   a. The noise surprised the chair.
      b. The noise angered the chair.
      c. The chair is eating.
      d. The chair liked the noise.

Similarly, the fact that being *tall* is a persistent state rather than a transitory event explains why sentence (6b) is unnatural, but also why a variety of sentences like the following are unnatural as well:

(8) a. He'll be tall at five o'clock.
b. He's being tall.

What is significant is the fact that concepts like *inanimate* and *persistent state* are concepts of broad relevance in the determination of semantic constraints. While parallel concepts such as *potential barker* might be recognized in an attempt to explain the limitations on the subject of *bark*, that concept would serve one purpose and no other. Concepts like *inanimate* and *persistent state* are capable of explaining a great variety of specific limitations, and thus enable the linguist to account for many specific constraints on the basis of a small number of semantic units of this kind. In later chapters we shall see how the role of such units can be formalized. The point is that it does seem fruitful for linguists to concern themselves with constraints based on universal human knowledge so long as these constraints are describable in terms which have some general applicability.

8.13 Contemporary linguists nearly always make certain assumptions, of a kind not yet discussed, in dealing with topics like those of the following chapters. The assumptions to which I refer run counter to the approach that will be followed here; thus, it is necessary that these differences be made explicit before we proceed. The currently accepted point of view might be referred to as the "*X is really Y* syndrome." The following two surface structures may serve as a preliminary illustration:

(9) a. I lengthened the string.
b. I caused the string to become longer.

A kind of statement that is common among linguists would be to the effect that (9a) is really, or really means, or comes from (9b). That is, there is an assertion that "X is really Y." Typically both X and Y are acceptable surface structures, although it is not essential that Y be fully acceptable in its own right. It would usually be admitted that this kind of assertion is only a loose way of speaking, and that what is really meant is something more like this: "X and Y are both derived from one and the same deep structure, and X differs more radically from that deep structure than does Y." Thus, for example,

George Lakoff has discussed at length the following two surface structures:[14]

(10)   a. Seymour sliced the salami with a knife.
      b. Seymour used a knife to slice the salami.

He has suggested that they are derived from the same deep structure, which, for example, contains two verbs. Both verbs, *use* and *slice*, are represented in the surface structure of (10b), but only one of them, *slice*, appears in (10a). It is in ways such as this that the surface structure (10a) can be said to differ more radically than (10b) from the deep structure which both hold in common. I am not so much concerned with the view that one member of a set of surface structures, all derived from the same deep structure, reflects that deep structure more closely than another. What I want to question is the more fundamental assumption that examples of this sort do indeed illustrate several surface structures which are derived from one and the same deep (or semantic) structure.

8.14   I shall question this assumption on two grounds. The first involves the over-willingness of present-day linguists to assign identical meanings, and therefore identical deep structures, to different surface structures. My position will be that in at least a great many cases of this kind the surface structures do not, in fact, have identical meanings but only very similar meanings. I believe that recent linguistic theory has suffered considerably from a most unsubtle view of meaning identity. The view has been essentially that two sentences (or surface structures) have the same meaning if, wherever one would be a true statement, the other would be also. All of the following sentences might fulfil that criterion:

(11)   a. Elephants like peanuts.
      b. An elephant likes peanuts.
      c. All elephants like peanuts.
      d. Every elephant likes peanuts.
      e. Any elephant likes peanuts.

Perhaps it is the case that the truth of one of these sentences entails the truth of all the others. By that criterion, then, all five sentences would be said to mean the same thing and to be derived from the same deep structure. I would assert, however, that the criterion mentioned is misleading, and that the only valid criterion for sameness of meaning must be whether one surface structure conveys

[14]Lakoff 1968.

exactly the same message, thoughts, concepts, or ideas as another. I believe it is only on a very unsophisticated level of conceptualization that all the sentences of (11) can be said to fulfil this criterion, and these sentences in fact have different meanings, even if the differences are small and difficult to describe. In Chapter 14 I shall have more to say about these particular examples. At the moment I hope that some readers will appreciate, introspectively, that the sentences of (11) convey thoughts which are not completely identical.

8.15   My other basis for questioning the *X is really Y* point of view is even more contrary to present assumptions. It is my belief linguistic theory should allow for the possibility that two surface structures, even when they may convey identical meanings (meaning being taken in the sense of conceptual manifestation) nevertheless may have different—perhaps quite different—semantic (or deep) structures. A geometric analog may be helpful in making this point. Suppose there are four distinct semantic units, which we may label W, X, Y, and Z. Suppose, in addition, the manifestations of these four units are such that they can be pictured in the manner given in (12), just as

(12)

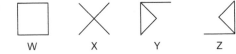

     W   X   Y   Z

the manifestations of various color concepts can be pictured as in (1) above. That is, the thoughts, experiences, or perceptions associated with these four semantic units are such that they can be represented geometrically in these four ways. Then suppose it is possible to combine W with X to yield the result pictured in (13) on the left, and it is also possible to combine Y with Z to produce the result on the right. In (13) we see the manifestations of the semantic configurations WX and YZ. But these manifestations are identical.

(13)

    WX   YZ

While the semantic units themselves are entirely different, the manifestations of their combinations turn out to be the same. We can say that the two different semantic configurations WX and YZ have identical meanings.

8.16   The preceding example was artificial, but I believe that language is
full of analogous situations. Consider, for example, sets of surface
structures like the following:

(14)   a. Chris
        b. my oldest son
        c. my wife's oldest son
        d. Doug's older brother
        e. my sister-in-law's oldest nephew
        f. the member of my family who was born in 1952

(15)   a. bachelor
        b. unmarried man
        c. unmarried adult male human being
        d. man who has never married
        e. man who has never had a wife
        f. human being who is adult, male, and has never had a wife

The members of such sets are usually called *paraphrases* of each other.
I am not at all sure that it is correct to say that these, or most other,
paraphrases have completely identical meanings, but let us assume
for the sake of argument that they do. It is true that, if I were to
utter any of the surface structures in (14), I would have the same
person in mind. (It is also true that I would be focusing on this
person in different ways, but it is potential meaning differences of
this sort that we may ignore here.) It should be noted that the
membership of these sets is not exhausted above. There is, in fact,
no apparent limit to the paraphrases that might be included in (14).
One could, for example, take any number of circuitous routes
through the English kinship terminology to arrive at my oldest son.
Nor is there an obvious limit to the paraphrases that might be
included in (15). If one and the same semantic structure underlies all
the paraphrases that might be included in (14) or in (15), then
postsemantic processes must have the following property: they must
be capable of operating on a single semantic structure to convert
it into a large, possibly limitless number of highly varied surface
structures. It seems to me that it is difficult to accept the idea that
postsemantic processes should have this function, and that it
would be a difficult if not impossible function to make explicit if all
of its possible ramifications were taken into account. It is unnecessary
to take a position of this kind. Instead, it is feasible and I think
considerably more satisfying to take the position that the surface
structures in (14) and (15) are all derived from different semantic
structures. More or less by accident, it happens to be the case that all

the semantic structures represented in (14) and all those represented in (15) are manifested in the realm of thoughts or ideas in the same or (more likely) almost the same way, as are WX and YZ in (13). Such, it seems to me, is the nature of paraphrase. A similar situation would exist on the phonetic side of language if there were certain distinct configurations of phonetic units which turned out to be manifested in the same sound. I know of no such cases, and perhaps there is good reason why they do not exist on the phonetic side. Considering the large number of semantic units, however, the fact that the manifestations of many of them overlap, and the limitless possibilities that exist for the formation of semantic structures, it is not surprising that the manifestations of numerous semantic structures should come close to being the same, or should in some or many cases be identical. All this need·not be taken to imply that one and the same semantic structure can never lead to more than one surface structure; I am suggesting only that this situation is much less prevalent than is commonly thought.

8.17 The formalism employed in the following chapters for the presentation of structural diagrams and the statement of rules has one important feature that may prove especially confusing to the reader unless it is clarified at the outset. In diagraming semantic (and postsemantic) structures, I shall assume that a particular semantic (or postsemantic) unit is either present or absent in a particular case. If it is present, its label will be written in the proper place in the diagram. If it is absent, its label will not be written. Thus, (16a) shows a verb that is specified as a state and (16b) one that is not so

(16)   (a)   (b)
         V   V
         state

specified. This notation will be adequate so far as structures themselves are concerned; however, in the statement of rules which form semantic structures or which convert them into postsemantic structures it is often necessary to say something specific about the absence of a particular unit. In the next chapter, for example, we shall want to say that a verb which is not a state must be a process and/or an action. To indicate "a verb which is not a state" in the manner shown in (16b) would not be sufficient. The incorrect rule shown in (17) must be read as applying to any verb, without regard to whether it is a state or not. In the statement of rules, therefore,

(17)
$$V \longrightarrow \left(\begin{array}{c} \text{process} \\ \text{action} \end{array} \right)$$

and only there, the notation "−state" will be used, with the meaning "not specified as a state." The rule in question will thus be written as shown in (18). It must be understood that a semantic

(18)
$$V_{-\text{state}} \longrightarrow \left(\begin{array}{c} \text{process} \\ \text{action} \end{array} \right)$$

unit like *state* is intended as a singulary unit which is either present or not present; it is not to be interpreted as a binary unit which has a positive and a negative value. Thus, the minus sign means "not present" rather than "minus," and no positive and negative values for semantic units will be assumed. This use of a singulary rather than binary kind of semantic unit is only tentative, and binary units may ultimately prove to be more acceptable. Having experimented with both possibilities, however, I have decided to make use of the singulary format throughout the rest of this work.

part two

In particular

9

States, Processes, and Actions

9.1   In this chapter and those which follow, some rather specific suggestions regarding the semantic structure of English will be made, and in Chapter 17 there will be some similar suggestions regarding the semantic structure of another language. The reader should keep in mind that these suggestions are tentative in the extreme. A vast amount of hard and detailed work will be necessary before anyone can feel even moderately secure regarding the matters that will be discussed. It is necessary, however, to begin somewhere, and it is in that spirit that the following chapters are presented.

9.2   Syntactic description has usually taken the *sentence* to be its basic unit of organization, although probably no one would deny that systematic constraints exist across sentence boundaries as well. From time to time some attention has been given to "discourse" structure, but the structure of the sentence has seemed to exhibit a kind of closure which allows it to be investigated in relative, if not complete, independence. If we look at language from a semantic perspective, intersentential constraints play a role that is probably more important than under other views of language, for a number of the limitations which cross sentence boundaries are clearly semantic in nature. Even so, it remains possible for us to focus on the semantic structures which underlie sentences, so long as we keep in mind that this focus is artificially narrow and that many things will be explainable only when we extend our view beyond it. From time to time we will look briefly across sentence boundaries, but most of our discussion will be limited to sentences. At first the limitation will be even narrower: to sentences which contain only one occurrence of what I shall call a *verb*.

9.3   I shall take the position that every sentence which is of interest to us is built around a *predicative* element. Usually, though not always, this predicative element is accompanied by one or more *nominal* elements. For example, in the sentences *The clothes are dry* there is a predicative element involving the meaning *(be) dry*, and it is accompanied by the nominal element *the clothes*. In the sentence *Harriet sang* there is a predicative element *sang* accompanied by the nominal element *Harriet*. Henceforth I shall refer to predicative elements as *verbs* and to nominal elements as *nouns*. These terms have been used most often for elements of surface or syntactic structure, not for semantic elements. In discussing semantic structure I could very well—and perhaps more comfortably—use terms like *predicate* and *argument* for *verb* and *noun* respectively. The reason I shall not do so is that what I am calling semantic verbs and nouns are reflected typically—in a distorted way, to be sure—in surface verbs and nouns. It is unnecessarily awkward to start with one set of terms, say *predicate* and *argument*, and have to change to another, *verb* and *noun*, at some unmotivated point along the path from semantic to surface structure.

9.4   My assumption will be that the total human conceptual universe is dichotomized initially into two major areas. One, the area of the verb, embraces states (conditions, qualities) and events; the other, the area of the noun, embraces "things" (both physical objects and reified abstractions). Of these two, the verb will be assumed to be central and the noun peripheral. There are various kinds of evidence which are best explained by assuming centrality for the verb. I shall mention a few general points now, but the entire exposition which follows I think will tend to confirm this assumption. It is of some interest, first of all, that in every language a verb is present semantically in all but a few marginal utterances. While it is accompanied typically by one or more nouns, we will shortly discuss some sentences in which only a verb is present. Utterances which semantically have no verb, like *oh* or *ouch* perhaps, seem best regarded as relics of the prehuman kind of communication discussed in Chapter 2, in which the direct symbolization of unitary messages was the rule. Otherwise, I would assert, a verb is always present, though it may in some instances be deleted before a surface structure is reached. A somewhat more interesting assertion is that the nature of the verb determines what the rest of the sentence will be like; in particular, that it determines what nouns will accompany it, what the relation of these nouns to it will be, and how these nouns will be semantically specified. For example, suppose the verb is specified as an *action*, as we shall see is true of the verb in *The men laughed*. Such a verb dictates that it be accompanied by a noun, that the noun be related to it as *agent*, and that the noun be specified as *animate*, perhaps also as *human*. Thus I am taking the position that it is the verb which dictates the presence and character of the noun, rather than vice versa.[1] The correctness of this view is suggested by such facts as the following. If we are confronted with a surface structure such as *The chair laughed* and forced to give it a meaning of some kind, what we do is to interpret *chair* as if it were abnormally *animate*, as dictated by the verb. What we do not do is to interpret *laugh* in an abnormal way as if it were a different kind of activity, performed by inanimate objects. Numerous examples of this sort can be contrived, and they apparently show that the semantic influence of the verb is dominant, extending itself over the subservient accompanying nouns.[2] It is relevant to observe also that when units which I shall later call *inflectional* are added to the verb in semantic structure, it is impossible to say whether they have been added to the verb or to the entire sentence. In *The men laughed* we find a semantic unit *past*. Does the presence of this unit mean that the laughing took place in the past—that *past* applies to *laugh*—or that the men's laughing took place in the past—that *past* applies to the configuration of *laugh* with *the men*? I believe that the question has no significance, that any unit like *past* which is added semantically to a verb is added simultaneously to the entire sentence which is built around that verb, in the same way that anything which happens to the sun affects the entire solar system. In contrast, we may note that the fact that *men* is *plural* is relevant only to that noun; it is not a meaning that extends over the sentence as a whole. A noun is like a planet whose internal modifications affect it alone, and not the

[1] Essentially the opposite position is taken in Chomsky 1965 and Fillmore 1968.
[2] Cf. McIntosh 1961:337. Although examples which appear to show the opposite may also be found, there are usually and perhaps always additional considerations which keep them from being counterexamples.

solar system as whole. As we proceed we shall see other evidence that the verb is central, the accompanying noun or nouns peripheral to it. In fact, although the term *sentence* provides a convenient way of referring to a verb and its accompanying nouns (and to more complex structures containing several verbs), the status of *sentence* as an independent structural entity is doubtful. There seems no need for some independent symbol *S* as the starting point for the generation of sentences; the verb is all the starting point we need. What we may call for convenience a sentence is either a verb alone, a verb accompanied by one or more nouns, or a configuration of this kind to which one or more coordinate or subordinate verbs have been added.

9.5   **States.** A good way to begin is by trying to account for certain basic differences between the semantic structures of the following four sets of sentences:

(1)   a. The wood is dry.
        b. The rope is tight.
        c. The dish is broken.
        d. The elephant is dead.

(2)   a. The wood dried.
        b. The rope tightened.
        c. The dish broke.
        d. The elephant died.

(3)   a. Michael ran.
        b. The men laughed.
        c. Harriet sang.
        d. The tiger pounced.

(4)   a. Michael dried the wood.
        b. The men tightened the rope.
        c. Harriet broke the dish.
        d. The tiger killed the elephant.

In set (1) a certain noun (*wood, rope, dish, elephant*) is said to be in a certain state or condition (*dry, tight, broken, dead*). I shall say of such sentences that the verb is specified as a *state* and that, as is typically true of such a verb, it is accompanied by a noun which is its *patient*. The patient specifies what it is that is in the state. The remaining sentences, those of sets (2), (3), and (4), contain verbs which are not specified as states. As a rule of thumb, nonstates can be distinguished from states by the fact that they answer the question

What happened?, *What's happening?*, and so on. A nonstate is a "happening," an event:

What happened?
    The wood dried.
    The men laughed.
    Harriet broke the dish.
but not (for example)
    *The wood was dry.

Various other rough tests can be applied to distinguish nonstates from states.[3] In many instances, for example, a nonstate can occur in the "progressive" form, which is not available to a state:

    The wood is drying.
    The men are laughing.
    Harriet is breaking the dish.
but not
    *The wood is being dry.

Such rules of thumb are presented only as rough, practical guides, not as "discovery procedures." They are not necessarily always accurate, nor do they necessarily provide unfailing criteria for decisions in doubtful cases. In general, there is no reason to think that a particular semantic fact will be mirrored with 100 percent consistency by some other fact. To indicate that a verb may or may not be specified as a state, a rule of the following form can be used:

(S9-1)   V ——» state

The fact that the arrow has a broken shaft means that its application is optional. The fact that it has a double head means that it must be read *is further specified as*, and not *is rewritten as*, *is replaced by*, or the like. A rewrite rule, several of which we shall encounter shortly, will be given with the usual single-headed arrow. In the convention of numbering rules which I shall follow, the designation (S9-1) means that this is the first semantic structure rule to be introduced in Chapter 9. This rule says that a verb, abbreviated V, may be specified optionally as a state. By implication, if a verb is not so specified it is a nonstate or, informally, a "happening" or event.

9.6   **Processes and actions.** But there are major differences between the sentences of (2), (3), and (4) which show that nonstates are not all of the same kind. In the sentences of (2) we seem to be dealing with

[3] Cf. Lakoff 1966.

processes, where the noun is said to have *changed* its state or condition. I shall say, therefore, that the verb in such sentences has been further specified as a process. Since a process still involves a relation between a noun and a state, it still seems valid in the sentences of (2) to say that the noun is the *patient* of the verb. The verbs in (3), however, are of a different sort. They have nothing to do with either a state or a change of state; instead, they express an activity or *action*, something which someone *does*. A rule of thumb which helps to distinguish an action from a process is that an action sentence will answer the question *What did N do?*, where N is some noun:

What did Harriet do?
    She sang.
but not (for example)
    *She died.

Conversely, it is often the case that a simple process sentence will answer the question *What happened to N?*, to which a simple action sentence is not an appropriate answer:

What happened to Harriet?
    She died.
but not
    *She sang.

The noun in an action sentence like those of (3) can no longer be said to be the patient of the verb. It specifies something which is neither in some state nor (in the same sense as above) changing its state; rather, it specifies something which performs the action. Such a noun can be said to be the *agent* of the verb. Thus states and processes are accompanied by patients, but actions by agents. If we now turn to the sentences of (4), it appears that the verb in these sentences is, simultaneously, both a process and an action. As a process it involves a change in the condition of a noun, its patient. As an action it expresses what someone, its agent, does. The agent is still someone who does something, but in (4) the agent does it *to* (or sometimes *with*) something, the patient of a process:

What did Harriet do?
    She broke the dish.
What happened to the dish?
    Harriet broke it.

In summary, a verb which has not been specified as a state by rule (S9-1) can be specified in either or both of two other ways. It may be a process, as in (2), it may be an action, as in (3), or it may be both a process and an action, as in (4). These three possibilities are captured in the following rule, where the parentheses indicate an inclusive disjunction—either *process* or *action* or both may be chosen. The solid shaft on the arrow shows that the rule is obligatory; the designation "−state" is intended to mean, not that a semantic unit "nonstate" is present, but that the semantic unit *state* is absent:

(S9–2) $\text{V} \atop \text{−state}$ $\longrightarrow$ $\left(\begin{matrix} \text{process} \\ \text{action} \end{matrix} \right)$

Rules (S9–1) and (S9–2) together provide the following four semantic specifications for a verb:

(1)	(2)	(3)	(4)
V	V	V	V
state	process	action	process
			action

9.7   **Ambient**. Now we need to indicate how verbs of these four types come to be accompanied by patient and/or agent nouns. Before we do, however, it might be well to consider the possibility that no noun at all need be present in some sentences:

(5)   a. It's hot.
       b. It's late.
       c. It's Tuesday.

The meaning of sentences like these seems to involve nothing but a predication, in which there is no "thing" of which the predication is made. It should be evident that the *it* in these sentences may be a surface element only; it need not reflect anything at all in the semantic structure. (Of course, there is another sentence in which the *it* of *It's hot*, for example, does reflect the presence of some semantic element.) Apparently the verb in each of these sentences is specified as a state. These sentences do not answer the question *What's happening?*, nor can they be made *progressive*: **It's being hot* is ruled out. What seems to be the case is that the particular states in (5) are all-encompassing states. They cover the total environment, not just some object within it. I shall say that the verb in these sentences is specified as *ambient*. In addition we might consider sentences like the following:

(6)   a. It's raining.
       b. It's snowing.

Here too the surface element *it* reflects nothing in the semantic structure. These sentences, however, evidently do not express states, for they answer the question *What's happening?* Furthermore, they seem to express actions rather than processes, for they also answer the question *What's it doing?*, where the *it* in the question does not reflect any item in the semantic structure either. If they express actions, the sentences of (6) do so without assigning any agent. Again we can say that the verb is *ambient*; it involves an all-encompassing event which is without reference to some particular "thing" within the environment. It would appear that a verb may be specified as ambient if it is a state or an action, but not if it is a process, a situation we can state with the following rule:

(S9-3) V
     -process $\longrightarrow$ ambient

That is, a verb which is not specified as a process may be specified optionally as ambient. If we now look at the results of (S9-1, 2, 3) applied, of course, in that order, we find verbs specified in the following six ways, as illustrated in the sets of sentences indicated by the numbers:

(1)	(2)	(3)	(4)	(5)	(6)
V	V	V	V	V	V
state	process	action	process	state	action
			action	ambient	ambient

9.8   **Patient and agent.** We are now in a position to discuss the manner in which each of these six kinds of verb dictates the presence of accompanying nouns, as well as the relation (patient or agent) which such nouns bear to each verb. In the first place, a verb which is specified as a state or process requires the accompaniment of a patient noun, provided the verb is not specified as ambient at the same time. This requirement can be stated in the following way:

(S9-4)

                                          pat
V $\longrightarrow$ V   N
$\left\{\begin{array}{l}\text{state}\\\text{process}\end{array}\right\}$ $\left\{\begin{array}{l}\text{state}\\\text{process}\end{array}\right\}$
-ambient

In these diagrams *pat* will be used as an abbreviation for *patient* and N for noun. The single-headed arrow means that the configuration on the left *is replaced by* that on the right. It is understood that whichever member of the exclusive state/process disjunction (indicated by the braces) is present on the left of the arrow, that same member must be present on the right also. We need to provide also for the addition of an agent noun to an action verb, again provided the verb is not ambient:

(S9–5)

```
                            ┌──────────┐
                                    agt
V              ⟶    V            N
action              action
−ambient
```

Agt, of course, is used as an abbreviation for *agent*. In the sentences of (4) above, where the verb is both a process and an action, rules (S9–4) and (S9–5) both apply. In that case, various kinds of evidence suggest that the resulting configuration (perhaps by a universal convention) should be diagramed as in (7), where the patient relation is more "internal" than the agent relation:

(7)

```
        ┌──────────┐
┌──────│───────┐  │
        pat      agt
V        N        N
process
action
```

For one thing, it may be noted that under certain circumstances an action verb may be *pronominalized* ("proverbalized" would be a more appropriate term), in which case it will be reflected in the surface structure in the form *do it*:

Harriet sang.
She did it (that is, sang) beautifully.

Now, if the action verb is at the same time a process, and thus has a patient noun, "proverbalization" affects the entire configuration of verb plus patient, not simply the verb alone:

Harriet broke the dish.
She did it (that is, broke the dish) accidentally.

This observation suggests that the verb plus patient configuration behaves as a unit in a way that the verb plus agent configuration does not, for there is no "proverbal" form analogous to *do it* which substitutes for the verb plus agent as a unit. Second, it seems to me that "adverbs" like *accidentally* in the example just given can have as their domain of modification only the total verb plus patient configuration and never the verb alone, independently of the patient. In *Harriet broke the dish accidentally* the adverb *accidentally* modifies *broke the dish* as a unit. Apparently it cannot modify *broke* alone, a fact which might explain why *Harriet broke accidentally the dish* is deviant. This observation, then, also confirms the special internal coherence of the verb plus patient configuration. It is interesting to note also that idioms are often literalized as verb-patient configurations (*break-the-ice*, for example), but never, so far as I know, as verb-agent configurations. When we come later to a discussion in Chapter 15 of how a sentence distinguishes new from old information, other evidence relevant to this matter will be pointed out.

9.9   By way of recapitulation, rules (S9-1) through (S9-5) create the following six semantic configurations, given with an example for each:

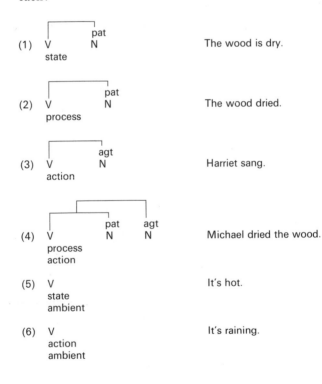

(1)   V   pat
     state   N   The wood is dry.

(2)   V   pat
     process   N   The wood dried.

(3)   V   agt
     action   N   Harriet sang.

(4)   V   pat   agt
     process   N   N   Michael dried the wood.
     action

(5)   V   It's hot.
     state
     ambient

(6)   V   It's raining.
     action
     ambient

10

Lexical Units

10.1   In the last chapter, specifically in rules (S9–1), (S9–2), and (S9–3), we saw how a verb may be specified in terms of semantic units like *state*, *process*, *action*, and *ambient*. Henceforth I shall use the term *selectional* to refer to such units. This term has already been used in linguistics in a not altogether unrelated way, and I see it as having a double justification here. For one thing, units like these have a primary role in the selection of accompanying nouns and of the relations which such nouns bear to the verb. This role is captured in rules like (S9–4) and (S9–5) above. (There are also more specific characteristics of accompanying nouns which may be determined in a similar way.) For another thing, selectional units have to do directly with the selection of units within the verb like *dry*, *laugh*, and so on, and it is with units of this kind that we shall be concerned first.

10.2   It is already evident that some semantic units are related to each other in a hierarchical fashion. Highest in the hierarchy are the all-inclusive units, *verb* and *noun*. The selectional units are intermediate in inclusiveness, covering somewhat narrower areas of conceptual space like *state*, *process*, and *action*. As we move down the hierarchy from that which is more inclusive to that which is less so—from *verb*, let us say, to *action*—at some point we come to units which include no others, which are maximally specific. For units of this kind I shall use the term *lexical*. Thus, *sing* and *laugh* are lexical units within the more general area of conceptual space which I have labeled *action*, as indicated in (1). Lexical units have several

(1)

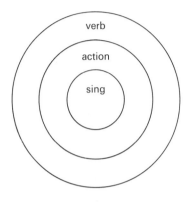

properties which distinguish them from semantic units of other kinds. The number of such units in a language is extremely large, perhaps in the tens of thousands. Because of the much lower probability of occurrence of any one lexical unit, such a unit carries by far the greatest burden of "information" in a sentence; it is the lexical units which principally determine what a sentence is about. The inventory of lexical units in a language may have a fairly stable core which changes only gradually with time, but it is constantly shifting at the edges, with new items being added and old ones lost at a pace that is unusually rapid with relation to the pace of language change as a whole. Furthermore, each speaker of a language has his own idiosyncratic stock of lexical units, the core of which he shares with other speakers of that language but some of which vary not only from one speaker to another but also for the same speaker over his lifetime. It is the inventory of lexical units which is most responsive to nonlinguistic influences and most influenced by personal linguistic histories. Lexical units can be introduced into a semantic structure by rules of the following general type, although later these rules will be modified in important ways (the square brackets indicate specifications which are present simultaneously):

(S10–1)   a. $\begin{bmatrix} \text{state} \\ -\text{ambient} \end{bmatrix}$ $\longrightarrow$ dry, tight, broken, dead, . . .

b. $\begin{bmatrix} \text{process} \\ -\text{action} \end{bmatrix}$ $\longrightarrow$ dry, tighten, break, die, . . .

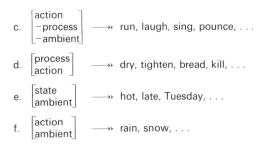

c. $\begin{bmatrix} \text{action} \\ -\text{process} \\ -\text{ambient} \end{bmatrix}$ ⟶» run, laugh, sing, pounce, . . .

d. $\begin{bmatrix} \text{process} \\ \text{action} \end{bmatrix}$ ⟶» dry, tighten, bread, kill, . . .

e. $\begin{bmatrix} \text{state} \\ \text{ambient} \end{bmatrix}$ ⟶» hot, late, Tuesday, . . .

f. $\begin{bmatrix} \text{action} \\ \text{ambient} \end{bmatrix}$ ⟶» rain, snow, . . .

The number of lexical units introduced on the right side of rules of this type is often very large. These rules, added to those of the preceding chapter, produce semantic configurations like those shown in (2), where the lexical units are underlined. The notation under

(2)

(a)	(b)	(c)	(d)	(e)	(f)
V	V	V	V	V	V
state	process	action	process	state	action
dry	break	sing	action	ambient	ambient
			kill	late	rain

(2c) shows the way I shall represent, in diagrams of semantic structure, the situation pictured in (1) above. The notation under (2d) actually represents the situation shown in (3), where *kill* is found within the intersection of *process* and *action*. A more accurate way of

(3)

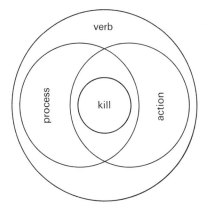

representing this situation in semantic structure diagrams would be that shown in (4), where it is made clear that *action* is not included within *process*, as (2d) might suggest, but that *process* and *action* intersect, with *kill* included within the intersection. It turns out,

(4)

```
              V
            /   \
          /       \
    process      action
          \       /
            \   /
             kill
```

however, that in our discussions and manipulations of semantic structures it will be enough for us to know, for example, that *kill* is a process and an action. The further information given in (4) will turn out to be superfluous for our purposes, so that a simpler notation like that shown in (2d) will enable us to deal with semantic structure diagrams in a more concise format. Whether the information lost is required, in the long run, remains to be seen. That is, ultimately it may prove necessary to include more elaborate structures below the V's and N's which are given in the diagrams in this work, but the necessity is not now clearly apparent.

10.3   It will prove convenient to have a special term for the lexical unit which occurs within a verb. I shall use the term *verb root*. Thus, the units like *kill* and *laugh* introduced on the right of rules like those in (S10-1) will be called verb roots. There are, of course, *noun roots* also: the lexical units which are found within nouns. But before we can consider the introduction of noun roots into semantic structure, we must give some attention to the selectional units which are found within a noun, just as we had to consider selectional units of a verb (*state, process,* etc.) before anything could be said about verb roots. As was the case with verbs, the discussion for the moment will be oversimplified and provisional. Let us consider as initial examples the nouns used in sentences (1) through (4) in the last chapter: *wood, rope, dish, elephant, Michael, men, Harriet,* and *tiger*.

10.4   **Count nouns.** A dichotomy which seems as significant within a noun as does the state vs. nonstate distinction within a verb is the distinction between a *count* noun and a noun which is not a count noun (usually called *mass* noun). A noun may be specified as having a meaning which involves a class of separate individuals, as is true of all the nouns in the above list but *wood,* whose meaning involves an undifferentiated mass. (There is a noun root *rope* which is not a count noun, but it is not the one used in the examples of 9.5.) As the name implies, it is only count nouns which can be counted. Thus, *three dishes* and the like can be said, but not **three woods*. There is a sense, to be sure, in which the latter is quite possible (when it means *three kinds of wood*), but *wood* has become a count noun in that case (see 11.14). It is also true that some count nouns cannot be counted, as is true of *Michael* and *Harriet* in the list above. Such nouns are specified in an additional way (10.7) which explains this fact. (It is certainly possible to say *three Michaels* in the sense of *three people named Michael,* but such phrases also have a special kind of semantic structure.) Before we formulate a rule which states that a noun may be specified optionally as *count*, let us examine another way in which a noun may be specified.

10.5   **Potent.** It appears that only some nouns are eligible to occur as agents of action verbs. Thus, while it is possible to say that *Michael, Harriet, the men, the tiger,* or *the elephant* did something, the same is not possible for *the rope* or *the dish* (barring such fanciful events as the dish running away with the spoon). The ability of a noun to occur as an agent depends on its semantic specification as a thing which has the *power* to do something, a thing which has a force of its own, which is self-motivated. To a large extent, as the examples so far given suggest, this concept of self-motivation coincides with the concept of animateness; that is, it is largely animate beings which are conceived of as having their own internal motivating force. There seem to be some nouns, however, which are not animate but which may nevertheless occur as agents:

(5)   a. The heat melted the butter.
        b. The wind opened the door.
        c. The ship destroyed the pier.

Here *the heat, the wind,* and *the ship* have a force of their own which enables them to "perform" certain actions. (It has been suggested that such nouns are instruments rather than agents,[1] but that does not seem to me to be the case. One would not say, for example, *Michael opened the door with the wind,* and while one could say *The captain destroyed the pier with the ship,* the meaning is different from that in [5c].) On the basis of these observations, I shall suggest that a noun may be specified optionally as *potent,* meaning that it has, or is conceived to have, its own internal power. We can now state a rule which combines the introduction of *potent* with that of *count*:

(S10–2) N $\longrightarrow$ $\begin{pmatrix} \text{count} \\ \text{potent} \end{pmatrix}$

[1] Fillmore 1968.

This rule says that a noun may be specified optionally as count and/or potent. We thus have four possibilities which can be diagramed as shown in (6).

(6) N   N   N   N
         count   potent   count
                           potent

10.6 **Animate.** The further specification of a noun is a complex and little understood affair, and there are many paths we could follow at this point. Since my intention is to suggest ways of attacking problems rather than to provide exhaustive solutions, I shall content myself here with a consideration of several narrower specifications which can be applied to *potent,* and one such specification that can be added to count. The concept *animate* has already been mentioned. It was suggested in the last paragraph that it was not a broad enough concept to account for all nouns which are found as agents, and *potent* was introduced for the purpose. We can now recognize, however, that a semantic unit *animate* probably exists as well. There are a number of verbs, for example, whose patients normally must be animate. They must, that is, be conceived of by the speaker, though not necessarily by a biologist, as belonging in the category of animals. For example, (7a, b) are natural things to say, while (7c, d) are not:

(7) a. The elephant is tired.
     b. I frightened the elephant.
     c. *The dish is tired.
     d. *I frightened the dish.

These and other observations suggest the usefulness of hypothesizing that a noun which has been specified as potent may be further specified optionally as animate. As it happens, this specification seems to be possible only when the noun is also a count noun. It is within the intersection of *potent* with *count,* in other words, that *animate* may occur:

(S10–3) $\begin{bmatrix} \text{count} \\ \text{potent} \end{bmatrix} \longrightarrow$ animate

A noun which has been specified as animate may or may not be further specified as *human*. The concept human, for the most part, has to do with human beings as opposed to other animate creatures. The presence of this semantic unit has various surface structure manifestations. For example, a noun which contains it may be represented in surface structure by pronouns like *he*, *she*, or *who*, while a nonhuman noun is represented by *it* or *which* under corresponding circumstances:

(8)   a. They found the elephant <u>which</u> escaped.
          <u>It</u> was gone three days.
        b. They found the man <u>who</u> escaped.
          <u>He</u> was gone three days.

It is interesting that an intrinsically nonhuman noun root (like *elephant*, for example) can be anthropomorphized so that it is conceived of as having certain human attributes:

(9)   They found the elephant who escaped.
        He was gone three days.

We shall return to this possibility below. For the moment, it is a simple matter to state that an animate noun may optionally be human:

(S10–4) animate —→» human

The examples above illustrate that a human noun is given "gender"; that is, its sex is specified. There are certain complexities in this area, but I shall assume here that a human noun, if not otherwise specified, is understood to be what we would normally term *masculine*. In other words, I shall take masculine to be the unmarked state of a human noun, and feminine, then, to be the marked state. In general, not knowing the sex of a human noun, we treat it conceptually as male. Let us, then, add a rule which says that a human noun may optionally be specified as feminine:

(S10–5) human —→» feminine

Rules (S10–3, 4, 5) add to the list of possible noun specifications given in (6) the three shown in (10).

(10)   N   N   N
        count   count   count
        potent   potent   potent
        animate   animate   animate
                       human   human
                                      feminine

10.7 **Unique.** Let us note finally that *Michael* and *Harriet* differ from the other nouns in the examples given earlier in that they involve only a single individual, a class of one member. For that reason, although they are count nouns, they are not amenable to counting, since counting depends on the existence of more than one individual in the class. It must be understood that while there are many individuals named Michael, each one of these individuals is a separate concept. All such concepts have nothing significant which groups them together except for the fact that they are all symbolized *Michael*. "Proper names" provide examples of homonymy on a grand scale. When I refer here to a semantic unit *Michael*, I am referring to one particular concept that is given that symbolization, not to the semantically arbitrary and uninteresting class of all such concepts. Let us say, then, that a human noun may be further specified as unique:

(S10–6) human $\longrightarrow$ unique

This rule is clearly inadequate, but it will serve for present purposes. In particular, it does not allow for nonanimate unique nouns like *San Francisco*. A more adequate statement would apparently allow count nouns to become unique if they were either human or nonanimate. In 14.12 certain other factors associated with unique nouns will be mentioned. But taking it as stated above, we can say that (S10–6) adds the possibilities shown in (11) to the list of noun specifications given at the end of (6) and (10).

(11)   N   N
        count   count
        potent   potent
        animate   animate
        human   human
        unique   feminine
                         unique

10.8 Now we have nine ways in which a noun may be specified, so far as selectional units are concerned. To these nine, particular noun roots can be added by means of rules like the following:

(S10–7) a. $\begin{bmatrix} \text{N} \\ -\text{count} \\ -\text{potent} \end{bmatrix}$ $\longrightarrow$ wood, sand, water, . . .

         b. $\begin{bmatrix} \text{count} \\ -\text{potent} \end{bmatrix}$ $\longrightarrow$ rope, dish, chair, . . .

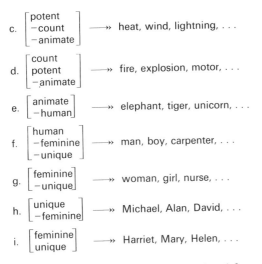

c. $\begin{bmatrix} \text{potent} \\ -\text{count} \\ -\text{animate} \end{bmatrix}$ —→ heat, wind, lightning, . . .

d. $\begin{bmatrix} \text{count} \\ \text{potent} \\ -\text{animate} \end{bmatrix}$ —→ fire, explosion, motor, . . .

e. $\begin{bmatrix} \text{animate} \\ -\text{human} \end{bmatrix}$ —→ elephant, tiger, unicorn, . . .

f. $\begin{bmatrix} \text{human} \\ -\text{feminine} \\ -\text{unique} \end{bmatrix}$ —→ man, boy, carpenter, . . .

g. $\begin{bmatrix} \text{feminine} \\ -\text{unique} \end{bmatrix}$ —→ woman, girl, nurse, . . .

h. $\begin{bmatrix} \text{unique} \\ -\text{feminine} \end{bmatrix}$ —→ Michael, Alan, David, . . .

i. $\begin{bmatrix} \text{feminine} \\ \text{unique} \end{bmatrix}$ —→ Harriet, Mary, Helen, . . .

Redundant selectional units are omitted from the left side of these rules. Thus, for example, in (S10-7g, h, i) both *feminine* and *unique*, according to earlier rules, imply the simultaneous presence of *human, animate, potent,* and *count.* The kind of total structure which is arrived at through the application of rule (S10-7i), to take one example, can be diagramed in the manner shown in (12a), but the simpler and more ambiguous kind of listing shown in (12b) will be relied on in this work.

(12) a.

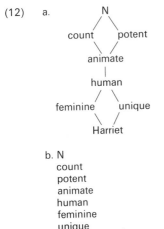

b. N
count
potent
animate
human
feminine
unique
Harriet

10.9 We thus arrive at more fully, but still incompletely, specified semantic configurations of the type shown in (13). This structure underlies the sentence *The explosion awakened Michael*. So far the discussion

(13)

	pat	agt
V	N	N
process	count	count
action	potent	potent
awaken	animate	explosion
	human	
	unique	
	Michael	

has implied that the generation of a semantic structure proceeds in the following way. At the outset the verb is assigned selectional units like *process* and *action*. These units, once assigned, determine the rest of the structure in two ways. First, they limit the choice of a verb root, as *process* and *action* permit the choice of *awaken* but not of *dead*, for example. Second, they determine the number and relation of accompanying nouns, as *process* requires the accompaniment of a *patient* noun and *action* of an *agent*. So far the discussion might lead to the conclusion that these nouns are now completely free to be specified in their own way, subject only to the constraints expressed in rules (S10–2) through (S10–7). In other words, we have not accounted for the fact that selectional units within the verb determine not only the number and relation of accompanying nouns but also, to a limited extent, the selectional units within those nouns. That the verb does have such an influence means that the verb, through its selectional units, ultimately limits not only the choice of its own verb root but also the choice of accompanying noun roots. In (13), for example, the *agent* noun is constrained by the verb to be potent, although the choice of human or nonhuman, for example, is free. The *patient* noun, because of the verb, must be animate and therefore both count and potent, although the choice of human or nonhuman, or of unique or non-unique, is again free. How can we account for such constraints? The fact that the agent must be potent here stems from a fact of considerable generality, a fact which was the reason for assuming the existence of the unit *potent* in the first place. That is, it is usually true that an agent noun must be specified as potent, although it is not true that every potent noun must be an agent. Thus, in addition to (S10–2), which allows any noun to be specified as potent optionally, we need some statement to the effect that this specification is *required* for an agent noun. One possible device would be to add a rule like the following to accompany (S10–2):

(S10–8) agt   agt
         N   ⟶   N
                      potent

That is, whenever the configuration on the left is generated in a semantic structure, it must be replaced by the configuration on the right. Ultimately, the fact that such a noun is potent goes back to the fact that its verb was specified as an action. To be sure, there are a few verb roots which seem not to require potent agents: verbs like *frighten* and *amuse* which involve the instilling of emotions. Apparently someone can be frightened or amused by a tree or a house as well as by an explosion or a clown. Perhaps such verb roots should be marked as exempting their agent nouns from rule (S10–8).

10.10 To account for the fact that the patient noun in the sentence *The explosion awakened Michael* must be animate requires, it would seem, a different device. The requirement that a process or state verb have an animate patient is much less general than the requirement that an action verb have a potent agent, and it seems more closely dependent on the idiosyncrasies of particular verb roots. The very similar sentence *The explosion broke the window* has an action-process verb, as does the sentence we have been considering, but its patient is not animate. Such constraints appear to call for the introduction into the verb of a new kind of selectional unit. The unit in question here might be labeled *animate patient*. Essentially it is a way of saying that the application of rule (S10–3), which introduces *animate,* is obligatory for the patient noun. By implication the full application of (S10–2), which introduces *count* and *potent,* is obligatory also, since the presence of these two units is a necessary condition for the presence of *animate.* A rule which introduces the selectional unit *animate patient* must introduce it as a further specification of the selectional units *process* or *state,* since it is only verbs of this kind which have patients. We might, then, write the rule as follows:

(S10–9) $\left\{ \begin{array}{l} \text{state} \\ \text{process} \end{array} \right\}$ ⟶ animate patient

That is, either *state* or *process* may optionally be further specified as *animate patient*. Like other selectional units of the verb, this one has two roles. Its role in the selection of the verb root can be formalized by including it on the left side of rules by which verb roots are introduced. Thus, among rules of the general type illustrated in (S10-1) we might find the following:

$$\begin{bmatrix} \text{process} \\ \text{animate patient} \\ \text{action} \end{bmatrix} \longrightarrow \text{frighten, amuse, awaken, } \ldots$$

The other role of the selectional unit *animate patient* is to insure that the patient of this verb is specified as *animate*. One way in which this can be accomplished is through the addition to rules (S10-2, 3) of statements to the effect that their application is obligatory in the environment of a verb which is specified as *animate patient*. Thus, (S10-2) can be rewritten:

(S10-2)   N $\longrightarrow \begin{pmatrix} \text{count} \\ \text{potent} \end{pmatrix}$

$$\underset{\substack{\text{full application obligatory/V} \\ \text{animate patient}}}{\underline{\qquad\qquad\qquad\qquad\qquad}} \overset{\text{pat}}{\underset{\text{N}}{}}$$

where the stipulation below the rule is to be read, "The application of this rule in full (that is, specification of the noun in terms of both *count* and *potent*) is obligatory if the noun in question is a patient noun attached to a verb that is specified as *animate patient*." Rule (S10-3) can then be rewritten:

(S10-3) $\begin{bmatrix} \text{count} \\ \text{potent} \end{bmatrix} \longrightarrow \text{animate}$

$$\underset{\substack{\text{obligatory/V} \\ \text{animate patient}}}{\underline{\qquad\qquad\qquad\qquad}} \overset{\text{pat}}{\underset{\text{N}}{}}$$

This rule is the heart of the matter; the stipulation means that it must be applied if the environment is as indicated. In this or some similar way we can account for the fact that certain verbs require animate patients, and for the numerous other facts of a similar kind.

10.11   It is apparently necessary to recognize that some lexical units are able to function alternatively as selectional units. For example, let us suppose that rule (S10-7e) is rephrased so that it does not introduce directly noun roots like *elephant* and *tiger* but only a small number of roots like *animal* and *bird*. (Perhaps a bird may be a kind of animal in biological terms, but in ordinary usage we conceptualize bird and animal as separate and coordinate concepts.) Such a unit may then function as the root of its noun. Alternatively, however, it may go on to be more narrowly specified, in accordance with optional rules such as:

(S10–10) a. animal ——» elephant, tiger, bear, . . .
          b. bird ——» robin, bluebird, hawk, . . .

in which case this narrower unit will be the noun root, and *animal* or *bird* will be, in effect, a selectional unit. Still narrower degrees of specification may be found. For example, *bear* may be subject to further specification as:

(S10–11) bear ——» brown bear, grizzly bear, polar bear, . . .

Thus, nouns whose lexical units are *animal, bear,* and *grizzly bear,* respectively, can be diagramed as indicated in (14).

(14)   N   N   N
       count   count   count
       potent   potent   potent
       animate   animate   animate
       animal   animal   animal
                      bear   bear
                                     grizzly bear

In this way we are able to account for a variety of semantic observations. For example, if there are semantic constraints which apply specifically to *animal*, the same constraints will apply automatically to *tiger, bear, grizzly bear,* and any other unit for which *animal* may serve as a selectional unit. It is chiefly through this device that we can account for the redundancy of (15a, b) and the contradictoriness of (15c):

(15)   a. A bear is an animal.
       b. A grizzly bear is a bear.
       c. A bear is a bird.

In (15a, b) the semantic structure includes the same information in two places, once within the patient noun and again within the "predicate noun" (see 11.16). In (15c) the semantic structure of the patient noun is inconsistent with the semantic structure of the predicate. The mutually exclusive nature of *animal* and *bird* is implied by the revised version of (S10–7e) described at the beginning of this paragraph. A particularly interesting phenomenon that lends itself to explanation in these terms will be discussed in (14.10). It appears, in summary, that a language contains many semantic units which function both as lexical units and as selectional units; to put it another way, much of the lexical inventory of a language is hierarchically or taxonomically organized. Units which have this dual function might be labeled *classificatory* units. Thus, *animal, bird,* and *bear* are classificatory noun roots, as is also, for example, *game,* since it may be further specified optionally as *chess, tennis,* and so on. Although they may be less numerous, classificatory verb roots are not uncommon. *Sing,* for example, may be more narrowly specified as *chant, croon,* and so forth. The study of these lexical hierarchies coincides to a large extent with the study of what ethnologists have identified as "folk taxonomies."[2]

[2] See, for example, Sturtevant 1964.

11

Derivation

11.1 Before the principal topic of this chapter is introduced, it will be helpful for us to examine and try to account for a basic difference between the two sentences of (1):

(1) a. The door is open.
b. The road is wide.

By and large, the state of being open is an absolute or fixed concept while the state of being wide is a relative one. Wideness has to do with the distance between the sides of an object; when we say that something is wide, we say that this distance exceeds a certain norm. The norm, however, is not fixed by the concept *wide* itself but is determined by the patient:

(2) a. The road is wide.
b. The table is wide.
c. The board is wide.

In each of these sentences the absolute distance between the sides of the object which qualifies it as wide is different. What is wide for a board is not wide for a table, and what is wide for a table is not wide for a road. The same kind of variability is not observable with openness:

(3) a. The door is open.
b. The window is open.
c. The box is open.

We do not find a continuum of openness such that there is a norm for doors, beyond which a door qualifies as open, a different norm for windows, and still another for boxes. The difference between (1a) and (1b) can be visualized as in (4), where X represents the

(4)   a.

position of the patient within conceptual space. In (1a) the patient is in the absolute position of being open, as indicated by the single point in (4a). In (1b) the patient is located along a continuum of wideness, represented by the line in (4b). Its position on this continuum may be anywhere to the right of (that is, in excess of) a norm represented by N (the distance between its sides which is normal for that object), but the location of this norm varies with the patient. It is true that there are degrees of openness. We can say, for example:

(5)   a. The door is slightly open (partly open, open a crack, etc.).
       b. The door is completely open (open all the way, wide open, etc.).

The parameter here is not like that represented by the line in (4b), however. There is no question of a norm which varies with the patient. Rather, the sentences of (5) suggest degrees of approximation to an ideal. The concept of openness evidently is one which has a maximum, with an object qualifying as open even if it is not in this maximum state, but qualifying as more or less open with reference to it. A relative state like wideness does not show this characteristic. It is odd to say:

(6)   a. *The road is partly wide.
       b. *The road is completely wide.

(We are not, of course, concerned here with the meanings paraphrasable as *The road is wide in part* and *The road is wide along its entire length*.) There is no maximum, no ideal state or "ending point" so far as wideness is concerned; the parameter illustrated by the sentences in (5) does not exist. Conversely, it is possible to specify the closeness along the continuum of wideness which an object exhibits with respect to the norm:

(7)   a. The road is rather wide.
       b. The road is very wide.

In (7b), for example, the meaning is that X lies relatively far to the right of N. It would be odd to say:

(8)   a. *The door is rather open.
        b. *The door is very open.

since openness does not have the parameter which makes this kind of specification possible. For the same reason (9a) is a normal sentence and (9b) a peculiar one:

(9)   a. The road is wider than the sidewalk.
        b. *The door is more open than the box.

(I shall return to sentences like [9a] in 11.12.) Let us say that while the verbs in both (1a) and (1b) are specified as states, only that in (1b) is further specified as *relative*. The possibility of a relative state can be introduced with the following rule:

(S11–1) state $\longrightarrow$ relative

The introduction of the two types of verb root can then be accomplished in roughly the following manner (replacing rule [S10-1a] in Chapter 10):

(S11–2)
a. $\begin{bmatrix} \text{state} \\ -\text{relative} \\ -\text{ambient} \end{bmatrix} \longrightarrow$ open, red, deaf, . . .

b. $\begin{bmatrix} \text{relative} \\ -\text{ambient} \end{bmatrix} \longrightarrow$ wide, loud, old, . . .

11.2 If we now turn to process sentences like those of (10) below, we find that we are dealing with a change, one which may take place gradually or suddenly, through either time or space:

(10)   a. The door opened.
        b. The road widened.

In (10a) the change is one in which the patient goes from not having the quality concerned to having the quality. In (10b) the change is one in which the patient moves some distance along the continuum of wideness, from having a lesser degree of that quality to having a greater degree. The difference between (9a) and (9b) can be visualized as in (11). In the first case the door simply moves from the state of being not open to the state of being open. In the second case the road becomes, not *wide,* but *wider*; that is, the position of

(11)   a.
       b.

W and X on the continuum of wideness is unrelated to the location of the norm N in (4). After the change communicated in (10b) it may or may not be true that *The road is wide.*

11.3   **Inchoative.** There is reason to think that the verbs (more specifically the verb roots) in (10) are "derived from" those in (1), that the process *open* is derived from the state *open*, the process *widen* from the state *wide.* In the case of *wide* there is the obvious surface structure evidence in the fact that *widen* has a suffix, a fact which might be taken to reflect its derivative nature. In addition, it seems to me, introspection suggests some knowledge on the part of a speaker as to which items in his language are derived and which not. The independence of this knowledge from surface considerations (such as the presence of a suffix) is suggested by the fact that we know the process *open* to be derived from the state (if we do know this), even though no suffix is present, but even more by the fact that we evidently know that *tired* (as in *Michael is tired*) is basic and *tire* (as in *Michael tires easily*) derived from it, even though the surface evidence—the fact that it is *tired* which has a suffix—perversely suggests the opposite. When introspection and surface evidence are contradictory, it is the former which is decisive. It may occur to the reader that *tired* simply crops up more often in everyday speech than *tire*, and that that is the reason why we feel the first to be basic, the second derived. I suspect, however, that there is a correlation between frequency of occurrence and the property of being basic or underived which reflects ultimately a greater cognitive salience of the state as opposed to the process in these examples. Perhaps the concepts involved here are intrinsically states rather than processes because of the nature of the human conceptual universe. In any case, a possible way of formalizing the derivation of a process from a state is with a rule of the following kind:

(S11–3) state   —→   process
        root   root+inchoative

The designation *root* is a cover symbol for any verb root of the appropriate type; the verb root on the right is understood to be the same as the one on the left. The configuration *root* + *inchoative* is one that will be referred to as a *derived* root. The element *inchoative* is a semantic unit of a new kind, one which can be called a *derivational* unit. One function of such a unit is to convert a lexical unit of one type into a lexical unit of another; in this case, to turn a verb root which is intrinsically a state into one that is derivatively a process. Besides having this function, a derivational unit usually also contributes a particular meaning of its own; here it is the meaning which differentiates (4) from (11) above. I use the term *inchoative* for this derivational unit, although in its etymological sense this term ought to convey a notion of "beginning" rather than "becoming," because to some extent it has been established in this technical usage.[1] In rule (S11-3), as in rules (S9-4, 5) of Chapter 9, the single headed arrow indicates a conversion of one configuration into another, but in this case the conversion is optional. To describe its effect discursively, rule (S11-3) allows a verb root which is intrinsically a state to be converted optionally into one that is derivatively a process through the addition to it of the derivational unit *inchoative*. In the surface structure of English the presence of this unit is sometimes reflected by the suffix *en*, sometimes in a different way (as *heat* from *hot*), sometimes not at all (as with *open*), and occasionally, as with *tired* and *tire,* there may be a perverse postsemantic development. One important fact about derivational rules like (S11-3) is that they do not usually apply to all verb roots of the relevant type. Thus, (S11-3) does not apply to all verb roots which are intrinsically states; it does not apply, for example, to *heavy, wet,* or *deaf.* Since (S11-3) is a rule of wide applicability nevertheless, it seems advisable as a descriptive device to mark roots like *heavy,* for example, as having the special property of not being subject to this rule. As we discuss other derivational rules, it should always be kept in mind that particular roots are likely to be idiosyncratically immune to their effects.

11.4   The following sentences show a different situation from that discussed above:

(12)   a. The dish is broken.
        b. The dish broke.

---

[1] It has been used, for example, in modern studies of Iroquois languages such as Lounsbury 1953:78.

Here again we have both a state—in (12a)—and a process—in (12b)
—but the direction of derivation is different. In (12) it appears to
be the state which is derived from the process, rather than the other
way around: *broken* is derived from *break*. Part of the evidence is
again to be found in the surface structure: it is *broken* which has a
suffix. Again, however, I believe that introspective evidence sup-
ports the same view, and I would suggest again that this situation
may reflect the greater cognitive salience of the process *break* as
opposed to the state *broken*, as earlier it was the state *wide* which
was more salient than the process *widen*. There are, then, some verb
roots (*wide, open*) which are intrinsically states, but others (*break*)
which are intrinsically processes.

11.5   **Resultative.** Recalling that intrinsic states may be either relative or
not, we are led to ask whether the same option is available to
intrinsic processes. The example given in (12), *break*, clearly is not
relative. The process is not, like *widening*, a change along a continuum; it is rather, like *opening*, an entering into a new condition.
Furthermore, the state *broken*, derived from it, is not a relative
state. In fact it may be the case that intrinsic processes are never
relative—at this writing I know of no counterexample—in which
case rule (S11-1) above was correct in allowing only a state to be
further specified as relative. This observation does not mean there
are no relative processes; *widen* obviously is one. What it means
is that relative processes are always derived from relative states, as
permitted by rule (S11-3). Since, then, in introducing verb roots
which are intrinsically processes there is no need to specify whether
the process is relative or not (it never will be), only one rule is
necessary instead of two rules parallel to those in (S11-2):

(S11-4) $\begin{bmatrix} \text{process} \\ -\text{action} \end{bmatrix} \longrightarrow$ break, melt, sink, . . .

The kind of derivation responsible for *broken* in (12a) can be
described with the following rule, which is essentially the reverse of
(S11-3):

(S11-5) process ——→ state
         root   root + resultative

The item labeled *resultative* is, like *inchoative*, a derivational unit,
which in this case converts a verb root which is intrinsically a
process into one which is derivatively a state. The following list

provides a summary of the kinds of verbs that have been discussed
so far:

V state <u>open</u>	The door is open.
V process <u>open + inchoative</u>	The door opened.
V state relative <u>wide</u>	The road is wide.
V process relative <u>wide + inchoative</u>	The road widened.
V process <u>break</u>	The dish broke.
V state <u>break + resultative</u>	The dish is broken.

The diligent reader may notice that rules (S11-3, 5) as they stand
create an endless loop which generates an infinite number of
monstrosities such as:

V
process
<u>open + inchoative + resultative + inchoative + resultative + inchoative</u>

(Such a result depends on the fact that the term *root* in these rules
covers—as it must—not only a simple verb root like *open*, but also
a derived combination like *open + inchoative*.) Since, as we shall see
in the next paragraph, there is reason not to stipulate that (S11-3,5)
cannot both be applied to the same root, the best way to avoid
this endless shuttling back and forth between states and processes
is probably through a stipulation which forbids the application
of (S11-5) to the immediate output of (S11-3) and vice versa. It
may be noted that if *inchoative* and *resultative* are actually opposite
polarities of the same derivational operation, then it is possible to
regard a combination like *inchoative + resultative* as equivalent to
zero, so that the application of (S11-3) and (S11-5) to each other's
outputs would be vacuous in any case.

11.6 **Absolutive and relativizer.** The matter to which we shall now turn requires that the reader exercise his introspective powers to their full capacity. The following sentences will serve as illustrations:

(13) a. The soup is hot.
      b. The soup is heating.
      c. The soup is hot.
      d. The soup is heating.
      e. The soup is heated.

Although some of these sentences have identical surface structures, the intended semantic structures of all five are different. Sentence (13a) expresses a relative state and is thus parallel to (1b), *The road is wide*. A continuum of temperature is involved. With this meaning of *hot* it is possible to say things like *The soup is very hot, The soup is hotter than the coffee*, and so on. The structure of the verb in this case is the following:

(13a) V
       state
       relative
       hot

Sentence (13b) is the inchoative derivation based on (13a), through the application to the latter of rule (S11-3). It is thus parallel to sentence (10b), *The road widened*. Its meaning can be paraphrased *The soup is getting hotter*. The structure of the verb is:

(13b) V
       process
       relative
       hot + inchoative

With (13c), however, we encounter a new phenomenon. Although its surface structure is identical to that of (13a), the meaning of (13c) is intended to be that which is roughly paraphrasable as *The soup has reached the intended temperature*. In other words, the verb in (13c) is no longer relative, as were those in (13a, b). Instead, there is an absolute goal of hotness which the soup is said to have attained, presumably the temperature at which the soup is ready to serve. It appears, then, that some intrinsically *relative* verb roots can be converted into nonrelative roots through the addition of a derivational unit I shall call *absolutive*. The rule can be stated as follows:

(S11-6) relative ⟶ root + absolutive
        root

If this kind of derivation is applied to the verb structure of (13a), it yields the following, which is hypothesized as the structure of the verb in (13c):

(13c) V
       state
       hot + absolutive

But a verb root which is subject to (S11–6) in its stative role will also be subject to it in its derived process role. That is, (S11–6) will apply not only to (13a) to yield (13c), but also to (13b) to yield (13d), whose meaning is intended to be that which is paraphrasable as *The soup is getting hot* (not *hotter*). The soup is approaching the temperature at which it is ready to serve. The structure of the verb in (13d) is thus:

(13d) V
       process
       hot + inchoative + absolutive

which is identical with that of (13b) except for the loss of *relative* through the addition of *absolutive*. We noted at the end of 11.5 that the resultative derivation, (S11–5), cannot be applied to the immediate result of (S11–3), that is, to a verb whose outer layer of derivation is inchoative. The outer layer of derivation in (13d), however, is not inchoative but absolutive, a fact which explains why (S11–5) can now be applied to it to produce (13e), even though, through a previous stage of derivation, *inchoative* is present. The structure of the verb in (13e) is the following:

(13e) V
       state
       hot + inchoative + absolutive + resultative

It may be observed that the meaning of (13e) is very similar, though not identical, to the meaning of (13c). It is interesting to see that (13e) differs from (13c) only in possessing both *inchoative* and *resultative,* whose combined effect on the meaning we would expect to be minimal. One other fact that should be pointed out is that the verb in (13c) seems eligible for the application of (S11–3), which would turn it into a derived process with the structure of (14).

(14)   V
       process
       hot + absolutive + inchoative

The only difference between (14) and the structure of (13d) is that the order of *relative* and *absolutive* is reversed. The distinction between the structure just given and that given for (13d) may be a meaningless one, in which case (S11-3) could be said to apply to (13c) in a vacuous manner. Alternatively, the absolutive derivation could be regarded as ordered to apply after the inchoative one. In this paragraph we have seen that an intrinsically relative verb root can be converted derivationally into one that is nonrelative. It would appear that it is also possible for an intrinsically nonrelative verb root like *deaf* or *red* to be converted derivationally into one that is relative, as in the sentences:

(15)   a. Roger is very deaf.
       b. Roger is deafer than Harry.
       c. The sky is very red.
       d. The sky is redder now than it was a moment ago.

Thus a rule like the following may also be valid:

(S11-7) state   ⟶   state
        −relative   relative
        root   root + relativizer

This rule is the reverse of (S11-6) in the same sense that (S11-5) was the reverse of (S11-3).

11.7   **Causative.** It is important that we consider also sentences of the following type:

(16)   a. Linda broke the dish.
       b. Linda opened the door.
       c. Linda is heating the soup.

Each of these sentences seems to contain as one part of it a configuration of process verb with patient, of the type already discussed:

(17)   a. The dish broke.
       b. The door opened.
       c. The soup is heating.

In addition, however, the sentences of (16) identify someone as the cause of the process, the instigator of the change. In other words, these sentences contain not only a patient but also an *agent*, and their verbs are not only processes but also *actions*. It seems correct to say, furthermore, that the processes—illustrated in (17)—are basic, and that the actions result from an added layer of derivation.

Thus we can posit another kind of derivation whose essential nature can be stated as follows:

(S11–8) process   ——→   process
          <u>root</u>   action
                           <u>root + causative</u>

Causative is a derivational unit similar to *inchoative*, but this time one that converts a verb root which is a process (either intrinsically or as the result of a prior derivation) into one that is derivatively both a process and an action. Such a derived verb will then require the accompaniment not only of a patient but also of an agent by rule (S9–5) of Chapter 9. The essential structure of (16a) can be diagramed as in (18).

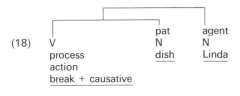

(18)
    V   pat   agent
    process   N   N
    action   <u>dish</u>   <u>Linda</u>
    <u>break + causative</u>

Here there is only one layer of derivation, the causative, but in (16b) this causative derivation is applied to a process verb whose root is already derived inchoatively. The structure of the verb in (16b) can thus be diagramed:

(16b)   V
          process
          action
          <u>open + inchoative + causative</u>

Sentence (16c) is actually ambiguous. Linda may be simply raising the temperature of the soup, making it *hotter*, or she may be raising the temperature toward the goal of servability, making it *hot*. In the first case the verb is relative, in the second case it is not. The first meaning exhibits a verb like that of (16b), with the addition of *relative*:

(16c–1) V
           process
           relative
           action
           <u>hot + inchoative + causative</u>

The second meaning shows an intervening *absolutive* derivation,

whereby the process has been made nonrelative prior to the application of the causative derivation:

(16c–2) V
process
action
hot + inchoative + absolutive + causative

It is worth noting that certain intrinsically stative verb roots—we
might take *deaf* as an example—cannot be converted into simple
processes but must be converted into action-processes, if they
undergo any derivation at all. That is, they cannot be made simply
inchoative but must be made both inchoative and causative. If
(S11–3) is applied to them, (S11–8) must be also, so that we cannot
say simply *Roger deafened* but must say something like *The explosion
deafened Roger*. This example demonstrates again that the behavior
of a particular verb root with respect to derivational rules often is
idiosyncratic and calls for special marking. At the end of 11.3 we
observed that some roots are immune to some rules, and now we
see that some roots require the application of a sequence of two
rules whenever the first of the two is applied.

11.8   We saw earlier that some verb roots are intrinsically states but,
through inchoative derivation, can be made into processes. Others,
intrinsically processes, through the resultative derivation can be
made into states. Most recently we have seen that either intrinsic or
derived processes, through causative derivation, can be made into
action-processes. The obvious question at this point is whether there
are also verb roots which are intrinsically action-processes. I believe
that sentences like the following provide evidence that there are:

(19)   a. Roger is cutting paper.
       b. Roger lifted the rock.
       c. Roger kicked the door.

That is, verb roots like *cut, lift,* and *kick* appear to be intrinsic
action-processes and to appear as such in these sentences. If so, the
essential structure of (19a) can be diagramed as in (20).

(20)
```
           ┌────────────────┐
      ┌─────────────┐       │
      │        pat       agt
      V         N         N
   process    paper     Roger
   action     ─────     ─────
   cut
   ───
```

The only reason for hesitancy here is the question whether the semantic relation between *cut* and *paper* in (19a) is the same as the relation between, say, *open* and *door* in *Roger is opening the door*. In the latter the causing of a change of state is apparent: Roger is "causing the door to become open," and the patient-state relation between *door* and *open* is clear. In (19a), in parallel fashion, it is possible to say that Roger is "causing the paper to become cut," but there seems to be more emphasis on the action of causing than on the ultimate result. Even so, we can say when Roger is finished that *The paper is cut*. I would suggest, therefore, that the difference in salience here between the action and the resultant state stems from the fact that *cut* is intrinsically an action-process while *open* is intrinsically a state. The verb root in (19a) is underived, as is the root in *The door is open*. The verb root in *The paper is cut*, however, is derived. This particular derivation is a common one, and there is nothing especially unusual about the sentence just quoted. On the other hand, if we consider the somewhat odd sentences *The rock is lifted* and *The door is kicked* with relation to (19b, c), we see that some verb roots which are intrinsically action-processes are converted less satisfactorily into states. The parallelism of all three sentences, nevertheless, is apparent and seems to justify us in regarding *paper, rock,* and *door* in (19) as, all three, patients of their respective verbs. If this view is correct, we can introduce verb roots like those in (19) with a rule like the following (replacing [S10–1d] in Chapter 10):

(S11–9) $\begin{bmatrix} \text{process} \\ \text{action} \end{bmatrix} \longrightarrow$ cut, lift, kick, ...

11.9 **Deactivative.** Sentences like those of (21) below suggest that, at least under limited circumstances, an intrinsically action-process verb root can be converted derivationally into one that is simply a process:

(21) a. The paper cuts easily.
b. The rock lifts easily.

Suppose we posit a new derivational unit *deactivative* which performs this function. The derivation in question can then be stated as:

(S11–10) process $\longrightarrow$ process
action   root + deactivative
root

Sentences like *The paper is cut,* mentioned in the preceding paragraph, can then be seen as the result of applying (S11-5), the resultative derivation, to the output of (S11-10). The structure of the verb in such a sentence is thus:

V
state
root + deactivative + resultative

The major derivational processes discussed so far, disregarding those which add or subtract the unit *relative*, are related to states, processes, and action-processes in the manner outlined in (22).

(22)

	inchoative		causative	
	$\longrightarrow$		$\longrightarrow$	
	(S11-3)		(S11-8)	
state		process		action-process
	resultative		deactivative	
	$\longleftarrow$		$\longleftarrow$	
	(S11-5)		(S11-10)	

11.10 **Deprocessive.** Figure (22) does not mention, and nothing has been said so far in this chapter concerning, a fourth major type of verb that was discussed in Chapters 9 and 10. I refer to verbs which are actions but not processes, and which therefore are accompanied by an agent but not by a patient. Verb roots like *laugh* and *dance* belong intrinsically to this type:

(23)   a. Roger laughed.
        b. Linda danced.

Such verb roots can be introduced by the kind of rule already cited as (S10-1c) in Chapter 10:

(S10-1c) $\begin{bmatrix} \text{action} \\ -\text{process} \\ -\text{ambient} \end{bmatrix} \longrightarrow$ laugh, dance, sing, . . .

In the present chapter, however, the question arises as to whether some verb roots which are not intrinsically of this type can be converted into it through derivation. It would appear, in fact, that this possibility is open to certain intrinsically action-process verb roots, as suggested by the sentences of (24) below. The point is that these verbs occur here without patients and thus are actions only:

(24)   a. Roger is cutting.
        b. Roger is lifting.
        c. Roger is kicking.

Verbs like these can be created with a derivational rule like the following:

(S11–11) process ——→ action
          action   root + deprocessive
          root

That is, a verb root which is intrinsically an action-process can be converted into one that is derivatively simply an action through the addition to it of the derivational unit *deprocessive*. It is interesting to observe that this deprocessive derivation can be applied only to a verb root which is *intrinsically* an action-process, not to one that has become an action-process through a prior causative derivation. We do not find sentences like the following:

(25)   a. *Linda is opening.
        b. *Linda is breaking.

The verb roots *open* and *break* are intrinsically a state and a simple process respectively. The causative derivation makes them action-processes, as in (16), but they are ineligible for further conversion into simple actions by means of (S11–11). Hence they are not found without a patient noun. It is necessary to stipulate, then, that (S11–11), the deprocessive derivation, cannot apply to the output of (S11–8), the causative derivation. Having now seen that intrinsic action-processes can be converted into derived simple actions, we might wonder whether there is an opposite kind of derivation which converts intrinsic simple actions into derived action-processes. Examples like the following might suggest that there is:

(26)   a. Roger laughed a hearty laugh.
        b. Linda danced the minuet.

Further reflection on the meanings of these sentences, however, may serve to dispel this idea, since the nouns *laugh* and *minuet* are evidently not related semantically to their respective verbs as patients. They are not said to be in a state or to have undergone a change of state. We shall return to sentences of this type in 12.7. If it is the case that these sentences do not qualify, and in fact that there is no way in which verb roots which are intrinsically simple actions can be converted into action-processes, the right side of (22)

(27)   deprocessive
        . . . action-process ————————→ action
                       (S11–11)

can be extended only in the fashion shown in (27), that is, in one direction only.

11.11 **Antonymy.** Two major topics which deserve more extended discussion than will be accorded here are the matters of antonymy and comparison. It is readily observable that most of the examples of intrinsically stative verb roots given above can be paired with corresponding antonyms, *wide* with *narrow, open* with *shut, hot* with *cold* . . . If the verb root is relative, its antonym indicates a reversal of direction along the continuum involved. Thus, to say *The road is narrow* is to say that the distance between its sides is below, rather than above, the norm determined by the patient *road.* If the verb root is not relative, its antonym indicates a state of not being in the condition involved. Thus, to say *The door is shut* is to say that it is not open. It seems to me likely that an antonym should be treated as derived from the basic verb root through the addition to the latter of a derivational unit which can be labeled *antonym.* The structure of *narrow* can then be formalized as *wide + antonym,* and so on. This formalization captures the fact that *narrow* is more "marked" than *wide,* as evidenced by the fact that we normally talk about a continuum of wideness or width, in contrast to the somewhat unusual alternative of talking about a continuum of narrowness. The well-known fact that *How wide is it?* is the usual question, rather than *How narrow is it?*, is another manifestation of the unmarked vs. marked character of *wide vs. narrow.*

11.12 **Comparison.** The other matter just mentioned was comparison, whereby we arrive at surface structure representations such as *wider, hotter,* and so on. Only enough will be said about this topic to enable us to discuss its relevance to a different issue that will be mentioned subsequently. Suppose we begin by considering the sentence:

(28)   The road is wider.

This sentence has no clear meaning as it stands. It is helpful to visualize its meaning in terms of a diagram such as was given for sentence (1b), *The road is wide,* at the very beginning of this chapter. Figure (29) is a repetition of that part of (4) which had to do with relative verbs, except that N is replaced by C. Sentence (1b) said

(29)   C   X
       ———————•———•———————

that the width of the road, represented by X, exceeds the norm for roads, represented by N. Sentence (28) says that the width of the road exceeds some point along the continuum of wideness; we might call this point the standard of comparison. It is represented in (29) by C. We can regard X in (29) as representing the width of the road at the time (28) is uttered, and C as representing the point which this width exceeds. What distinguishes (28) from (1b) is the manner in which the location of N and C are determined. In (1b) the location of N was determined by the patient *road*. In (28) the determination of C is left open; its position along the continuum is, as it were, movable. Hence the vagueness in (28) when this sentence is uttered in isolation; we do not know the location of C. How can C be pinned down? Its position can evidently be established through either the context or an explicit statement. If, for example, we have been driving along a road and I suddenly utter (28), the context makes it clear that C is the width of that part of the road which lies behind us. I am saying that the width of the part we are on now exceeds the width of the part we were on before. If, as another example, we have just returned after a long period of time to a once-familiar road on which some construction has been performed in the meantime and I now utter (28), the context makes it clear that C is the width of the road at the earlier time. I am saying that the width now exceeds the width then. Suppose, on the other hand, we had just been measuring both the road and the sidewalk and I utter (28)—this time probably with a higher pitch on *road* than in the earlier examples, for a reason which will be discussed in Chapter 15. In this context it would be clear that C is the width of the sidewalk, and that I am saying that the width of the road exceeds that of the sidewalk. It is often the case, however, that the context does not make clear the location of C on the continuum. If so, it is necessary to state explicitly where C is located, and that is done in English by means of a following clause beginning with *than*:

(30)   a. The road is wider than it was back there.
         b. The road is wider than it used to be.
         c. The road is wider than the sidewalk (is).

The initial clause of each sentence establishes that we are talking about the location of X along a specified continuum, and in particular that X exceeds some point C. The second clause, beginning with *than*, establishes the location of C. I shall assume here that there is a semantic unit *comparative* which is a derivational unit, and which may be added to a verb root that is intrinsically a relative state to produce a derived verb root that is like the one in (28) and (30):

(S11–12) state   ⟶   state
         relative   relative
         root   root + comparative

Comparative is unlike the derivational units so far discussed in that in itself it does not change any of the selectional units of the verb. Thus it is not impossible for a derived verb root to occupy the same semantic slot as the underived root on which it is based. Within a more detailed picture than that represented in (S11-12), however, *root + comparative* would be seen not to be interchangeable with a simple root of the same relative and stative type. We have already seen that a comparative verb depends on the establishment of a standard of comparison (C), either contextually or through the addition of another clause to the semantic structure. The same is not true, of course, of a noncomparative verb. Furthermore, most noncomparative states can be changed to processes through the inchoative derivation. Such a derivation is not possible for a comparative state and, in fact, we can make the general statement that once (S11–12) has applied, no further derivational rules can apply. Thus (S11–12) has the function of changing the nature of the verb root in significant ways, although this fact is not apparent as the rule is stated here.

11.13 **Paraphrases.** We cannot leave the subject of verb root derivation without considering the relationship between sentences like the following. They are examples of a widespread linguistic phenomenon, the fact that different surface structures may reflect meanings that are very similar if not identical:

(31)   a. The road widened.
        b. The road became wider.
        c. The road got wider.

Two views concerning these sentences are possible. One is that only a single semantic structure is present in all three. The surface differences are then explainable by positing an optionality in certain transformations. A description of English based on this view would aim toward a statement of English transformations such that different paths through them, resulting from certain optional choices, would lead to the three different surface structures. The other possible view is that three different semantic structures are present in (31). The extreme form of this view would hold that different surface structures *always* reflect different semantic structures, that there is never any such thing as complete synonymy or complete paraphrase. A less extreme position, such as I adopt here, is that different surface structures reflect identical semantic structures much less often than is customarily assumed, but that the situation is not ruled out on principle. There may well be some instances in which nothing more than the application or omission of a certain optional transformation accounts for a surface difference—instances where it may be valid to assert that no difference in semantic structure exists, even though there is a surface difference. I wish to suggest, however, that such is not the case with the sentences of (31), and that the semantic structures underlying these three surface structures are in fact different. Naturally this position carries the obligation to explain what the differences are, for unquestionably the meanings of these three sentences are very similar. What I shall suggest is that differences of two wholly distinct kinds are present. One kind of difference distinguishes (31a, b) from (31c); the other kind distinguishes (31a) from (31b, c). The first kind is what would usually be called a difference in "style." It seems to me that in normal, uninhibited, colloquial conversation I would hardly ever use either (31a) or (31b), but only (31c). Conversely, in writing, unless I were quoting a colloquial conversation, I would not normally use (31c). That is, the difference between (31a, b) on the one hand and (31c) on the other is simply the difference between what might be called *literary* and *nonliterary* style. Style, in this sense, is surely a semantic matter; it is part of what is communicated. We can say that a semantic unit *literary* is attached to the semantic structures of (31a, b), but that it is absent from the semantic structure of (31c). It may be the case that the only semantic difference between (31b) amd (31c) is this literary-nonliterary one, but the difference between these two sentences on the one hand and (31a) on the other is another kind of difference which it is necessary to discuss at greater length. To begin with, we may note that *become* (or *get*) is found in the surface structures of certain other sentences, for example:

(32)   a. The road became wide.
       b. The road became very wide.

Such possibilities suggest that *become* has a broader function than that of the *inchoative* unit exemplified in (31a), since the inchoative derivation cannot be used to produce anything parallel to the sentences of (32). One gains the impression that the range of uses of *become* simply happens to include one use whose meaning co-incides (more or less) with the meaning of (31a). How can we des-cribe this broader semantic function of *become*? Using the same type of diagram that was used in earlier figures in this chapter, we can represent the meanings of (31b) and (32a), as compared with the earlier (1b) and (28), in the manner of (33), where the arrows indicate entry into the condition represented by X.

(33)   (1b)   The road is wide.

       (32a) The road became wide.

       (28)   The road is wider.

       (31b) The road became wider.

Furthermore, the relation between *The road is very wide* and (32b), *The road became very wide*, is the same as that illustrated in (33) for the pair (1b)—(32a), except that in addition the location of X is understood to be relatively far from N. It is evident that the function of *become*—more properly, of the semantic unit reflected in the surface unit *become*—is to create a process from a state, a process which involves an entry into that state. The dashes to the left of N in the second line of (33) indicate that before the change the road may have been of normal or of less than normal width (it may have been *narrow*). The function of *become* is, then, similar to that of *inchoative*, and we might want to introduce it in a similar way:

(S11–13) state —→ process
        root   root + become

Become, however, differs from *inchoative* in that the range of roots to which it can be applied is much broader. While *inchoative* can be added perhaps only to an underived state, *become* can be regarded as a kind of outer layer of derivation which can be added with relative freedom to both simple and derived states. Thus, it can be added not only to *wide*, as in (32a), but also to the comparative result of the application of (S11-12), as in (31b), as well as to the intensive *very wide*, as in (32b), which is probably also the result of derivation. The meaning of *become* cannot be regarded as identical with the meaning of *inchoative*. We noted earlier that what *inchoative* does semantically is to convert a situation like that diagramed in the first line of (33) into a situation like that shown in (34), which is a repetition of (11b) above. That is, it converts a state in which X

(34)   W $\longrightarrow$ X
$$\underline{\hspace{3cm}\bullet\hspace{1cm}\bullet\hspace{2cm}}$$

is said to exceed a certain norm into a process in which X is said to change from one position to another along the continuum, without relation to a norm. That is not the meaning of *become*. Rather, *become* involves simply an entry into a state, of whatever kind. How does it happen, then, that (31a) and (31b), one with *inchoative* and the other with *become*, appear to have the same (or much the same) meaning? The answer should be apparent in a comparison of (34), which represents (31a), with the last line of (33), which represents (31b). Both sentences say that X comes to exceed some earlier point, either W or C, along the continuum of width. The meanings of the two sentences still would differ if the location of W and C differed. But evidently W and C are both points which, in these sentences, have a location no more exact than "a lesser degree of width than X." A more specific location for C can only be derived from the context, for example through a *than* clause:

(35)   The road became wider than the sidewalk.

No comparable device is available to (31a). But without such a clause, (31b) is no more specific than (31a), and both sentences consequently "say the same thing." The point is that the sameness here is not a sameness in the semantic units involved—or at least not in all of them—but a sameness in the final conceptual situation which results, the coincidence of the last line of (33) with (34). We have here, then, a detailed illustration of the point made at the end of Chapter 8: that different semantic structures may converge on a single meaning.

11.14 **Derivation based on noun roots.** Before we leave this chapter it is necessary to point out that derivation can be applied to noun roots as well as verb roots. That is, there are a number of derivational units which can be added to noun roots to produce noun roots of a different kind, or even to produce verb roots. For example, the noun root *beer* is intrinsically noncount. That is, its presence in a noun depends on the absence of the selectional unit count. One clue to the recognition of a noncount noun is the fact that it is not subject to being counted. Yet we find sentences like the following:

(36)   I ordered three beers.

Here it would seem that *beer* has been converted into a count noun through the addition of a derivational unit, to which the not entirely happy label *countizer* might be given. This possibility can be described as follows:

(S11–14) N   —→ N
         −count   count
         root   root + countizer

That is, a noun root which is intrinsically noncount can be converted into one that is derivatively *count* through the addition to it of the derivational unit *countizer*. The relevant structure of the noun in (36) can be diagramed as in (37).

(37)   N
        count
        beer + countizer

There are many rules of a similar kind that might be mentioned. For example:

(S11–15) animate —→ animate
         −human   human
         root   root + anthropomorphizer

This rule says that a root which is intrinsically animate but non-human may be converted into one that is derivatively human through the derivational unit *anthropomorphizer*. Nouns of the intrinsically animate but nonhuman type, listed above in (S10–7e), include *elephant*. If such a noun is anthropomorphized through (S11–15) it will be referred to as *he* (or *she*) rather than *it*. Furthermore it is subject to additional specification as *unique* by (S10–6), an option not available to it in its underived state. Semantic units which involve unique elephants can then be listed:

(S11–16) $\begin{bmatrix} \text{unique} \\ \text{elephant + anthropomorphizer} \end{bmatrix}$ —→ Jumbo, . . .

(It may be noted that *elephant* is here a classificatory noun; cf. 10.11.)

Thus we are able to explain the fact that pets and other animals which are given proper names are referred to as *he* or *she*, and not as *it*:

(38)   a. The elephant broke his leg.
       b. The elephant broke its leg.
       c. Jumbo broke his leg.
       d. *Jumbo broke its leg.

In (38a), but not in (38b), the elephant has been anthropomorphized by (S11–15). Only if it has been anthropomorphized can the elephant also be unique and thus specifiable in terms of lexical units like *Jumbo*. Thus, while (38c) is possible, (38d) is not. Other rules of a similar sort include:

(S11–17) a. human   ⟶   human
            −feminine   feminine
            <u>root</u>   <u>root + feminizer</u>

          b. feminine   ⟶   <u>root + defeminizer</u>
            <u>root</u>

By (S11–17a), for example, the intrinsically nonfeminine noun root *actor* is converted in the derivatively feminine noun root *actress*. In this case the derivational unit is reflected in the surface structure suffix which is symbolized *ess*. Feminizer does not always receive a symbolization, however. Probably it is also present in a sentence like *My neighbor killed herself*, where *neighbor*, being intrinsically nonfeminine, is also derivatively feminine by (S11–17a). An intrinsically feminine noun root like *nurse* may be converted into a derived root which is no longer feminine through the addition of *defeminizer*, as stated in (S11–17b).

11.15   A noun root can also be converted into a verb root:

(39)   a. Roger watered the lawn.
       b. Roger skinned the lion.

Instead of a single derivational unit *verbalizer*, there are probably several which perform this function, each of them restricted to a certain subset of noun roots. Thus, the noun root *water* can be converted into a derived verb root through the addition of a particular verbalizer which adds a meaning something like *apply to*: *Roger applied water to the lawn*. The noun root *skin*, on the other hand, is subject to verbalization through a different derivational unit, one which adds a meaning something like *remove from*: *Roger removed the skin from the lion.* Instead of one verbalizer, then, we might better speak of verbalizer$_1$, verbalizer$_2$, and so on. The formalization of the means by which derived verb roots like those in (39) are introduced into a semantic structure presents a special problem. A rule like (40) is apparently impossible, as the system for the formation of semantic structures has been developed so far:

(40)   N $\longrightarrow$ V
        root   process
                        action
                        root + verbalizer

The reason is that the generation of a sentence has been viewed as beginning with the verb, to which satellite nouns are eventually added after selectional and other units within the verb have been established. A rule like the above, however, suggests that nouns are established and provided with roots before derived verbs are formed from them. It would seem, therefore, that structures like (41), which

(41)   V
        process
        action
        water + verbalizer$_1$

might be posited for the verb in (39a), are better generated within the verb itself, perhaps by extending the rules which introduce verb roots to include those which are derived from noun roots:[2]

$$\begin{bmatrix} \text{process} \\ \text{action} \end{bmatrix} \longrightarrow \ldots, \text{noun root} + \text{verbalizer}_1, \ldots$$

The several ambient actions like *rain* and *snow*, originally introduced in Chapter 10 as simple verb roots by (S10–1f), are probably also derived from noun roots. I am assuming, with some justification from introspection as well as from a comparison of surface structures in various languages, that *rain*, *snow*, and the like are intrinsically noun roots. Rule (S10–1f), therefore, might be better stated as follows:

$$\begin{bmatrix} \text{action} \\ \text{ambient} \end{bmatrix} \longrightarrow \text{noun root} + \text{verbalizer}_3$$

[2]Actually, however, this situation is one of several which suggest that the ordered rule format for the generation of semantic structures—a format which I have retained from Chomskyan linguistics, where such rules are applied to the generation of base structures—is not in the end appropriate, and that it should be replaced by a set of statements expressing "well-formedness constraints." Cf. n. 2 in chap. 18, and the brief discussion of this alternative in 20.6.

where the noun roots which participate in this rule are limited to a few of the *rain* and *snow* type. In some languages the derivational unit *verbalizer₃* has a surface representation of one kind or another. It may, for example, be converted postsemantically into a full-fledged verb root.

11.16 **Predicate nouns.** A special kind of derivation is that which is involved in sentences like:

(42)   Roger is a student.

The verb in this sentence is a state. Its root is not some intrinsically stative verb root, however, but one that is derived from a noun. What is special is that, unlike the derived verb roots mentioned in 11.14 and 11.15, that in (42) is not derived from a noun *root* but from an entire noun, a noun which is subject to further specification in terms of other, nonlexical semantic units. For example, it is also possible to say *Roger is the student, Roger and Harry are students*, and so on. (This kind of further specification will be discussed in Chapter 14, and particularly in 14.15.) Apparently we must supplement rule (S10–1a), the rule in Chapter 10 which introduces nonambient states, as follows:

$$\begin{bmatrix} \text{state} \\ -\text{ambient} \end{bmatrix} \longrightarrow \ldots, \text{N} + \text{predicativizer}, \ldots$$

The noun which is thus introduced can then be further specified in the usual way (with certain restrictions occasioned by its peculiar environment). The verb in sentence (42), then, can be diagramed as in (43):

(43)   V
       state
       N + predicativizer
       count
       potent
       animate
       human
       student

12

Other Relations of Noun to Verb

12.1   I have tried to establish a picture of semantic structure in which the typical configuration is that of a central verb accompanied by one or more nouns, each of which stands in some particular semantic relation to the verb. The only noun-verb relations that have been mentioned so far have been those of patient and agent. These two, in fact, do appear to play a more fundamental role in semantic structure than any others, a role which is tied to the basic specification of a verb as a state, process, action, or action-process. They are, however, by no means the only relations which a noun can bear to a verb, and in this chapter we shall take a look at what some of the others might be. The suggestions below are hardly meant to be final or complete, but they may have some use as tentative hypotheses.[1] In attempting to formalize the semantic structures involved, I shall assume a classification of verbs into states, processes, actions, and action-processes as a starting point. Attention then will be given to how the new relations fit with these four types of verbs, and to what new specifications of verbs may also need to be posited.

12.2   **Experiencer.** Let us first consider sentences like the following:

(1)   a. Tom wanted a drink.
       b. Tom knew the answer.
       c. Tom liked the asparagus.

[1] This chapter owes a great deal to Fillmore 1968.

Although *Tom* in each of these sentences looks as if it were an agent from the point of view of surface structure (cf. *Tom cut the paper*), there seems good reason to say that it is not an agent. Tom is not the instigator of an action, not someone who did something. Rather, he is one who was mentally disposed in some way, one with respect to whose mental experience a drink was wanted, an answer known, or the asparagus liked. I shall say that the verb in sentences like these is an *experiential* verb, and that such a verb must be accompanied by a noun which, for want of a better term, I shall call the *experiencer*. The experiential verbs illustrated in (1) appear to be states, as suggested by the fact that they do not answer the question *What happened?* It is also true that they do not occur with the progressive specification; we would not normally say *Tom was wanting a drink* or the like. As is usual for states, each of them is accompanied by a patient noun (*drink, answer, asparagus*) in addition to the experiencer *Tom*. These nouns specify the object that is wanted, known, or liked. The following sentences suggest that experiental verbs are not limited to states but may be processes as well:

(2)   a. Tom saw a snake.
        b. Tom heard an owl.
        c. Tom felt the needle.
        d. Tom learned the answer.
        e. Tom remembered the answer.

Such sentences evidently involve events rather than states, since they appear to be acceptable answers to the question *What happened?* They seem not to involve actions, however, since (in the intended meaning) they do not say that Tom did something. Evidently, then, they qualify as processes. Again Tom is an experiencer, one whose mental disposition or mental processes were affected. Sentence (2a) might be roughly paraphrased *A snake became visible with respect to the experience of Tom.* It must be pointed out that some of these verbs do not readily accept the progressive specification in the way that process verbs normally do. It is odd to say *Tom was seeing a snake*, with Tom as an experiencer. I believe that this fact has to do with an incompatibility between the meaning of progressive (see 13.9 below) and the nature of sensory perception (including seeing, hearing, etc.), which is not conceived of as something that takes a certain amount of time for its accomplishment. Sentences (2d; e) call for special comment, in that their verb roots probably are to be regarded as derived from stative roots. In fact, both of these roots might be regarded as derived from a configuration containing *know*, as in (1b). The configuration *know + inchoative* then would be reflected in the surface item *learn*, while the surface item *remember* would reflect the addition of another layer of derivation, accomplished through a second derivational unit which might be labeled *again* or something of the sort. A natural question at this point is whether experiential verbs can be actions as well as states and processes. Sentences like these suggest that they can:

(3)   a. Harry showed Tom the snake.
      b. Harry taught Tom the answer.
      c. Harry reminded Tom of the answer.

All the examples of this kind that I am aware of, however, lend themselves to the hypothesis that they are causatively derived from processes of the kind illustrated in (2): in these examples, from (2a), (2d), and (2e), respectively. If we leave the generation of sentences like those in (3) to a derivational rule like (S11–8) in Chapter 11, it may be possible to say that only nonaction verbs are intrinsically experiential, a hypothesis which can be expressed as follows:

(S12–1) V   ⟶ experiential
        −action

Experiential verb roots can then be introduced by rules like:

(S12–2)
    a. $\begin{bmatrix} \text{state} \\ \text{experiential} \\ \text{−ambient} \end{bmatrix}$ ⟶ want, know, like, . . .

    b. $\begin{bmatrix} \text{process} \\ \text{experiential} \\ \text{−ambient} \end{bmatrix}$ ⟶ see, hear, feel, . . .

Another rule is needed to indicate that an experiential verb requires the accompaniment of a noun which is related to it as experiencer (abbreviated *exp*):

(S12–3)

        V   ⟶   V   exp
        experiential   experiential   N

The relevant aspects of the semantic structure of sentence (1a) can then be diagramed as in (4). Rule (S12–1) leaves open the possibility

(4)

		pat	exp
		N	N
V		drink	Tom
state			
experiential			
want			

that an experiential state may also be *ambient*, by rule (S9–3) in
Chapter 9. That is evidently the situation in sentences like:

(5)   Tom is hot.

Here no patient is present, but only the experiencer *Tom*. The sentence might be paraphrased *It's hot with respect to the experience of
Tom*. It contrasts with two homonymous sentences in which Tom
is the patient rather than the experiencer, and which mean either
that Tom's temperature is higher than the norm for humans or (very
improbably) that he is ready to be eaten, as in *The soup is hot* (11.6).
The relevant semantic structure of sentence (5) can be diagrammed as
in (6).

(6)

	exp
	N
V	Tom
state	
experiential	
ambient	
hot	

12.3   **Beneficiary.** To illustrate another relation of noun to verb we can
make reference to the following sentences:

(7)   a. Tom has (or Tom's got) the tickets.
        b. Tom has (or Tom's got) a convertible.
        c. Tom owns a convertible.

Obviously in these sentences Tom does not reflect a semantic agent,
any more than he did in the sentences of (1). On the other hand,
there are reasons for thinking that Tom is not an experiencer either.
No mental experience or disposition on Tom's part is involved in
these sentences. Instead, there is a kind of "benefactive" situation
in which Tom can be said (in a broad sense) to be the one who bene-
fits from whatever is communicated by the rest of the sentence.
I shall call the verb in such a sentence a *benefactive* verb, and the
noun which specifies the person benefited I shall call its *beneficiary*.
Aside from the apparent meaning difference between experiencer

and beneficiary, the hypothesis that the two relations are distinct is supported by the fact that some languages represent them in different ways in surface structure. In addition, we shall see presently that there are certain differences in semantic functioning which are best explained by assuming that experiencer and beneficiary are not the same. I stress this point because it has been suggested elsewhere that both relations can be subsumed under a heading such as "dative."[2] The meaning of (7a), then, might be paraphrased *The tickets are (in the state of being) in the temporary possession of Tom.* In many languages the surface structure of a benefactive sentence reflects this kind of semantic configuration more closely, as we find surface configurations literally translatable as *The tickets are to Tom* or the like. In any case, it would seem that *tickets* and *convertible* in (7) can be regarded validly as patients, as is normally required by stative verbs like these. We may note that the meanings of the verbs in (7b, c) are in one sense closer to each other than those of the verbs in (7a, b), although the surface structures do not reflect this fact. The following are possible paraphrases of the meanings of the verb roots in all three sentences:

(7a)   be in the transitory possession of
(7b)   be in the nontransitory possession of
(7c)   be the private property of

The distinction between nontransitory possession and private ownership is small. It might be suggested on the other hand that the verb roots in (7a, b) are identical and that the difference in the kind of possession is determined by a difference in the nature of the patients: tickets are normally possessed only temporarily while convertibles are possessed for a longer period. There are, however, many patients which can easily be imagined as possessed in either way (*Tom has a watch*, for example), where the ambiguity (he may simply be holding a watch or he may own one) has to be attributed to the verb. A thorough discussion of benefactive states would also have to take into account the important distinction between alienable and inalienable possession, but I shall pass over that subject here in order to turn to the question of whether benefactive verbs may be processes as well as states. The following sentences will serve to illustrate such a possibility:

[2] Fillmore 1968.

(8)   a. Tom lost the tickets.
        b. Tom found the tickets.
        c. Tom won the tickets.
        d. Tom acquired a convertible.

Here, as was not the case in (7), something happened; an event took place. The event was not, however, an action; Tom did not do something. It was simply a process, a change in the disposition of the patient (*tickets, convertible*). The process clearly seems to have been a benefactive one, with Tom again as the beneficiary. Some problem arises, however, in deciding whether the verbs in sentences like these are simple or derived. It is certainly plausible that *find*, as in (8b), should be considered the antonym of *lose*—the surface reflection of the semantic configuration *lose + antonym*. Its meaning is what we would expect as the meaning of *unlose*, if there were such a surface item. (There is a different verb root *find* whose meaning is similar to that of *discover*, but it is not the one intended in (8b).) More interesting is the verb root reflected in the surface item *acquire* in (8d). A case might be made for regarding it as an inchoative derivation from the verb root of (7b), *be in the nontransitory possession of*. If it is, however, there still remain simple verb roots like *lose* (not a game but an object) in (8a) and *win* in (8c) which are candidates for intrinsic processes of the benefactive type. Next we might consider whether there are verb roots which are intrinsically benefactive action-processes. The following sentences are relevant:

(9)   a. Mary bought Tom a convertible.
        b. Mary sold Tom a convertible.
        c. Mary sent Tom the tickets.
        d. Mary gave Tom the tickets.

Here *Mary* functions as an agent; she is someone who did something. The sentences are therefore actions. Since they contain a patient as well, they qualify as action-processes, and they are in addition benefactive. Are these simple verb roots, or are they derived? The verb root in (9b) perhaps can be regarded as the antonym of that in (9a). It is likely, moreover, that the verb root reflected in surface structure as *give*, as in (9d), is causatively derived, perhaps from an inchoative formation, but ultimately from the simple stative verb root in (7a), *be in the transitory possession of*, or from that in (7b), *be in the nontransitory possession of*. We are left, still, with *buy* and *send* as candidates for intrinsic action-processes of the benefactive kind. It may be recalled that no experiential verb root was discovered which qualified as an intrinsic action-process, so it may be that the existence of benefactive verb roots of this type is one of the things that distinguishes benefactive from experiential verbs. Assuming that there are no benefactive verbs which are simple actions rather than action-processes, we can provide for the specification of a verb as *benefactive* with the following rule:

(S12–4) V $\qquad$ →→ benefactive
$$\begin{Bmatrix} \text{state} \\ \text{process} \end{Bmatrix}$$
$-$ambient

This formulation allows a benefactive action-process but excludes from the benefactive category an action which is not also a process. The next step is to introduce the several types of verb roots which this rule allows:

(S12–5)

a. $\begin{bmatrix} \text{state} \\ \text{benefactive} \end{bmatrix}$ →→ have (7a), have (7b), own, . . .

b. $\begin{bmatrix} \text{process} \\ \text{benefactive} \end{bmatrix}$ →→ lose, win, . . .

c. $\begin{bmatrix} \text{process} \\ \text{action} \\ \text{benefactive} \end{bmatrix}$ →→ buy, send, . . .

Finally, we need a rule to indicate that a benefactive verb requires the accompaniment of a beneficiary noun (abbreviated *ben*):

(S12–6)

V $\longrightarrow$ V   ben
benefactive   benefactive   N

As one example of what these rules accomplish, we can diagram the relevant semantic structure of sentence (9a) as in (10). It may be noted that the surface structure of the sentence *Mary bought a*

(10)

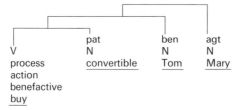

V   pat   ben   agt
process   N   N   N
action   convertible   Tom   Mary
benefactive
buy

convertible implies that she bought it for herself—that the beneficiary is identical with the agent. In such a case the beneficiary may be deleted postsemantically. The deletion is optional, however, since we may also say *Mary bought herself a convertible*. But what of sentences like these:

(11)   a. Mary knitted a sweater.
       b. Mary knitted Tom a sweater.
       c. Mary sang.
       d. Mary sang for Tom.

Several observations can be made. First, *Tom* seems to be a beneficiary in (11b, d), just as in the earlier sentences of this paragraph. Second, where no beneficiary appears in the surface structure, as in (11a, c), there is no reason to think that one was present in the semantic structure and subsequently deleted. In other words, (11a) is not like *Mary bought a convertible*, where a beneficiary identical with the agent is present semantically, since (11a) does not say whether Mary knitted the sweater for herself or for someone else. What we can conclude, I think, is that *knit* permits an optional beneficiary but need not have one. *Buy*, on the other hand, must always have a beneficiary, as was dictated by the rules above. It would appear that *sing*, too, may optionally be accompanied by a beneficiary, as in (11d). In fact, it may be correct to say that every action verb (whether it be a simple action or an action-process) can optionally have a beneficiary attached. In addition to rule (S12-6), therefore, which obligatorily adds a beneficiary noun to a verb which is intrinsically benefactive, we can also state a rule which will optionally add a beneficiary to any action verb:

(S12–7)
$$
\begin{array}{ccc}
 & & \overline{} \\
 & & \quad \text{ben} \\
\text{V} & \longrightarrow & \text{V}\quad\ \ \text{N} \\
\text{action} & & \text{action}
\end{array}
$$

A beneficiary noun will appear in surface structure as a subject so long as no agent is present, as in the sentences of (7) and (8). When an agent is present, as in the sentences of (9) and (11), a beneficiary will show up either as a noun directly following the surface structure verb, as in most of the examples given, or as a sentence-final noun preceded by the preposition *for*, as in (11d), an alternative which is possible for the other sentences as well. Which position it occupies depends largely on whether or not it conveys new information in the sentence, a matter to which we shall give some attention in Chapter 15.

12.4   **Instrument.** Another relation which a noun may bear to a verb appears to be that of instrument. There are various pecularities associated with this relation, not all of which will be accounted for in this discussion. Furthermore, what will be said here requires mention of a certain *inflectional* semantic unit. Such units have been awaiting detailed treatment in Chapters 13 and 14, but it will be necessary to mention one of them here. Our discussion can begin, however, in a simple way with the following sentences as illustrations:

(12)   a. Tom cut the rope with a knife.
       b. Tom opened the door with a key.

Knife and *key* in these sentences are certainly neither patients, agents, experiencers, or beneficiaries. Perhaps they seem to resemble agents most closely, since they have something to do with bringing about the change of condition which the sentences convey. Nevertheless, *Tom* is the real agent here; he is the one who did something. It might be thought that *with a knife* and *with a key* are simply adverbial elements tacked on to modify the verb. We shall see in Chapter 18, however, that such adverbial elements are normally derived from full-fledged verbs. Since we cannot say *N is with a knife* or anything of the sort, with N being specified in terms of some root, it is doubtful that *with a knife* is a verbal element. *Knife* and *key*, of course, are usually termed *instruments* in sentences like these, an instrument being some object which plays a role in bringing a process about, but which is not the motivating force, the cause, or the instigator. It is subsidiary to the agent—something which the agent uses. Let us, then, regard *instrument* as one of the possible relations between a noun and a verb. It differs noticeably from the relations *experiencer* and *beneficiary* in not being associated with a particular selectional unit within the verb. There is nothing parallel to *benefactive* or *experiential* which requires the verb to have an accompanying instrument. What *is* necessary, leaving aside certain instances to be mentioned shortly, is that the verb be specified as an action-process. Thus we can state the following optional rule:

(S12–8)

That is, an action-process verb optionally may be accompanied by a noun which is related to it as instrument (abbreviated *inst*). We may diagram the relevant semantic structure of sentence (12a) as in (13).

(13)

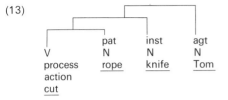

pat	inst	agt
N	N	N
rope	knife	Tom

V
process
action
cut

12.5   Although this fact may not be immediately apparent, sentence (12a)
is actually ambiguous. Its unmarked meaning, that accounted for
in the diagram just given, simply has to do with Tom changing the
condition of the rope, using a knife as an instrument. The sentence
may also mean, however, something which is paraphrasable as
Tom succeeded in cutting the rope with a knife. One has the impression
that there was some question as to how the rope could be cut, and
that Tom turned out to be able to do it with a knife. A similar
observation can be made for sentence (12b). It may have been the
case that attempts had been made to open the door in various ways,
and that Tom succeeded in doing it with a key. I shall account for
this additional possible meaning for the sentences in (12) by positing
the existence of a semantic unit which I shall label *successful*. In
considering how this unit should be introduced into a semantic
configuration it is necessary to observe that sentence (14) appears
not to have the ambiguity observed in the two earlier sentences:

(14)   The men widened the road with a bulldozer.

It would appear that this sentence has only the unmarked meaning,
and not one that might be paraphrased *The men succeeded in widening
the road with a bulldozer*. This and similar observations suggest that
the unit *successful* cannot be added to a verb which is specified as
relative, as is the case with *wide* (11.1). This conclusion makes
some sense if we think of the meaning of *successful* as involving the
achievement of some goal. A goal is present with a nonrelative
process but not with a relative one, where there is only a change from
one point to another along a continuum. The following rule
probably is not entirely adequate as a way to introduce this new
semantic unit, but it will serve our purposes here:

(S12–9)

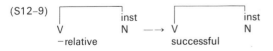

	inst			inst
V	N	—→	V	N
−relative			successful	

That is, a verb which is not specified as relative, but which does have an instrument noun attached to it, may be further specified as *successful*. However, *successful* is not a selectional unit like *state*, *process*, *experiential*, and the like, since it has nothing to do with the choice of a particular verb root. It can be added with apparent freedom to any verb which fulfils the specified conditions. It qualifies, therefore, as an inflectional unit, a type to which we shall turn our attention in the next chapter. In diagrams of semantic structure I shall list inflectional units below the verb (or noun) root. The alternative semantic structure underlying sentence (12a) is identical to that diagramed in (13), except that the verb is specified as in (15).

(15)   V
        process
        action
        <u>cut</u>
        successful

12.6   Now let us consider the following sentences:

(16)   a. The rope cut with a knife.
        b. The door opened with a key.

Two observations can be made. First, the verb in each of these sentences is a simple process, not an action-process as were the verbs accompanied by instruments discussed above. Second, these sentences are not ambiguous in the manner of the sentences of (12). The meaning which they have is not the unmarked meaning first discussed for the sentences of (12) but the alternative meaning accounted for by positing the additional semantic unit *successful*. That is, these sentences can be paraphrased *The rope was successfully cut with a knife*, and so on. What appears to be the case is that a verb specified as *successful* may be a process rather than an action-process, but that in order to be specified as *successful* a verb must be accompanied by an instrument. Sentences like those of (16) thus can be accounted for by adding the following rule to apply after rules (S12–8, 9):

(S12–10) $\begin{bmatrix} \text{process} \\ \text{action} \\ \text{successful} \end{bmatrix} \longrightarrow \begin{bmatrix} \text{process} \\ \text{successful} \end{bmatrix}$

That is, an action-process verb which is specified as *successful* optionally may be converted into a simple process verb. This rule must precede rule (S9–5) in Chapter 9 so that no agent will be added when it has applied. Since (S12–10) must follow the addition of an instrument by (S12–8), this sequence of rules suggests that not all nouns can be added to a verb at the same time; in particular, that an instrument is added well ahead of an agent. Rule (S12–10) has an effect similar to that of the *deactivative* derivational rule (S11–10) mentioned in the preceding chapter, but it seems to describe a somewhat different phenomenon. The relevant structure of sentence (16a) can be diagramed as in (17). A question arises as to whether

(17)

	pat	inst
V	N	N
process	rope	knife
cut		
successful		

sentences like the following have essentially the same semantic structure as those in (16):

(18)   a. The knife cut the rope.
       b. The key opened the door.

Perhaps the main difference between (18a) and (16a), for example, has to do with the distribution of new and old information (chap. 15). There are, on the other hand, sentences whose surface structures are much like those of (18), but whose meanings do not suggest the presence of the semantic unit *successful*, a unit which seems obligatory for sentences like those of (16):

(19)   The rock broke the window.

I am not entirely convinced, however, that *rock* in (19) is a semantic instrument; it seems to me at least likely that this noun is an agent. The noun root *rock* is not intrinsically *potent* and is not, therefore, normally eligible to occur within an agent noun (10.9), but it may be that any such noun can be given a derivative potency under circumstances like those imaginable for (19). I might mention in closing this brief discussion of instrument nouns that there are some sentences, for example *He jumped with a pole*, which suggest that rule (S12–8) sometimes does apply to a simple action verb, one which is not simultaneously a process. It does not do so regularly, however, and no attempt was made to account for this exceptional possibility in the rules above.

12.7   **Complement.** So far in this chapter we have considered the noun-
verb relations *experiencer*, *beneficiary*, and *instrument*. Nouns of all
three kinds share the property that they are at least sometimes
reflected as surface structure subjects:

(20)   a. Tom wanted a drink.
        b. Tom has the tickets.
        c. The knife cut the rope.

In (20a) the subject is an experiencer, in (20b) a beneficiary, in (20c)
an instrument. Surface structure *objects* in the examples which have
been given have all been assumed, tentatively at least, to reflect
semantic patients. It is doubtful, however, that the objects in the
following sentences should be so regarded:

(21)   a. Mary sang a song.
        b. The children played a game.
        c. Tom ran a race.
        d. The infantry fought the war.

Here the verb describes a certain action which, by its very nature,
implies the coexistence of a certain nominal concept. Singing, for
example, implies a song; playing implies a game. It is typical of cases
of this sort that the verb involves an action which causes something
to come into being—which creates something. The noun in question
then specifies what it is that is created: a rendition of a song, an
instance of a game, etc. In these cases I shall say that the verb is
completable and that the noun is its *complement*.[3] In using the latter
term I run the risk of engendering confusion because of the frequent
use of the term in other ways. It seems to me to be the ideal term
for this kind of noun, however, and there is a certain overlap
between this and other uses it has had. The relation of complement
appears to be quite distinct from that of patient, although the
surface representations of the two are identical in most languages
(just as are the surface representations of agent and experiencer).[4]
A complement noun does not specify something that is in a state
or that changes its state. It completes or specifies more narrowly the
meaning of the verb. It is important to realize that a complement
may involve a narrower specification than is evident from the
examples in (21):

[3] Equatable, mutatis mutandis, with Fillmore's "factitive case."
[4] Hockett 1958:235 implies that in Georgian the patient-complement distinction *is*
reflected in the surface structure.

(22)   a. Tom sang "The Star Spangled Banner."
         b. The children played touch football.

Here the complements are narrower specifications of *song* and *game* respectively, the latter functioning as classificatory nouns (10.11). Perhaps the nouns at the end of the following sentences should be regarded as complements also:

(23)   a. Tom won a television set.
         b. Tom read *War and Peace*.

Here *television set* is a narrowing down of a broader concept like *prize*, the broadest complement of *win*. *War and Peace* is a similar narrowing of a concept like *reading matter*, the broadest possible complement of *read*. So far the examples all have contained action verbs, but perhaps the following illustrate complements of states:

(24)   a. The book weighs a pound.
         b. The candy costs ten cents.

It would seem that *weigh* must be accompanied by a complement expressing a *weight*, *cost* by a complement expressing a *price*.

12.8   Certain states, then, require complements, while certain actions may have them optionally, as in (21), (22), and (23). At the moment I know of no process verb which is accompanied by a complement, either obligatorily or optionally. The fact that a nonprocess verb may optionally be specified as completable can be stated as follows:

(S12–11)   V
           $_{-process}$ $\longrightarrow$ completable

The relevant lexical units can then be introduced with rules like these:

(S12–12)
   a. $\begin{bmatrix} state \\ completable \end{bmatrix}$ $\longrightarrow$ weigh, cost, measure, . . .

   b. $\begin{bmatrix} action \\ completable \end{bmatrix}$ $\longrightarrow$ sing, play, win, . . .

It is then necessary to state that a completable verb either may or must be accompanied by a complement noun (to be abbreviated *comp*):

(S12–13)
           V $\longrightarrow$ V   comp
           completable   completable   N

Further study is necessary to determine the circumstances under which this rule is obligatory. Perhaps, for one thing, it is obligatory for all completable states; we can say *The book weighs a pound* but not *The book weighs*. In addition, however, it appears to be obligatory for actions of the *make* variety; we can say *He made a table* but not *He made* (cf. 17.3). For other actions, however, it is optional, since *He sang the Marseillaise* and *He sang* are equally possible. Once a semantic configuration containing a complement noun has been established, one further fact must be accounted for. It is apparent that the noun root which may occur within a particular complement noun is severely limited by the verb root. In fact, a completable verb root may dictate the presence of one and only one particular noun root in its complement—as *sing* dictates *song* and *play* dictates *game*—although that noun root may optionally, as a classificatory noun, go on to be more narrowly specified—as *game* may be further specified as *chess*, *tennis*, or *football*. It seems impossible to avoid the need for a large number of rules of the following type:

(S12–14)   comp
          a. N   ⟶⟩ song/V
                          sing

              comp
          b. N   ⟶⟩ game/V
                          play

Presumably each such rule could be included in a dictionary as part of the entry for each completable verb root. As an example of the kind of semantic structure that has been posited for a sentence containing a complement, diagram (25) can be suggested for sentence (22a), *Tom sang "The Star Spangled Banner."*

(25)

V	comp N	agt N
action	song	Tom
completable	Star Spangled Banner	
sing		

12.9   **Location.** The last relation between noun and verb that I shall discuss here is that which can be labeled *location*. We may take the following sentences as illustrative:

(26)   a. The knife is in the box.
       b. The cat is on the roof.
       c. The key is under the rug.

The suggestion I shall make about such sentences is that they contain state verbs which are further specified as *locative*, and that a verb which has been so specified is accompanied by a noun which bears to it the relation of *location*. In these examples the location noun is specified lexically as *box*, *roof*, and *rug*. Thus the semantic structure of sentence (26a) can be diagramed, in its relevant aspects, as in (27). A reason for placing the location noun closer to the verb

(27)

```
        ┌───────────────┐
  ┌─┐   │       │
  │     loc     pat
  V     N       N
  state box     knife
  locative ───
  in
```

than the patient will be given in 15.4. Rules for the formation of such a semantic structure are easily stated. First it is necessary to allow a state to be specified optionally as locative:

(S12–15) state ——→ locative

Then we can provide for the introduction of locative verb roots, essentially the list of what are usually thought of as locative "prepositions":

(S12–16) locative ——→ in, on, under, . . .

Finally, it must be stated that a locative verb requires the accompaniment of a location noun (abbreviated *loc*):

```
                      ┌───────────┐
                      │           loc
(S12–17)  V    ——→   V           N
          locative   locative
```

The result is the kind of surface structure diagramed for sentence (26a) above. It runs counter to traditions based on the study of surface structure to consider *in* a verb root, as in fact it does to consider *wide* a verb root, as we did earlier. In the surface structure of English and many other languages, *in* is traditionally regarded as a preposition and *wide* as an adjective. Both are typically preceded by forms of *be*, which plays the surface role of verb: *The knife is* in the box, The road *is* wide. This *be*, however, is surely not the *semantic* verb root in such sentences. Its function is to carry the tense and other inflectional units originally attached to roots like *in* and *wide* because the latter, as surface items in English, are incapable of being so inflected. In addition, we find in English surface phrases like *the knife in the box* and *the wide road* where *be* is not present and *in* and *wide* appear to be outside the context of verbs altogether. As many readers may realize, however, phrases like these are readily explainable on the basis of semantic structures in which *in* and *wide* again are verb roots. Structures of this type will be discussed in Chapter 18. It is significant to observe that there are languages in which such items do appear in surface structure in the form of verbs, not prepositions or adjectives. Iroquois. languages, for example, one of which was used for illustrative purposes in Chapter 4 and will be met again in Chapter 17, have verb roots translatable as *(be) in* and *(be) wide* whose surface representations are like those of other verb roots in the language. Thus, for example, the Onondaga word *wá·ta* "(it) is in" is not different in surface form from other verbs.

12.10   To return to our general discussion of locative verbs and their accompanying location nouns, we can recall that only locative *states* have so far been accounted for. Is it possible for verbs which are not states to be locative? Sentences like the following appear to communicate locative processes:

(28)   a. Tom fell off the chair.
         b. The ship sank into the sea.

That processes are involved is evidenced by the fact that these sentences are possible answers to the questions *What happened to Tom?* and *What happened to the ship? Chair* and *sea* seem to be location nouns. Perhaps, then, we should consider the verb roots in these sentences to be the locative processes *fall off* and *sink into.* Other sentences suggest that there are locative actions:

(29)   a. Tom sat in the chair.
         b. Tom crawled under the table.

These are surely actions; for example, they answer the question *What did Tom do?* The nouns *chair* and *table* appear to specify locations, and the verb roots might be considered to be the locative actions *sit in* and *crawl under.* Furthermore, many sentences contain what seem to be locative action-processes:

(30)   a. Tom threw the knife in(to) the box.
       b. Tom placed the book next to the telephone.

Here we have a patient *(knife, book)*, an agent (*Tom*), and a location
(*box, telephone*), and the verb roots might be thought to be the
locative action-processes *throw in* and *place next to*. There is
something special about all the verb roots hypothesized for (28–30),
however. They all seem to consist—not only in surface structure
but also semantically—of the verb roots *fall, sink* (processes), *sit,
crawl,* (actions), and *throw, place* (action-processes), combined in
some way with the locative verb roots *off, in(to), under,* and *next to*.
Each verb root of the first type (with the possible exception of *place*)
may also occur unaccompanied by a location:

(31)   a. Tom fell.
       b. Tom sat.
       c. Tom threw the ball.
          etc.

It seems possible, therefore, that there are no nonstative verb
roots which are intrinsically locative; that rule (S12–15) is correct
in its implication that only state verbs can be so specified. What the
sentences in (28–30) seem to show is that some verb roots which are
not states, and which cannot, therefore, be intrinsically locative,
can nevertheless be converted into locative verb roots derivationally.
Perhaps even stative verb roots which are not intrinsically locative
may be subject to this kind of derivation:

(32)   a. Tom is sitting.
       b. Tom is sitting on the table.

Sit is evidently a state in this kind of sentence, in spite of the fact
that it may occur in the progressive form, and (32b) is then an example
of a derived locative state. The derivation of locative from nonlocative roots can be described with the following rule:

(S12–18) V   ⟶ V
          −locative   locative
          root   root + locativizer

That is, a verb which is not inherently locative (whether it is a state
or a nonstate) may be converted optionally into a verb which is
locative through the addition to the verb root of a derivational

unit labeled *locativizer*. The nature of *locativizer*, however, makes this kind of derivation different from any encountered earlier. *Locativizer* is not a single semantic unit like *inchoative* or *causative*, but a class of units, any one of which will perform the same locativizing function. What is particularly worth noting is the membership of this class. It consists apparently of the various locative states, those verb roots introduced in (S12–16) and usually thought of as prepositions. Such verb roots are, then, genuinely different from other verb roots insofar as they perform two distinct roles within semantic structure: they may occur as independent locative states, as in the sentences of (26), or they may occur as derivational units attached to nonlocative verb roots, as in sentences (28–30). The result in the latter case is a derived verb root which is locative, and which is therefore subject to the accompaniment of a location noun in accordance with (S12–17). (The derivational rule [S12–18], of course, must be applied before [S12–17].) By this view the structure of (29b), to pick an example at random, can be diagramed as in (33).

(33)

	loc	agt
V	N	N
action	table	Tom
locative		
crawl + under		

12.11 It is important to realize that there are many sentences whose surface structures are parallel to those in (28–30) but whose semantic structures are of a quite different sort. Perhaps this fact is demonstrated most easily by presenting a few sentences which are clearly ambiguous, one meaning being explainable on the basis of the derivational rule (S12–18), the other not:

(34)   a. Tom fell in the kitchen.
       b. Mary danced under the tree.
       c. Tom threw the ball behind the house.

The meaning of (34a) which is explained by (S12–18) is that in which the preposition alternatively might be *into*. Perhaps Tom had been walking above the kitchen on a weak floor. This sentence might be an answer to the question *What did Tom fall in(to)?* The verb root is *fall + in(to)*. The other meaning is that in which Tom was in the kitchen when he fell. This sentence does not answer the question *What did Tom fall in(to)?* but rather *Where did Tom fall?* Its semantic structure actually contains two separate verb roots, one of which is the process *fall* and the other the locative state *in*. Discussion of semantic structures of this kind will be reserved for Chapter 18. Exactly the same kind of ambiguity obtains in (34b, c). These sentences may contain the derived verb roots *dance + under* and *throw + behind*, as allowed by (S12-18), or they may contain simply *dance* and *throw*, with *under* and *behind* not serving as locativizers but as locative states in their own right. It is of interest to observe that some languages give different surface treatment to the location noun, placing it in a different case according to whether the locative verb is an underived, intrinsically locative state or a derived nonstate, resulting from a rule like (S12-18). Thus, German uses the dative case in the first situation, the accusative case in the second. There are, obviously, many further details which are relevant to a more complete picture of locative verbs and their location nouns. I shall close the discussion here, however, by raising one last question. Is rule (S12-17), the rule which says that a locative verb must be accompanied by a location noun, correctly stated as obligatory, or should it be optional? The question arises from sentences like the following:

(35)   a. The key is inside.
        b. The key fell in(side).
        c. Tim crawled under(neath).
        d. Tim threw the key in(side).

It seems to me that such sentences may illustrate, not that a location noun may be missing from semantic structure, but that it may be deleted postsemantically from sentences in which its lexical specification is already known to the hearer from the context. None of the surface structures in (35) could be uttered unless the lexical specification of the location noun were already established. The speaker assumes in (35a), for example, that the hearer knows what it is that the key is in. I am inclined to believe, therefore, that rule (S12-17) is correct in making a location noun obligatory for a locative verb so far as semantic structure is concerned.

12.12   It may be helpful to provide a brief summary at this point of the various relations of noun to verb which were discussed in this chapter and in Chapter 9. These relations, not necessarily all that exist, were seven in number and included *patient, agent, experiencer, beneficiary, instrument, complement,* and *location*. The relations of patient and agent have a fundamental character which is lacking in the others. Every sentence contains a patient or agent noun, if not both, unless the verb is in the exceptional *ambient* category. Six of these relations—all but instrument—are determined by the presence within the verb of a certain selectional unit. A state or process verb dictates the presence of a patient noun. An action verb dictates an agent noun. An experiential verb calls for an experiencer, a benefactive verb a beneficiary, a completable verb a complement, and a locative verb a location. An instrument noun depends basically on the presence of an action-process verb, although such a verb does not require the accompaniment of an instrument; it is possible for *action* to be deleted if the verb is further specified as *successful*. These various selectional units within the verb can cooccur in somewhat complex ways that have been at least partially described, so that several different types of nouns may be attached to a verb at the same time. The question might well be raised at this point whether it is not uneconomical to posit the existence of selectional units like *experiential* within a verb, at the same time that we posit relations like *experiencer* as existing between a noun and the verb. Is it not redundant to treat the selectional unit and the relation which depends on it as separate items? It should be remembered that selectional units of this kind have two distinct functions. One is to dictate the presence of a noun related to the verb in a certain way. The other is to limit the choice of a lexical unit within the verb. Thus, a verb which has been specified selectionally as experiential is not only accompanied by an experiencer noun but is also limited to certain verb roots such as *want, know, see,* and so on. It might be suggested that a different procedure would be more economical in arriving at the kinds of semantic structures with which we are concerned. A verb might be allowed to be accompanied by any random combination of related nouns at the outset, before anything was specified regarding the internal content of the verb. Thus, one verb might have a patient, agent, and beneficiary, another a patient and experiencer, etc. When we came to the lexical specification of each verb, we could then say that a verb which has an experiencer attached to it can only contain a verb root like *want, know, see,* where, in effect, the statement "has an experiencer attached" replaces the statement "is selectionally experiential."[5] It is not clear, however, that this alternative is any more economical than that

[5] Cf. Chomsky 1965:93ff.

which has been proposed here. It seems, in fact, to do no more than replace the selectional unit *experiential* with another item, equivalent to a selectional unit, *experiencer attached*. The two alternatives might be diagramed as in (36). The choice of the root is then

(36)

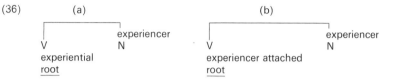

determined in identical fashion by either *experiential* or *experiencer attached*. One might argue that in (b), *experiencer* and *experiencer attached* are not two different semantic items but one and the same item with a relevance in two different places in the structure. But, it seems to me, one could with equal justification argue that *experiential* and *experiencer* constitute one semantic item, but one that has a dual relevance. Ultimately, then, the question raised here, for which I offer a solution opposite to that advocated by other linguists, rests on what determines what: does the nature of the verb determine the presence and relation of nouns, or does the presence and relation of nouns determine the nature of the verb? Throughout this work I take the position that the verb is the control center of a sentence, determining by its own internal specification what the rest of the sentence will contain—not completely, of course, but to a significant degree. I gave some reasons for this approach in 9.4, and will point out others below. In the context of the present chapter there is a further argument which seems to support this position. It will be recalled that both state and process verbs normally require the accompaniment of a patient. There is not, in other words, as there is in the case of experiencer, a single selectional unit within the verb that is always present when a patient noun is present. Suppose we were to start with nouns and let them determine the content of the verb. When there was a patient noun we would say that the verb was specified as *patient attached*. This specification, however, would not be equivalent to any specification suggested in this work, in the way that *experiencer attached* would be equivalent to *experiential*. It would still be necessary to specify whether the verb was a state or a process, for the ramifications of these two selectional units are many and varied, and much else in the verb and in the sentence depends on knowing which of these two specifications the verb has. That is, *patient attached* would have to be supplemented by the *state* or *process* specification in any case, and this specification is one that can only be made within the verb itself. But if we begin within the verb and make this specification there, we have no need for an additional selectional unit like *patient attached*; this specification is superfluous. It is enough to say that either a state or a process is accompanied by a patient noun, as was said in rule (S9–4). This kind of situation, then, adds support to our general hypothesis that the verb and not the noun is the controlling factor.

13

The Inflection of a Verb

13.1 Not only is a verb or noun specified in terms of certain selectional units and some particular lexical unit (perhaps a derived one), it may also be specified in terms of one or more *inflectional* units. As we have seen, the selectional units of a verb have two distinct functions. Operating outside the verb, they dictate the presence of accompanying nouns. Operating inside the verb, they limit the choice of a lexical unit, or verb root. In this latter function they can be thought of as narrowing the conceptual field within the verb until a lexical unit finally pins down the most specific concept of all. Once a lexical unit has been chosen, the selectional units that led to that choice are redundant, for each lexical unit implies by its own presence the concurrent presence of a certain combination of selectional units. The lexical unit *buy*, for example, implies the presence of the selectional units *process*, *action*, *benefactive*, and no doubt others. It is probably because selectional units are predictable, given a certain lexical unit, that usually they are not reflected overtly in the surface structure of a language. That is, units like *process* are not represented by prefixes or suffixes attached to a surface structure verb, or in some similar way. A verb or noun may also be specified, however, in ways that do not limit the choice of a lexical unit. Semantic units may be added to it whose presence *cannot* be predicated, given a certain lexical unit. For example, a verb, in addition to being specified as *process*, *action*, *benefactive*, and finally as *buy*, may also be specified as *past*. The presence or absence of *past* has nothing to do with limiting the choice of the lexical unit, nor does the presence of the lexical unit *buy* say anything about whether or not *past* is also present. It is semantic units like *past* to which I shall give the name *inflectional*. Inflectional units, then, do not influence the choice of a lexical unit, and are not redundant if the lexical unit is known. Typically, though not always, they have some overt surface structure representation.

13.2   One of the manifestations of the primacy of the verb in the semantic structure of a sentence is the fact that the inflection of a verb can as well be considered the inflection of the entire sentence, as mentioned in 9.4. Whether a verb is *past* or the entire sentence built around it is *past* is fruitless to ask. The verb in a sense *is* the sentence; whatever affects the verb affects the sentence as a whole. As we discuss the inflection of a verb in this chapter, therefore, it can be kept in mind we could be discussing just as well the inflection of a sentence. Recently there has been a spate of works dealing with the English verb, and particularly with those aspects of it which here I am calling inflectional.[1] At this point I could attempt to bring all the relevant factors discussed in those works—as well as other factors left undiscussed in them—within the framework being developed here. To do so, however, would mean replacing this chapter with a presentation rivaling in length the entire book. Hence, I shall do no more than indicate the general manner in which I think the inflection of a verb might be handled, at the same time providing illustrations of several inflections which are of particular importance to the English verb.

13.3   **Generic.** Many inflectional units receive some kind of surface structure representation, but the one we shall consider first does not. Perhaps, it might be surmised, this fact is attributable to the relatively late development of this semantic unit in language history, for its usefulness lies in the communication of abstract generalities. However that may be, it is an inflection of considerable importance in the English language, and one that is crucial to the discussion of noun inflection in Chapter 14. We can begin with the following illustrative sentences:

[1] E.g., as a far from complete list, Juilland and Macris 1962, Diver 1963, Joos 1964, Palmer 1965, Ehrman 1966, Allen 1966.

(1)   a. Bob sings.
        b. Bob opens the door.
        c. The door opens.

I believe the reader will easily recognize that surface structure (1a) is ambiguous. It may, on the one hand, be a stage direction or an on-the-spot reporting of a contemporaneous event. In such a case the event is a single, transitory occurrence. On the other hand, the meaning may be that of a general statement, more or less equivalent to *Bob is a singer*. In such a case no single, transitory event is communicated but rather a timeless propensity for an indefinite number of events to take place. The same kind of ambiguity can be observed in (1b). The sentence may be a stage direction, for example, or it may indicate that Bob regularly functions as the doorman. Similarly, in (1c) a single event may be involved, or a timeless propensity for the door to open. The first kind of meaning observable in each of these sentences, that which involves a transitory event, I shall assume to be inflectionally unmarked. The other kind of meaning, that of a timeless propensity, I shall explain in terms of the presence of a semantic unit *generic*, which is an inflectional unit. Although some verb roots may occur more often generically, others more often nongenerically, I suspect that it may be correct to say that the generic inflection may be added optionally to any verb that is not a state, as well as to any verb that is experiential or benefactive regardless of whether it is a state or not:

(S13–1) V $\longrightarrow$ generic
         $\left\{ \begin{array}{l} -\text{state} \\ \text{experiential} \\ \text{benefactive} \end{array} \right\}$

In diagrams of semantic structure an inflectional unit will be placed below the underline which identifies a lexical unit, whether verb root or noun root. The line under a lexical unit, therefore, now can be regarded as functioning to separate the units which are lexically relevant (selectional units plus the lexical unit itself) from those which are not (inflectional units). The two different semantic structures which underlie the surface structure (1c) can be diagramed as in (2). The fact that rule (S13–1) introduces an inflectional unit

(2)   V   V
        action   action
        sing   sing
                      generic

can be indicated by ordering it (and the other rules presented in this chapter) to apply after the rules which introduce lexical units, or in some other appropriate way.

13.4   What, now, of state verbs that are not experiential or benefactive? Do they also have the option of being either generic or nongeneric? At the beginning of Chapter 11 we were able to identify two different kinds of state verbs, nonrelative and relative, exemplified respectively by:

(3)   a. The door is open.
        b. The road is wide.

It would seem that for such state verbs the nongeneric vs. generic distinction is correlated with the nonrelative vs. relative one; in other words, a nonrelative state as in (3a) is necessarily nongeneric, a relative state as in (3b) necessarily generic. Some justification of this assertion is called for. On the basis of what was said above concerning nongeneric and generic verbs, we would expect a nongeneric state to be a transitory one, a generic state to be timeless. This distinction does appear in the sentences of (3), where the non-relative state *open* is normally temporary, while the relative state *wide* is not. We might guess that the transitory nature of a non-relative state results from the fact that the "ending-point" associated with such a state is not normally a permanent condition. In (3a) the door is understood to be open at the moment but, at least potentially, to be in a different state at other times. The same is not true of a relative state like *wide*, which is not conceived of as being transitory. Various kinds of more specific evidence can be called upon to confirm the nongeneric nature of (3a), the generic nature of (3b). Most convincing, perhaps, is that evidence which stems from the different effects which nongeneric and generic verbs have on accompanying nouns, a subject to be discussed in detail in Chapter 14. Under certain conditions a generic verb is accompanied by a noun which indicates the entire class of objects specified by the noun root. Under these conditions a nongeneric verb, on the other hand, is accompanied by a noun which indicates only some particular object or objects. Thus, when (4a) has the generic meaning, the noun refers to any bird whatsoever; when it has the nongeneric (stage direction) meaning, the noun refers to one particular bird:

(4)   a. A bird sings.
        b. A door is open.
        c. A freeway is wide.

If we look at the other two sentences of (4), the ambiguity of the noun in (4a) is not paralleled. In (4b) reference is to one particular door, confirming the nongeneric meaning for the verb in that sentence. In (4c), on the contrary, reference is to any freeway whatsoever, confirming the generic quality of the verb. If, then, we accept the observation that (3b) is necessarily generic, what may be called for is a rule which specifies that a relative state must be so inflected:

(S13–2) V   ⟶⟶ generic
        state
        relative

This rule, together with (S13–1), will place *generic* obligatorily or optionally in its proper semantic environments. Neither rule, it should be noted, allows a nonrelative state to be inflected as generic unless it is either experiential or benefactive.

13.5 **Perfective.** A different inflection of the English verb, one which, unlike *generic*, does have a clear surface structure reflection, can be illustrated with the following:

(5)   a. Bob has sung.
        b. Bob has opened the door.
        c. The door has opened.
        d. The door has been open.

The inflectional unit which these sentences exemplify traditionally has been called *perfective* (or *perfect*). Its meaning has always seemed difficult to characterize, and a variety of suggestions have been offered by different scholars. The fact that, under certain circumstances, it may or may not occur together with the semantic unit which I have called generic has been the cause of some confusion. Because *generic* has no surface representation, some perfective surface structures are ambiguous; they may be either generic or not. This is true of at least (5a, b) above. It is probably best to consider first the meaning of nongeneric perfective sentences. The easiest place to start may be with sentence (5d), since its meaning seems clear. The verb is a state and, as usual, the patient is said to be in that state at the time of reference. In this and the other sentences of (5) we may take the time of reference to be the moment when the sentence is uttered. How, then, does the perfective sentence (5d) differ in meaning from the corresponding nonperfective sentence *The door is open*? The difference seems to be that in (5d) it is understood that the door began to be open at some time prior to the time of reference. The perfective inflection adds the meaning that the present state had its origin in the past. What, then, can be said of sentences (5a, b, c), which describe not states but events? Here too certain situations are understood to obtain at the moment of utterance. In (5c), as in (5d), it is understood that the door is open. In (5b), not only is the door open but it is also understood that Bob is still alive and active. That is, (5b) would not be an appropriate thing to say if either the door were now closed or Bob were now dead. The difference between (5b) and the corresponding non-perfective sentence *Bob opens the door* (in the stage direction sense) is that it is understood that the event itself took place before the time of reference. In (5b, c) the events are derived from states; it is easy to see that the state still obtains at the time of utterance and that the event which produced the state came earlier. But what of (5a), where the event is not derived from a state? Any event, it would seem, has certain consequences. Events derived from states have the obvious consequence of placing the patient in that state. Other sorts of events, however, have consequences which are no less real, although they may be more dependent on the context of the event. Sentence (5a), for example, contains the event of Bob singing. Depending on the context, the consequence of this event may be that we are now aware that Bob can sing, having previously doubted it; that it is now possible for Bob to go home, since he has completed what he was here to do; that it is now time for the next act to take place; or something else. Whatever the particular consequence may be, sentence (5a) says that this resulting situation now obtains, but also that the event which produced this situation took place before the time of reference. As in (5b), it is understood also that Bob is still alive and active. In summary, the meaning of *perfective* in all these sentences seems to be that a certain situation exists at the time of reference—here, let us say, at the moment of utterance. If the situation is a state, *perfective* also means that the patient began to be in that state prior to the time of reference. If the situation is the consequence of an event, *perfective* means that the event took place prior to the time of reference. Perhaps the best way to characterize the meaning of *perfective* is to say that everything is understood to obtain at the time of reference, as in a nonperfective sentence, except that either the beginning of the state or the event which produced the situation is pushed back to an earlier time.

13.6   Let us now turn to the alternative meanings which are possible for surface structures (5a, b), at least. Perhaps the distinction which is relevant here can be clarified most easily through appeal to another sentence:

(6)   Bob has climbed Mt. Whitney.

According to the discussion above, this sentence means that the event of Bob climbing Mt. Whitney took place prior to the utterance of the sentence, but that the consequences of this event are present at the time of utterance. It may be that Bob's prestige is higher because of this feat, that he can now add another mountain to the list of 14,000-foot mountains he has climbed, or something else. It might be uttered to a third party when all three, the speaker, the hearer, and Bob, are at the summit of Mt. Whitney. But the reader should have no trouble in realizing that this surface structure might also be uttered on the New York subway and have reference to one or more events which took place years before. In that case a generic statement is being made, in contrast to the nongeneric statement described above in which the immediate consequence of one single event was being communicated. It is still true of the generic meaning of (6) that the sentence describes a situation which exists at the time of the utterance. The situation might again have to do with Bob's present prestige as a climber of high mountains, and it is still a situation which is the consequence of an event (or this time, possibly, events) which took place prior to the time of the utterance. What is different in the generic sentence is that the particularity of the event is replaced by a timeless nonparticularity. The difference between the two sentences thus seems parallel to the difference between the nonperfective *Bob climbs Mt. Whitney* as (an admittedly unusual) stage direction and the same surface structure as a description of what Bob habitually does.

13.7   It should now be apparent that the surface structures (5a, b) can also be interpreted in the generic way, rather than in the non-generic way earlier described. In (5a) the meaning may be, not that Bob has just finished singing, but that he has sung an indefinite number of times in the past. In (5b) the generic meaning may be a little unexpected, since the event of Bob opening the door habitually would be unlikely to have a consequence worth mentioning, but perhaps the speaker means that Bob has shown himself to be a capable opener of this door, or something of the sort. In any case, the parallel ambiguity of (5a, b) and (6) seems easy to appreciate. It is much less clear, however, that (5c, d) can have this kind of

ambiguity, and I shall take the position that they cannot. It seems
to me, that is, that these two sentences normally cannot have the
generic meaning. If that is true, it means that any action verb,
whether generic or not, may be inflected optionally as perfective,
while a nonaction verb (a state or a simple process) may be so
inflected only if it is nongeneric. A generic state or a generic simple
process cannot be made perfective. The rule which accounts for
this situation can be stated as follows:

(S13–3) V   ——» perfective
$$\left\{\begin{array}{l} \text{action} \\ \left[\begin{array}{l} -\text{action} \\ -\text{generic} \end{array}\right] \end{array}\right\}$$

That is, perfective is a possible inflection for an action verb, or for a
nonaction verb that is simultaneously nongeneric. This rule helps
to generate verb structures like those shown in (7), structures which
are present in the examples indicated.

	(5a)	(5a)	(5c)	(5d)
(7)	V	V	V	V
	action	action	process	state
	sing	sing	open + inchoative	open
	perfective	generic	perfective	perfective
		perfective		

13.8   It should be noted that this rule does not allow for a surface structure
like the following:

(8)   The road has been wide.

The verb in this sentence is relative and therefore necessarily inflected as generic according to (S13–2). Since it is a nonaction verb
but at the same time generic, it is excluded from the introduction
of perfective by (S13–3). It would not be too difficult either to
revise the rules already presented or to add a new rule in such a way
that sentences like (8) would be generated. It is by no means clear
that this should be done, however. Sentence (8), as it stands, is an
odd thing to say. To be sure, in a complex sentence like *The road
has been wide for a long time* this oddness vanishes. It may well
be the case, however, that the adverbial element *for a long time*
changes the specification of the verb containing *wide* in such a way
that it is able to accept the perfective inflection. Perhaps, for
example, *for a long time* erases the *generic* inflection from *wide*,
allowing it to be perfective in the same manner as *open* in (5d) or in
The door has been open for a long time.

13.9   **Progressive.** Another inflection of the English verb is illustrated
        by the following sentences:

(9)   a. Bob is singing.
        b. Bob is opening the door.
        c. The door is opening.

All three surface structures may be based on an inflection which
traditionally is called *progressive*. The first two may also be based
on a different inflection, one which will be discussed shortly. It is
important to note that the progressive inflection is available only
to nonstate verbs. There are no semantic structures which would
lead to surface structures like *The door is being open*, with a state
verb. (The fact that there are surface structures like *Bob is being
careful* does not contradict this assertion. The verb in this sentence
is not a state but an action; the sentence is paraphrasable as *Bob is
behaving carefully*.) As with *perfective*, the meaning of *progressive*
has been much discussed. As with *perfective*, again, confusion has
arisen because a progressive verb may be either nongeneric or
generic. Probably all that need be said about the meaning of a
progressive verb is that it indicates that the event or the indefinite
series of events (in the generic case) are spread out over a certain
period of time. This period, furthermore, is not unlimited in extent
but is understood to be subject to eventual termination. The meaning is one of *duration*, but just as importantly it is one of *limited*
duration. Unless there is some further specification, the event or
series of events is understood to be in progress at the time of reference, which, in the sentences of (9), again we can take to be the
moment when the sentence is uttered. If we consider first just the
nongeneric case, we can see that the event in the sentences of (9)
takes some time to occur, but that it will eventually stop. It is
understood to be in progress at the time of the utterance. The
fact that the event is understood to be limited in duration might
seem to follow from the nature of events themselves—that they
are inevitably limited to a certain time period—and not to be
determined by the unit *progressive*. As we turn to verbs which are
generic as well as progressive, however, we see that the limited
duration facet of the progressive meaning does have to be taken
into account.

13.10   That (9a) may be either nongeneric or generic should be apparent.
        In the nongeneric case the speaker is reporting on Bob's ongoing
        act. The alternative generic meaning can be appreciated if we think

of this sentence as an answer to the question *What is Bob doing these days?* Sentence (9a) then becomes a general statement, not restricted to a single event. In this case it is the series of events (rather than a single event) which is spread over a period of time. The fact that *progressive* also indicates that this period of time is limited appears clearly if we compare (9a) with the generic meaning of (1a), *Bob sings.* In the latter sentence we do not understand that the act of singing will terminate sooner or later, as we do under the generic interpretation of (9a), where Bob may be singing this month or this year, but not indefinitely. The fact that a single event by its very nature must terminate eventually does not explain the temporal limitation in this case, since it is now a sequence of events which is involved. The limitation must, then, be part of the meaning of *progressive.*

13.11 We have seen that (9a) may be either nongeneric or generic, but is the same true of (9b)? Apparently so. The sentence may mean either that Bob is at this moment opening the door—a single, transitory event—or that he is serving as the doorman these days—a general statement involving an indefinite number of events. Again it seems understood that eventually he will stop this activity, as is not understood, for example, in the nonprogressive generic sentence *Bob opens the door.* When we look at (9c), however, evidently we find a case where the progressive and generic inflections are incompatible. This surface structure, I think, can result only from a nongeneric semantic structure, unless some violence is done to our notion of what semantic possibilities exist in this area. The situation reminds us of what we found in the case of perfective: that any *action*, whether nongeneric or generic, was subject to the inflection, but that nonactions could be made perfective only if they were also nongeneric, as stipulated in rule (S13-3). Exactly the same seems to be true of the progressive inflection, except that it must be stipulated in addition that only a nonstate can be made progressive, never a state. Thus there is no progressive sentence parallel to the perfective sentence *The door has been open.* We can state the rule which introduces *progressive* as in (S13-4):

(S13-4) V   —→ progressive
        −state
        $\left\{ \begin{matrix} \text{action} \\ \left[\begin{matrix} -\text{action} \\ -\text{generic} \end{matrix} \right] \end{matrix} \right\}$

13.12 Rules (S13-3) and (S13-4) applied together allow a verb to be inflected as both perfective and progressive. This possibility exists for any verb that fulfils the conditions for progressive (which are narrower than those for perfective, being limited to nonstates), so that sentences like the following may be found:

(10) a. Bob has been singing.
      b. Bob has been opening the door.
      c. The door has been opening.

The single event (nongeneric) or the indefinite series of events (generic) is understood, because of the presence of *progressive*, to be spread over a limited period of time. The simultaneous presence of *perfective* indicates that there exists at the time of reference a situation which is the consequence of an event or series of events which took place at a time prior to the moment of utterance. These sentences say nothing about whether the event or series of events continues through the time of utterance; it may or it may not. What is significant, because of the presence of perfective, is that the present situation results from what happened prior to it.

13.13 **Anticipative.** Let me repeat two of the surface structures listed in (9) above:

(11) a. Bob is singing.
      b. Bob is opening the door.

We saw that each of these surface structures has two meanings, since each may stem from a nongeneric or a generic semantic structure. In fact, however, each of them has four meanings, for they may reflect a semantic structure which is *anticipative* rather than progressive. The anticipative sentences then may also be either nongeneric or generic. The meaning of *anticipative* seems to involve the current relevance of some action which the agent anticipates performing, and thus to be in a rough way the inverse of the meaning of *perfective*. Thus, (11a) might refer to the current relevance of a single action which Bob contemplates for tomorrow night, next week, or next year. Or, if it is generic, it might refer to an indefinite series of such actions. This kind of meaning is perhaps somewhat unusual for (11b), but the sentence can be imagined as indicating that it is now of some interest that Bob intends to act as the doorman (once or repeatedly) at some future time. Since the anticipative inflection involves some sort of intention on the part of an agent, an agent

must be present. The verb, therefore, must be an action. The anticipative inflection evidently is not compatible with *progressive*. In
general it seems to be incompatible with *perfective* also, although we
might imagine such a sentence as *I've been going* with the anticipative
meaning. If we exclude both progressive and perfective, the rule
which introduces *anticipative* can be stated as follows:

(S13–5) V   ——→ anticipative
         action
         −progressive
         −perfective

In summary, the four different semantic structures underlying the
surface structure verb in (11a) can be diagramed as in (12).

(12)   V   V   V   V
         action   action   action   action
         sing   sing   sing   sing
         ‾‾‾‾   ‾‾‾‾   ‾‾‾‾   ‾‾‾‾
         progressive   generic   anticipative   generic
                        progressive   anticipative

13.14 **Past.** Still another possibility, one which can be introduced with a
minimum of discussion, is that the verb may be inflected as *past*.
This inflection seems restricted in no way by any of the other inflections which have been mentioned, or by any of the selectional
units like *state* or *action* which we have found necessary to mention
as limiting environments for other inflections above. If we add *past*
to the semantic structures of some of the illustrations given earlier
in this chapter, we arrive at surface structures like the following:

(13)   a. Bob sang.
         b. Bob opened the door.
         c. The door opened.
         d. The door was open.
         e. Bob had sung.
         f. Bob had opened the door.
         g. The door had opened.
         h. The door had been open.
         i. Bob was singing.
         j. Bob was opening the door.
         k. The door was opening.
         l. Bob had been singing.
         m. Bob had been opening the door.
         n. The door had been opening.

The presence of *past* indicates that the time of reference is shifted from the moment of the utterance to some earlier time. This reference point in the past must be established in some way by the linguistic or nonlinguistic context. That is, when the speaker uses the *past* inflection he assumes that the hearer knows what the past reference point is. If he cannot make such an assumption he is constrained to add some device to the sentence to establish it. Thus, he might say *Last night Bob sang*, for example. The rule which introduces *past* evidently can be stated very simply:

(S13–6) V ——→ past

That is, a verb may be inflected optionally as *past* without further restrictions, apart from the contextual presupposition just mentioned. It may be noted that the surface structures of (13) are ambiguous in just the same way that they would be if they were not *past*. Thus (13a) may be either nongeneric or generic: either Bob sang once or he had a general propensity to sing. Four different semantic structures underlie (13i), identical with those diagramed at the end of the last paragraph except that *past* is also present. Perhaps, at some moment in the past, a single event was in progress; perhaps an indefinite series of events. Perhaps, at that time, Bob anticipated singing at some later time—either once or on an indefinite number of different occasions.

13.15   There are many other ways in which an English verb can be inflected. I would suggest, for example, that the surface structure items traditionally called "modals" reflect various semantic inflections of the verb. It would be too large a task to deal with the semantic origins of the modals here, but I shall outline the way in which one of them, at least, might be accommodated within this framework. The example I shall discuss is the surface structure item *must*. There are at least two distinct semantic units which this surface unit reflects. One has a meaning of obligation. The speaker says that it is obligatory for a patient to be in a certain state or for a certain event to take place at some time subsequent to the time of reference. Thus, *Bob must sing* may mean that the speaker finds it obligatory for Bob to sing at some future time. The other semantic unit reflected by *must* involves an inference. The speaker says that on the basis of evidence available to him he infers that a patient is in a certain state or that a certain event takes place. In this case *Bob must sing* means that the speaker infers that Bob sings. I shall hypothesize that two different inflections of the verb are present in these two cases. One of the inflectional units I shall call *obligational*, the other *inferential*. Let us begin with a discussion of *inferential*, which is the more commonly used of the two. In the immediately following examples, then, the possibility that *must* can also reflect obligation should be ignored.

13.16 **Inferential.** It will be easiest to begin with sentences which are neither perfective, progressive, nor past:

(14)   a. The road must be wide.
         b. The door must be open.
         c. The door must open.
         d. Bob must open the door.
         e. Bob must sing.

In each of these sentences the speaker is saying something similar to *I infer that the road is wide*, and so forth. I shall say that in each case the verb is specified inflectionally as *inferential*. Of some interest, however, is the relation between the nongeneric or generic character of these sentences and the occurrence of *inferential*. It appears that (14a) can have nothing but the generic interpretation. One confirmation of this assertion is the fact that *A freeway must be wide* has to refer to any freeway rather than to a particular one (cf. 13.4). On the other hand, (14b) can have only the nongeneric meaning. It can be observed by way of confirmation that *A door must be open* refers to a particular door, not to any door at all. This situation with regard to (14a, b) we should expect, for it was seen in 13.4 that a relative state like *wide* is necessarily generic, a non-relative state like *open* necessarily nongeneric. The examples (14a, b), then, present no surprises. If the reader reflects on (14c, d, e) from the same point of view, however, I think he will find that they cannot be anything but generic. Sentence (14e), for example, can only mean something like *I infer that Bob sings* in the generic sense; it cannot involve a single specific act of singing. The same observation can be made with respect to (14c, d). This situation is not what we would expect on the basis of the possibilities allowed for earlier. Without the inferential inflection, these verbs are free to be either generic or nongeneric. *Bob sings*, for example, can mean that Bob sings habitually, but it can also carry the stage direction kind of meaning. It is this stage direction or direct reporting meaning that is excluded when the verb is inferential. Perhaps we can understand why. Direct reporting involves immediate perception of the event by the speaker. He cannot say that he infers something to be happening when in fact he sees it happening before his eyes. This kind of nongeneric statement and the inferential meaning are experientially incompatible. It seems, then, that we can make a statement to to the effect that the inferential inflection is excluded from a verb which is a nongeneric nonstate.

13.17 The following examples will cause us to modify this statement, at the same time that they illustrate a peculiar fact about the surface representation of *inferential* in conjunction with other inflections:

(15)   a. The road must have been wide.
        b. The door must have been open.
        c. The door must have opened.
        d. Bob must have opened the door.
        e. Bob must have sung.

These surface structures suggest the semantic presence of *perfective*, and the perfective inflection indeed may be present here. One of the immediately recognizable clues to the presence of *perfective*, for example, is the fact that the agent in a sentence like (15e) must be alive at the time of reference. There is an interpretation of (15e) in which Bob must be alive. Given this same interpretation, and provided we take Caesar to be the ancient Roman, the following is odd:

(16)   Caesar must have climbed the Jungfrau.

This meaning is paraphrasable as *I infer that Caesar has climbed the Jungfrau* (or *that Bob has sung*). There is another interpretation, however, in which (16) is a perfectly natural thing to say, since it does not indicate that Caesar is still alive. This meaning is paraphrasable as *I infer that Caesar climbed the Jungfrau.* The verb in this sentence is not perfective but *past*. In other words, when the inflectional unit *inferential* is present in a semantic structure, postsemantic processes treat *past* as if it were *perfective*. We might say that the first postsemantic process that applies to *past* in an inferential verb is its conversion into *perfective*. The result is that on the basis of a surface structure we are unable to distinguish whether the verb was inflected semantically as inferential and perfective or as inferential and past. All the surface structures of (15) are ambiguous in this way. Sentence (15a), for example, may be paraphrasable as either *I infer that the road has been wide* or *I infer that the road was wide.*

13.18 But we must also look at the constraints involving *inferential* and *generic* in the sentences of (15). As we discussed the sentences of (14), we saw that there was an incompatibility between *inferential* and a nongeneric nonstate. Does the same incompatibility exist in (15)? Let us take first the perfective meaning of (15e) or of (16), assuming in the latter case that Caesar is the name of a person now alive. It seems evident that either a nongeneric or a generic interpretation is possible: *I infer that Bob has (just) sung*, or *I infer that Bob has (sometimes) sung.* If we turn to the past, rather than the perfective meaning attributable to these same surface structures, we find again that either a nongeneric or a generic meaning may be present: *I infer that Bob sang (once)* or *I infer that Bob sang (habitually).* What we can conclude, evidently, is that the incompatibility of *inferential* with a nongeneric nonstate, mentioned in 13.16, exists only in nonperfective, nonpast sentences. It is quite possible to make inferences about a single event, just as long as that event is not perceived immediately at the moment of the utterance. We have to modify our earlier statement, therefore, and say that the inferential inflection is excluded only from a verb which is at the same time a nonstate, nongeneric, nonperfective, and nonpast.

13.19 We must also look briefly at inferential sentences which are progressive:

(17) a. The door must be opening.
      b. Bob must be opening the door.
      c. Bob must be singing.
      d. Bob must have been singing.

Sentence (17d) is included to illustrate that an inferential statement may be inferential, progressive, and also either perfective or past. As previously, *perfective* and *past* lead to one and the same surface structure when *inferential* is present. Thus, the meaning of (17d) may be paraphrased as either *I infer that Bob has been singing* or *I infer that Bob was singing.* But let us examine whether (17a, b, c) may be either nongeneric or generic. Apparently they may. That is, (17c) may mean either *Bob must be singing (at the moment)* or *Bob must be singing (these days).* Thus, we can modify still further the statement at the end of the last paragraph: the inferential inflection is excluded only from a verb which is at the same time a nonstate, nongeneric, nonperfective, nonprogressive, and nonpast. It is also apparently the case that a verb which is both perfective and past cannot be made inferential. That is, a sentence like *Bob had sung* does not have available to it the inferential option. The rule which introduces the inferential inflection can be stated as in (S13-7). A

(S13-7) V $\longrightarrow$ inferential
$$\begin{pmatrix} \text{state} \\ \text{generic} \\ \text{progressive} \\ \begin{Bmatrix} \text{perfective} \\ \text{past} \end{Bmatrix} \end{pmatrix}$$

verb may be inflected as inferential if it is a state and/or generic and/or progressive and/or either perfective or past (but not both). This rule accounts for the restrictions on the occurrence of *inferential* noted above. By way of illustration, the relevant features of the four different verbs which are present in the semantic structures underlying (16), *Caesar must have climbed the Jungfrau*, can be diagramed as in (18).

(18)

V	V	V	V
action	action	action	action
climb	climb	climb	climb
perfective	generic	past	generic
inferential	perfective	inferential	past
	inferential		inferential

13.20 **Obligational.** The *obligational* inflection which is reflected in the surface structure item *must* can be disposed of more quickly. Surface structures like the following may reflect its presence:

(19)   a. The road must be wide.
       b. The door must be open.
       c. The door must open.
       d. Bob must open the door.
       e. Bob must sing.
       f. The door must be opening.
       g. Bob must be opening the door.
       h. Bob must be singing.

The following kinds of sentences, on the other hand, cannot be given the obligational interpretation but only the inferential one:

(20)   a. The road must have been wide.
       b. Bob must have sung.
       c. Bob must have been singing.

Evidently the obligational inflection is not available to a verb that is either perfective or past. Presumably the reason is that the meaning of *obligational* involves an obligation with respect to the future, whereas *perfective* and *past* both have to do with states or events which were initiated or took place in the past. It is also impossible for *obligational* and *inferential* to cooccur, probably because the latter is a historical outgrowth of the former. On the other hand, if the reader examines the sentences of (19) for occurrences of the generic inflection, he will find that no special constraints limit the cooccurrence of *generic* and *obligational* as they limit the cooccurrence of *generic* and *inferential*. For example, (19e), *Bob must sing*, means either that it is obligatory for Bob to sing on one particular occasion or that it is obligatory for Bob to sing in general. The rule which introduces *obligational* can be stated in this way:

(S13–8) V   ——→ obligational
         −perfective
         −past
         −inferential

That is, a verb which is neither perfective, past, nor inferential may be inflected optionally as obligational. The relevant structures of the verbs underlying (19e) can be diagramed as in (21), where the inferential possibility is included.

(21) V   V   V
      action   action   action
      sing   sing   sing
      generic   obligational   generic
      inferential   obligational

14

The Inflection of a Noun

14.1   The discussion in the preceding chapters was focused chiefly on the semantic specification of verbs.[1] Nouns, however, are also specified in terms of selectional, lexical, and inflectional units, which, I shall assume here, can be introduced in much the same way as the specifications of verbs. To a certain extent the selectional units of a verb determine what the selectional units of accompanying nouns will be, as was briefly discussed in Chapter 10. We shall see in this chapter that there is a way in which the *inflection* of a verb may influence the *inflection* of an accompanying noun. To a considerable extent, however, the selectional, lexical, and inflectional units of a noun can be chosen independently of what the verb may contain. Certain selectional units of nouns have already been discussed; mentioned in Chapter 10 were *count*, *potent*, *animate*, *human*, *feminine*, and *unique*. How these units determine the choice of noun roots was also sketched at that point. At the end of Chapter 11, furthermore, a few examples of derivation as it applies to noun roots were given. Since, therefore, we have already had these glimpses at the selectional and lexical specification of a noun, the present chapter will deal almost exclusively with noun *inflection*.

14.2   In Chapter 13 we looked at some verb inflections. The meanings of those inflections had to do above all with the temporal setting

[1] This chapter is based on Chafe 1968a.

of the state or event specified by the verb root. Nongeneric verbs, for example, involve transitory states or events, generic verbs a "timeless" state or propensity for the event to occur. Perfective verbs have to do with a condition existing at the time of reference which was initiated earlier or which is the consequence of an earlier event. Progressive verbs have to do with the limited duration of an event. The inflectional unit *past* sets the time of reference before the time of the utterance. Less obviously temporal verb inflections like *anticipative* and *obligational* are also associated in one way or another with the concept of time. In addition to communicating certain mental dispositions of the speaker, both have to do with what will be the case subsequent to the time of reference. Thus, most verb inflections have temporal implications. Doubtless this fact stems from the intrinsically temporal nature of states and events. Nouns are not dependent on time in this way. There is, however, something else about the meaning of nouns which is as basic to them as the concept of time is to verbs and which permeates the meanings of noun inflections in the same way that time permeates the meanings of verb inflections. In Chapter 10 we saw that a noun may or may not be specified selectionally as *count*. A noncount noun may contain as its noun root, for example, a lexical unit like *water*. A typical count noun root is *elephant*. Now, it is possible that one may wish to communicate about the general substance water, not some particular instance of that substance, and it is likewise possible that one may wish to talk about the entire class of elephants, not a particular member or particular members of that class. On the other hand, and probably more often, one may wish to talk about some particular water or some particular elephant or elephants. When the latter is true, another question arises: does the hearer know which water, which elephant or elephants the speaker is talking about, or is the speaker introducing a new instance of the substance, a new member or members of the class, whose identity was previously unknown to the hearer? It is the interaction of these two factors which seems to be as basic to noun inflection as time is to the inflection of a verb: (1) the totality of a substance or class vs. an instance of the substance or a member of the class, and (2) the question in the latter case of whether the hearer knows which instance or which member is referred to.

14.3   **Definite.** Our discussion of noun inflections can begin with the two sentences which follow:

(1)   a. An elephant likes peanuts.
        b. Water flows downhill.

In these sentences it is the entire class of elephants and the universal substance water which is being talked about. These nouns can be contrasted with those in:

(2)   a. An elephant stepped on my car.
        b. (Sm) water dripped onto the floor.

The notation (*sm*) will be used to indicate a surface structure item which is spelled *some*, but pronounced with weak stress. This item is distinct from the stressed *some*, as in *Some elephants like peanuts*, which has a different semantic origin (14.16). The unstressed *sm* seems always to be subject to optional deletion from a surface structure, and for that reason it is given in parentheses. That is, the semantic structure underlying (2b) can have two surface structures: either *Sm water dripped onto the floor* or *Water dripped onto the floor*, although the version which retains the *sm* is probably more common. The point to be made about the sentences in (2) is that the nouns which are specified lexically as *elephant* and *water* do not refer to the entire class of elephants or to all water, but to just one member of the class or one particular instance of the substance. The same is true in:

(3)   a. The elephant stepped on my car.
        b. The water dripped onto the floor.

What, then, is the difference between the sentences of (2) and those of (3)? It is evident that in (3) the speaker assumes that the hearer already knows which member of the class of elephants he is talking about, or which particular instance of water. In (3a) there may have been mention in conversation of an elephant, for example, or a particular elephant may already be visible to both speaker and hearer at the moment of utterance. The point is that the speaker believes that he can assume, for whatever reason, that the identity of the elephant is known not only to himself but to the hearer as well. Similarly, in (3b) the speaker assumes that the hearer knows what water is being talked about; it might be the water which both the speaker and the hearer know has collected on the roof, for example. If we contrast these sentences with those of (2), we see that in (2a) the speaker does not assume this prior knowledge on the part of the hearer as to the identity of the elephant, or in (2b) as to the identity of the water. He is introducing some particular elephant, some particular water, as new information. I shall say that the nouns in (3) are inflected as *definite*, since this inflection shows up in surface structure in the form of what is traditionally called the *definite article*. I shall treat the nouns in (2) as unmarked for definiteness and refer to them when necessary as *nondefinite*. There is, I think, some reason to avoid the connotation of the traditional term *indefinite*, which implies a kind of vagueness. There is nothing vague about the nouns in (2). The speaker is simply communicating his assumption that the hearer does not already know the particular item or the particular part of a substance which is at issue, and he is introducing this particular instance for the first time. The definite inflection can be introduced with a rule like the following:

(S14–1) N $\longrightarrow$ definite

Thus, the relevant semantic structures of the nouns in (2) and (3) can be diagramed as follows:

(2a)	(2b)	(3a)	(3b)
N	N	N	N
count	water	count	water
elephant		elephant	definite
		definite	

14.4 **Generic.** But what of the nouns in (1), where the entire class of elephants or the universal substance water is involved? The first question we might ask is whether the nouns in these sentences are definite. I believe the answer is no. The meaning of definite is that the speaker assumes that the hearer knows the identity of a particular member of the class or a particular instance of the substance. If an entire class or an entire substance is at issue, the definite meaning is inapplicable (although in 14.11 we shall meet a special situation where it is applicable nonetheless). The assumption that (1) and (2) share the negative property of being nondefinite also bears fruit when we turn to the question of what it is that distinguishes (1) and (2) from each other. As has already been noted, this difference can be described as one of whole class or substance for (1) vs. particular instance of class or substance for (2). I shall account for this difference by saying that the nouns in (1) are inflected as *generic*, while those in (2) are not.[2] How is this inflectional unit *generic* to be introduced? We might think of saying that a noun which is not inflected as definite by (S14–1) has the option of being inflected as generic. That is not quite what happens, however. Rather, the generic or nongeneric nature of a noun is not something that is established by a choice within the noun at all; it is something that is automatically determined for the noun by the verb to which the noun is attached. We can observe that the verbs in (1) are generic verbs while those in (2) are not. This fact suggests the hypothesis that a *nondefinite* noun is generic if it accompanies a generic verb, but nongeneric otherwise. The hypothesis is born out by further sentences. For example, we noted in 13.4 that the sentence *A bird sings* may have either a generic or a nongeneric (stage direction) verb. It was pointed out then that the meaning of the noun differs in a way that is correlated with the difference in the verb. If the verb is generic, the noun means something like *any bird*; if it is nongeneric, the noun has to do with a particular bird. We can see now that observations of this kind can be accounted for with the following rule:

(S14–2) $\text{N}_{-\text{definite}} \longrightarrow \text{generic}/\text{V}_{\text{generic}}$

That is, a noun, provided it is not definite, *must* be inflected as generic in the environment of a generic verb. Otherwise a non-definite noun will be nongeneric, as in (2).

14.5   A natural question to ask at this point is why the semantic choice should be thought to reside in the verb, which then determines the inflection of the noun. Why not posit the opposite: that the choice of generic or nongeneric is made within the noun, which then determines whether its verb will be generic or nongeneric? There are several reasons for preferring the alternative I have chosen. In the first place, a verb can be said to determine the genericness of the *nouns* which accompany it, not simply of one noun. Thus, in (1a),

[2] It has been suggested to me that the term *generic* would also be appropriate for the quite different specification of a noun found in sentences like *This is an excellent beer* or *The finest wines come from France*, where the meaning is paraphrasable as *kind of beer* or *kind of wine*. I do not deal with this rather restricted meaning in the present work. There is some precedent for using *generic* in the way I use it here, although I am not sure what alternative name to suggest for the other meaning.

Elephants like peanuts, it is not simply the noun *elephants* which is generic, but *peanuts* also. Only one choice with respect to the generic-nongeneric distinction can be made in any one simple sentence. If we localize this choice within one of the nouns, we have to say that it spreads from there not only to the verb but to other nouns as well. It is simpler and more natural to say that the choice is made within the verb and that it radiates from there to the accompanying nouns. As another example of the same point, we might take the following:

(4)   A bird sings songs.

If the verb here is generic, both the agent and the complement nouns are generic; if the verb is nongeneric, both the agent and the complement nouns are nongeneric (in which case the complement noun may have the alternative surface structure *sm songs*). There is no reason to attribute the choice of genericness to either the agent or the complement, and then to say that the inflection of the verb and of the other noun depends on that choice, just as there was no reason in (1a) to attribute the choice of genericness to either the beneficiary noun *elephants* or to the patient noun *peanuts*. There is another interesting observation relevant to this question. It appears that a generic or nongeneric verb forces a noun to be, respectively, generic or nongeneric, even when that noun is forced from some other direction to be the opposite. Consider, for example, the strangeness of the following:

(5)   *Any elephant stepped on my car.

In (14.17) we shall see that the "quantifier" *any* is regularly associated with a generic noun. *Elephant,* then, must be generic. The verb in this sentence, however, is difficult to interpret in any way but as nongeneric. Being nongeneric, it causes the noun to be nongeneric. In other words, the noun in (5) is forced by the *any* to be generic but by the verb to be nongeneric. Hence the schizophrenic effect which the sentence has. If it were the case that a noun, by its generic or nongeneric nature, caused the verb to be, respectively, generic or nongeneric, the genericness of the noun *elephant* should force the verb to be generic here, but it does not. It will be recalled also that I have suggested a general principle that semantic influence radiates from a verb to its accompanying nouns, not vice versa, and the arguments mentioned in this paragraph relate to and strengthen that hypothesis.

14.6   A summary may be helpful here. Let me repeat the sentences of (1), (2), and (3):

(1)   a. An elephant likes peanuts.
        b. Water flows downhill.

(2)   a. An elephant stepped on my car.
        b. (Sm) water dripped onto the floor.

(3)   a. The elephant stepped on my car.
        b. The water dripped onto the floor.

We have been concerned with the nouns which are specified lexically as *elephant* and *water*. I have suggested that the nouns in (3) differ from those in (2) by virtue of the fact that those in (3) are inflected as definite, in accordance with rule (S14–1). I have suggested in addition that the nondefinite nouns in (1) differ from the nondefinite nouns in (2) by virtue of the fact that those in (1) are generic. I have said that this difference is not one which is determined within the nouns themselves, but one which is determined by the generic or nongeneric nature of the verbs in these sentences, as set forth in rule (S14–2). We have, then, the following six possibilities:

(1a)	(1b)	(2a)	(2b)	(3a)	(3b)
N	N	N	N	N	N
count	water	count	water	count	water
elephant	generic	elephant		elephant	definite
generic				definite	

14.7   **Aggregate.** It was asserted at the beginning of 14.4 that *definite* and *generic* are incompatible, except in special circumstances to be mentioned in 14.11. How, then, can we explain the noun in a sentence like:

(6)   The elephant likes peanuts.

The surface structure makes this noun appear to be definite. The reader can easily recognize, however, that this surface structure is ambiguous. The noun can be interpreted in exactly the same way as the noun in (3a)—as definite—but it can also be interpreted in a generic way. The reference may be to the entire class of elephants. In the latter case, the question arises as to how this noun differs from the one in (1a), *An elephant likes peanuts*. What I shall suggest is that in (6) the class of elephants is regarded as an undifferentiated whole, not as composed of separate individuals as in (1a). As a name for the semantic unit which yields this undifferentiated meaning I shall use the term *aggregate*. *Aggregate* is clearly a subspecification of *generic* and hence can occur only when the verb is generic. This restriction explains why (6), where the verb is generic, is ambiguous, while (3a), where the verb is nongeneric, can have only the definite meaning, not the aggregate one. It also seems to be true that only a count noun can be inflected as aggregate. The rule which introduces this inflection therefore can be written:

(S14–3) generic $\longrightarrow$ aggregate/count

The structure of the noun in (6) which has the aggregate inflection can then be diagramed:

N
count
elephant
generic
aggregate

Postsemantic processes will lead to an identical surface structure representation for both *aggregate* and *definite*.

14.8 **Plural.** Still we have not considered the following possibilities, which are also open to count nouns of the types we have been considering:

(7) a. Elephants like peanuts.
b. (Sm) elephants stepped on my car.
c. The elephants stepped on my car.

These sentences contrast minimally with (1a), (2a), and (3a), the only difference being that in the earlier sentences one elephant was involved while here it is more than one. This difference seems entirely clear in the case of the nongeneric sentences (7b, c) as contrasted with (2a) and (3a): *(sm) elephants* vs. *an elephant* and *the elephants* vs. *the elephant*. But how can this distinction between one and more-than-one apply in the case of a generic noun, as in (7a)—*elephants*—vs. (1a)—*an elephant*? That is, how can we distinguish between one and more-than-one when it is the entire class of elephants which is involved in the first place? The answer, I think, is that *an elephant* in the generic sense means that we are considering one elephant at a time, but that no matter which one we consider, it will fit the rest of the sentence equally well. *An elephant likes peanuts* means that any elephant whatsoever that we may select from the entire class will turn out to like peanuts. The other case, *Elephants like peanuts*, means that all the individual elephants taken together—not one at a time—like peanuts. The third possibility for a generic noun— *The elephant likes peanuts*, as discussed in the last paragraph— means that the class is not viewed as consisting of individuals at all, but rather as an undifferentiated whole. Let us, then, say that the nouns in (7) are inflected as *plural.* Plurality is possible for a count noun which is not unique (for obvious reasons), and which is not inflected as aggregate:

(S14–4) N   ——→ plural
         count
         −unique
         −aggregate

14.9   Rules (S14–1) through (S14–4) have generated seven different noun inflections, three of which are available to both count and non-count nouns and four of which are available to count nouns only. These inflections are listed below together with the surface structures which result from them:

(1b)   N   water (flows downhill)
       water
       generic

(1a)   N   an elephant (likes peanuts)
       count
       elephant
       generic

(7a)   N   elephants (like peanuts)
       count
       elephant
       generic
       plural

(6)   N   the elephant (likes peanuts)
       count
       elephant
       generic
       aggregate

(2b)   N   (sm) water (dripped onto the floor)
       water

(2a)   N   an elephant (stepped on my car)
       count
       elephant

(7b)   N   (sm) elephants (stepped on my car)
        count
        <u>elephant</u>
        plural

(3b)   N   the water (dripped onto the floor/flows downhill)
        <u>water</u>
        definite

(3a)   N   the elephant (stepped on my car/likes peanuts)
        count
        <u>elephant</u>
        definite

(7c)   N   the elephants (stepped on my car/like peanuts)
        count
        <u>elephant</u>
        definite
        plural

The surface structure representations of these various inflections are not entirely straightforward, although perhaps not as complex as may appear from a first glance at the list above. The semantic units *definite* and *aggregate* fall together postsemantically to become the surface *definite article*. The surface item known as the *indefinite article* actually can be regarded as a reflection of the selectional unit *count*; that is, it appears in the surface structure whenever there is semantically a count noun which is neither definite, aggregate, nor plural—precisely in those situations where there is no other surface article or suffix. The optional surface item *(sm)* identifies a noun which is neither generic nor definite in those cases where the indefinite article is not present. Finally, the semantic unit *plural* is represented in surface structure by the well-known sibilant suffix, or in less regular ways with certain noun roots. *Generic* has no direct surface reflection.

14.10 **Shifted norm.** At the beginning of Chapter 11 we saw that certain states are specified as *relative*. The verb root *wide* was given as an example of a relative state, while nonrelative states were exemplified by *open*. The special feature which characterizes a relative state was said to be the existence of a variable norm, the location of which is determined by the patient of the state. Thus, in *The road is wide* we understand that *wide* means *wide for a road*. We are now able to make an interesting observation with regard to the relative state *big* in the following sentences:

(8)   a. An elephant is big.   (1a)
       b. Elephants are big.   (7a)
       c. The elephant is big.   (6)
       d. The elephant is big.   (3a)
       e. The elephants are big.   (7c)

It is intended that the first three sentences have generic, the last two nongeneric nouns, and thus that these nouns have the same semantic structures as those in the sentences referred to in parentheses— structures which were diagramed in the last paragraph. The new fact which we can observe here is that *big* means *big for an elephant* only in sentences (8d, e), the sentences in which the noun is nongeneric (because it is definite). In sentences (8a, b, c) the norm for bigness is not the norm for elephants; these sentences do not say that an elephant is big for an elephant, for example. Rather, it appears that the norm which is relevant to the meaning of *big* in the first three sentences is the norm for *animals*, or something of the sort. Similarly, in (9a) the norm is that for automobiles, not for Cadillacs, and in (9b) it is that for mouselike animals, not for rats:

(9)   a. A Cadillac is big.
       b. A rat is big.

The following generalization can be made on the basis of these and similar examples. While the norm for a relative state is indeed established by the patient of that state, something further needs to be said when the patient is generic. Specifically, in that case the norm is not the norm for the patient noun root itself but for the next semantic unit above it in a taxonomic hierarchy. In other words, above the noun root *elephant* in (8a, b, c) there is a classificatory unit *animal*, and it is this higher unit, not *elephant*, which determines the norm for *big*. In (9a) there is a classificatory unit *automobile*, in (9b) a classificatory unit *mouselike animal*, and it is these units, not *Cadillac* or *rat*, which determine the norms for big.[3] Why this shifting of the norm takes place is easy to understand. It would be contradictory to say that all members of a class have a certain quality which is defined as exceeding the norm for the members of that same class—that elephants are big with respect to the norm for elephants, for example. Whenever such a situation would otherwise exist, apparently there is an automatic conceptual switch by which the norm is shifted to that established by the higher taxonomic unit.

[3] Katz (1967:186–88) comes to a similar conclusion.

There is nothing contradictory about saying that elephants are big with respect to the norm for all members of the class of animals. Suppose we identify a new semantic unit, *shifted norm*. This unit can be introduced by a rule like (S14-5). The rule says that a verb

$$\text{(S14-5)} \quad \underset{\text{relative}}{V} \longrightarrow \underset{\text{generic}}{\overset{\text{pat}}{\text{shifted norm}/N}}$$

which contains the selectional unit *relative* must be further specified (inflectionally, it would seem) as *shifted norm* in the environment of a patient noun which is inflected as generic. We seem to have here an instance of a noun exerting an influence back on its verb, contrary to the usual pattern. In sentence (8a) it is first established that the verb is generic. Then, because it is nondefinite, the patient noun is made to agree in genericness. Once that has happened, however, the noun takes the initiative and, by (S14-5), forces the verb to take on the shifted norm inflection.

14.11 **Bounded.** It was asserted above that the definite and generic inflections are incompatible, but we can now look at some examples which show that this assertion needs to be qualified. The following surface structures are of interest:

(10)   a. The elephants like peanuts.
        b. The Indians like corn.

Example (10a) is unambiguous. *The elephants* can only be definite and plural; it cannot be generic. Example (10b), however, reflects two different semantic structures. In one of them *the Indians* is interpreted in the same way as *the elephants*. It has the same meaning we would find, for example, in a sentence like *The Indians who live in New York like corn*. In the other meaning of (10b), however, *the Indians* seems to have a generic meaning. All Indians are involved. This is the meaning we might normally attribute to a surface structure like *The Indians migrated into North America from Siberia*, although, to be sure, the ambiguity of (10b) is present here as well. Let us recall our earlier explanation of the incompatibility between *definite* and *generic*. It was suggested that *definite* means that the speaker assumes that the hearer already knows which member or members of the class are being talked about. If *generic* means that the entire class is being talked about, then no such assumption by the speaker is possible. Or at least this is so in the case of *elephants*. There seem to be certain noun roots, among them *Indian*, which designate a class whose boundaries are implicitly known. It is evidently part of our conceptual apparatus that the class of Indians is well defined in a way that the class of elephants is not. Obviously we cannot call every Indian by name, but we seem to think of Indians as constituting a bounded set. Many noun roots of this kind are spelled with a capital letter, but not all are. The ambiguity of (10b) is present also in (11a, b) but not in (11c):

(11)   a. The hippies have long hair.
         b. The computers have been overrated.
         c. The typewriters have been overrated.

Presumably *typewriter* was once a noun root that had this bounded quality. As the number of typewriters became vast and vague, *typewriter* must have joined *elephant* in the unbounded group. *Computer* may be expected to pass into that group before long; perhaps it has done so already for many speakers. Let us posit the existence of a semantic unit which can be labeled *bounded*. It must be a selectional unit, not an inflectional one, since it influences the choice of a noun root. It seems to be a specification that can be added only to a count noun, so that a rule like the following can be included among those which introduce the selectional units of nouns:

(S14–6) count —→ bounded

What (10b) and (11a, b) illustrate is that a bounded noun *can* be definite and generic at the same time. Evidently this is the case because the speaker is able to assume that the hearer knows which members of the class he is talking about even when he is talking about the entire class. One way of allowing for the generic meanings of (10b) and (11a, b) is through the following inflectional rule:

(S14–7) N   —→ generic/V
         bounded   generic
         definite
         plural

That is, a noun which has already been inflected as definite and plural, if it is specified selectionally as bounded, may be further inflected as generic (provided the verb is generic). One of the meanings of the noun in (10b) therefore can be diagramed as follows:

```
N
count
bounded
Indian
definite
plural
generic
```

In bookstores I continue to be startled occasionally by the existence of a book titled *A Field Guide to the Birds*. The title may have resulted from the truncation of a longer one, but as it stands it implies one of two things, neither of which appears to be true. Either a subset of birds has already been identified to the hearer (the bookstore browser)—in which case *bird* is inflected as definite but not generic—or else *bird* is a bounded noun root which can be both definite and generic. The first possibility is surely not the case, for one wants to ask "What birds?" But the second seems not to be the case either. *Bird* is normally unbounded, like *elephant*, and not a bounded noun like *Indian*.

14.12   **Unique.** It may be valid to regard *unique*, first introduced in Chapter 10, as the extreme manifestation of *bounded*. Some nominal concepts are so narrowly limited that they constitute a class of one member. Rather than introducing *unique* in some such manner as was suggested in (S10–6), therefore, we might find it desirable to make mention of *bounded*; for example (and still incompletely):

(S14–8) $\begin{bmatrix} \text{human} \\ \text{bounded} \end{bmatrix} \longrightarrow$ unique

However that may be, we should take note here that only one inflection is possible for a unique noun. Since there is only one member of the class, the hearer automatically knows which member is being talked about; hence a unique noun must be definite. The other inflections introduced above seem irrelevant for such a noun. The following rule is thus in order:

(S14–9) N $\longrightarrow$ definite
         unique

That is, a unique noun must be inflected as definite. This rule can be regarded as related disjunctively to the other inflectional rules above, so that a unique noun receives only this inflection. With regard to surface structure representations, it can be noted that some unique noun roots allow *definite* to be represented in the usual way as the definite article, while others cause it to be postsemantically deleted. Thus, we find *the sun* and *the Attorney General*, but simply *Bob* and *Roger*.

14.13 **Random.** There seems to be another semantic unit which bears some resemblance to *generic*, both in meaning and in the manner of its introduction into a noun, but which nevertheless appears to be something different. It can be illustrated with the following sentences, each of which is ambiguous:

(12) a. I'm looking for an elephant.
      b. I'm looking for (sm) elephants.
      c. Bob wants a book.
      d. Bob wants (sm) books.

We may assume that the verb in each of these sentences is nongeneric. The patient nouns, specified lexically as *elephant* and *book*, therefore are nongeneric too, as well as being nondefinite. That they are indeed nongeneric is confirmed by the fact that *sm* can be present in the surface structures of the plural nouns, as in (12b, d). *Sm* can never be added when the noun is semantically generic. Each of the patient nouns, however, can be interpreted in two distinct ways. In (12a) I may be looking for some particular elephant, as we would normally expect with a nongeneric inflection, but I may also be looking for whatever elephant I can find. In the first case I might follow this sentence with one beginning *When I find it* . . . In the second case I would have to say *When I find one* . . . Parallel observations can be made for (12b), with the necessary adjustments for plurality. Either I am looking for some particular elephants or I am looking for any subset of elephants I can find. In the first case I might add *When I find them* . . . In the second case I would have to say *When I find some* . . . Again, in (12c) Bob may want some particular book. We might add *Its title has escaped me.* On the other hand Bob may want a book of any kind. We might add *Any book will do.* Similar observations can be made for (12d). What is noteworthy about such cases is that the ambiguity exists only for the patients of a certain narrow range of verb roots. It would seem, therefore, that these roots are dependent on the presence within the verb of a selectional unit which might be labeled *random*.[4]

---

[4]Baker (Ms.), in effect, equates *random* with *generic*, but the verbs in (12) are nongeneric and must have nongeneric patients. Furthermore, as was noted, *sm* could not occur in (12b, d) if these nouns were generic.

Looking for and wanting are (at least potentially) random concepts. It is then possible for this unit *random* within the verb to be extended into the patient noun as an inflectional unit. When the noun does contain this unit it acquires the random meaning. Thus, a rule such as the following is called for (in addition to a rule introducing *random* as a selectional unit within verbs):

(S14–10) patient
$$\begin{array}{c} \text{N} \\ -\text{definite} \\ -\text{generic} \end{array} \longrightarrow \begin{array}{c} \text{random}/\text{V} \\ \text{random} \end{array}$$

That is, a patient noun which is neither definite nor generic may be inflected optionally as random in the environment of a random verb.

14.14   There are many special restrictions which apply to noun inflections of the types discussed above. It would be impractical to consider all of them here, but a few examples can be cited. As one of these examples we may note that the aggregate inflection seems to be impossible for the patients of many action-process verb roots. Thus (13c) and (13f) are ruled out if the verb is generic:

(13)   a. Bob smokes a cigar.
         b. Bob smokes cigars.
         c. *Bob smokes the cigar.
         d. A gopher digs a tunnel.
         e. A gopher digs tunnels.
         f. *A gopher digs the tunnel.

Evidently action-processes like smoking and digging cannot be applied to a total undifferentiated class but only to a class of individual items.[5] The reader perhaps may wonder whether *a cigar* and *cigars* in (13a, b) are really generic, as our earlier explanation requires them to be when the verb is generic. Does Bob really smoke the entire class of cigars? The crucial factor seems to be that his smoking is directed at cigars in general, not at some proper subset of cigars, and that fact is what is communicated by *generic* in this case. The generic nature of *cigars* in (13b) is substantiated by the fact that we cannot add *sm* to it, as we could if it were non-

[5]That the noun also has something to do with this phenomenon, however, is suggested by the acceptability of sentences like *Bob smokes the hookah*. Evidently the restriction described here does not apply to nouns which are selectionally specified as *exotic*.

generic: *Bob smokes sm cigars* is possible only if the verb is non-generic. Probably it is the "distributive" nature of Bob's smoking (or a gopher's digging) that leads both to a hesitation in accepting the generic nature of these patient nouns and to the impossibility of (13c, f). In any case, rule (S14–3), which introduces the *aggregate* inflection, needs to be constrained in order not to allow the addition of aggregate to these nouns. There are other verb roots, however, which appear to rule out a generic patient which is not either plural or aggregate. That is, if such verb roots have a generic patient it must be plural or aggregate:

(14) a. Bob is studying elephants.
      b. Bob is studying the elephant.
      c. *Bob is studying an elephant.

Evidently studying (when generic) cannot affect the members of a class one at a time but must apply to the entire class at once. Of course, (14c) is perfectly possible when the verb is nongeneric, and when *an elephant* is therefore nongeneric. Still other verb roots appear to require a generic patient (which is, furthermore, either plural or aggregate) but at the same time a nongeneric agent. This is true, for example, of the verb root *discover* whose meaning is paraphrasable as *bring to public attention* (as in *Columbus discovered America*). (There is another verb root *discover* whose meaning is paraphrasable as *find* or *come upon* (as in *Columbus discovered a fire in the forecastle*) and whose properties are different from those of the one that concerns us here.) The *discover* in question has properties parallel to those of *study* in (14), except that its agent must be nongeneric:

(15) a. A scientist discovered neutrons.
      b. A scientist discovered the neutron.
      c. *A scientist discovered a neutron.

Presumably a person can discover something in this way only once, but he may discover an entire class of things. Restrictions of the sort that have been illustrated in this paragraph can be accounted for through the assignment of additional selectional units to the verb, which then serve to influence the introduction of noun inflections under various circumstances.

14.15 Predicate nouns. In 11.16 brief mention was made of so-called predicate nouns, which were seen to be state verbs derived from nouns through a derivational unit that was labeled *predicativizer*. Thus, the relevant structure of *Roger is a student* was seen to be as shown in (16). Such a predicate noun, however, is subject to inflec-

(16)

```
              ┌─────────────────┐
                                pat
V                               N
state                           Roger
N + predicativizer
count
potent
animate
human
student
```

tion like other nouns, although the particular inflections which are available to it are much more limited than those available to other nouns. In fact, we shall see that the only inflectional *choice* which can be made within a predicate noun is the choice of whether it is or is not definite. Let us use the following sentences as examples:

(17) a. The boy is a student.
      b. The boy is the student.
      c. The boys are students.
      d. The boys are the students.
      e. An ouzel is a bird.
      f. An ouzel is the bird.
      g. Ouzels are birds.
      h. Ouzels are the birds.
      i. The ouzel is a bird.
      j. The ouzel is the bird.

It may be noted that the patient nouns of (17a—d) are nongeneric, while those of (17e—j) are generic. Evidently, however, the predicate nouns are all nongeneric. None of them refers to the universal class of students or birds. (This is evidently true in spite of the fact that [17c] does not have an alternative surface structure *The boys are sm students*, or [17g] the alternative surface structure *Ouzels are sm birds*; apparently the *sm* alternative is simply not available to a predicate noun.) If it is indeed the case that predicate nouns are never generic, this fact might be seen as a necessary consequence of the relation between a patient noun and a state verb. The noun is said to be in the condition specified by the verb, but the result is that with a predicate noun the patient is said to constitute a proper subset of the objects specified by the root of the predicate noun. *The boys* are said to be a proper subset of all *students*. The notion of a proper subset is incompatible with the meaning of generic; hence the unavailability of the generic inflection in these cases. Looking again at (17), we see that sentences (17c, d, g, h) have patients which are inflected as plural. The predicate nouns in these sentences are also plural, and must be so, while they cannot be made plural in the other sentences. Our conclusion must be that the patient and predicate nouns necessarily agree as to plurality. The choice of this inflection, furthermore, appears to reside in the patient rather than in the predicate noun. If that is so, then a rule is called for which automatically extends the plurality of a patient into the predicate:

(S14–11)

```
┌──────────────────┐    pat          ┌──────────────────┐    pat
│                  │    N      ──→    │                  │    N
V                       plural         V                      plural
N + predicativizer                     N + predicativizer
                                       plural
```

Thus, predicate nouns may be inflected as plural, but this inflection is determined for them by the patient. We can now take note of the fact that the predicate nouns in (17b, d, f, h, j) are inflected as definite, while those in the other sentences are not. There appears to be no relation between the definiteness or nondefiniteness of these predicate nouns and the inflection of the patient nouns. That is, the choice of definite is evidently a choice which can be made within the predicate noun itself. When the noun is definite, it indicates that the subset of the objects which the patient is said to constitute is a subset already known to the hearer, or at least that the speaker assumes this to be the case. Thus in (17b), *The boy is the student*, the speaker assumes that the hearer already knows the identity of the student being talked about. A predicate noun is thus subject to rule (S14–1) above, the rule which introduces the definite inflection, but to no other inflectional rules except (S14–11).

14.16 **Quantifiers.** Finally, a word needs to be said concerning the place of so-called quantifiers within the framework of noun inflection as described in this chapter. I refer to those semantic elements which are reflected in surface structure items such as *all, any, some, certain, a few,* and so on. I shall suggest that the semantic origin of such words lies in a class of inflectional units which have rather special properties. Suppose we label one such unit *all*, since it is reflected in surface structure by the word which is symbolized *all*. Apparently this unit may occur with a noun that already has been inflected as generic and plural. The question to be asked, then, is how the following two sentences differ semantically:

(18)   a. Elephants like peanuts.
       b. All elephants like peanuts.

The meanings of these sentences are certainly very similar, and it is difficult to find that the meaning of *all* does anything except to make more prominent or explicit the meaning of the generic plural inflection. In other words, the conjunction of *generic* and *plural* which is present in both sentences means that the entire class of elephants is involved, but (18b) gives a prominence and explicitness to that fact which is lacking in (18a). In (15.15) we shall see that there is something more to this prominence that it is related to the distribution of new information in the sentence. The very fact that it is the *entire* class of elephants which is being talked about is communicated as something new by the speaker in (18b), as it is not in (18a). Although there will be more to say about this matter in the next chapter, we can say now that a noun which has been inflected as generic and plural may be further inflected optionally as *all*:

(S14–12) $\begin{bmatrix} \text{generic} \\ \text{plural} \end{bmatrix} \longrightarrow$ all

Thus the difference between the experiencer nouns in (18a) and (18b), to be augmented in 15.15, for the moment can be diagramed as:

(18a)   (18b)
N   N
elephant   elephant
generic   generic
plural   plural
             all

14.17 Typically, a quantifier does more than make prominent (and present as new information) the inflection of a noun. Consider, for example, the following:

(19)   a. An elephant likes peanuts.
       b. Any elephant likes peanuts.
       c. Every elephant likes peanuts.

The noun in (19a) is inflected as generic but not plural. The meaning is that whatever elephant we may choose from the entire class, that individual will fit what is said in the rest of the sentence. In both (19b) and (19c) a quantifier has been added to this generic nonplural inflection, and each of these two quantifiers adds a unique meaning of its own. In (19b) there is evidently a prominence given to the fact that one elephant is randomly selected at a time, but in (19c) to the fact that *all* the individuals are being talked about. The difference seems to be between an emphasis on the random individual elephant vs. an emphasis on the entire class made up of these separately selected individuals. We might, then, formulate another rule as follows:

S14–13) $\begin{bmatrix} \text{generic} \\ -\text{plural} \end{bmatrix} \longrightarrow \begin{bmatrix} \text{any} \\ \text{every} \end{bmatrix}$

As another example of the additional meanings which may be contributed by quantifiers, we can look at the following:

(20) a. (Sm) elephants stepped on my car.
     b. Some elephants stepped on my car.
     c. Certain elephants stepped on my car.
     d. A few elephants stepped on my car.

In all these sentences the agent noun is nondefinite, nongeneric, and plural. In (20a) there is nothing more to say. In (20b), however, the noun is inflected with the quantifier *some* (which shows up phonetically with a higher pitch and greater amplitude than the optional surface unit represented as *sm*). In this sentence there seems to be an explicit vagueness as to the identity of the elephants; the speaker is not particularly concerned with which individual elephants were involved in the event. In (20c), on the other hand, where the noun is inflected with the quantifier *certain*, the speaker does show more concern for which elephants they were. In (20d), inflected as *a few*, there is the added information that this is a relatively small subset of elephants. Actually, the occurrence of *some* and *certain* is different from that of *a few*, since the latter requires the presence of plural while the first two do not. Hence we can have (21a, b) but not (21c):

(21) a. Some elephant likes peanuts.
     b. A certain elephant likes peanuts.
     c. *A few elephant likes peanuts.

14.18 But these sentences with *some* and *certain* illustrate still another semantic function which quantifiers may have. Earlier in this chapter we saw that the nature of a noun as generic or nongeneric is determined by the generic or nongeneric nature of the verb to which it is attached. The verb in both sentences of (21) is generic and therefore the nouns ought to be generic. But clearly they are not, and in fact the quantifier *some* is found only in nongeneric nouns. It will be remembered, however, that we have already encountered one case where the noun is not required to be generic in the presence of a generic verb; namely, when the noun has already been inflected as definite. Thus, *The elephants like peanuts* has a nongeneric experiencer noun, even though it has a generic verb. We accounted for this fact by saying that the nature of a noun as definite or nondefinite is determined first, by (S14–1), and that a noun which is left as nondefinite is then subject to the rule which makes it automatically generic in the presence of a generic verb—rule (S14–2). A definite noun is not subject to that rule, and remains nongeneric no matter what the verb may be. It now appears that a noun inflected with the quantifier *some* behaves in exactly the same manner as a definite noun; that is, it is immune to rule (S14–2) and is never made generic, even with a generic verb. This situation can be accounted for by introducing *some* (and *certain*) at the same point as *definite* in the sequence of rules, and by adding to (S14–2) the stipulation that it does not apply if the verb is inflected as either *definite* or *some* (or *certain*). Thus, in summary, the quantifier *some* really has three semantic functions: it gives prominence to the nongeneric nature of the noun, it adds a meaning of its own (perhaps a meaning of vagueness, in contrast to *certain*), and it prevents the noun from becoming generic even when attached to a generic verb.

14.19 There are, then, certain inflectional units—among them *definite*, *some*, *certain*, as well as *a few*—which allow a nongeneric noun to cooccur with a generic verb. There are apparently no inflectional units which allow the reverse; that is, which allow a generic noun to cooccur with a nongeneric verb. Thus, the quantifier *any* can only be introduced into a noun after that noun has been made generic through the influence of a generic verb. It requires the prior application of (S14–2), and there is simply no way that it can be introduced into a noun whose verb is nongeneric. Hence the already noted strangeness of sentence (5), *Any elephant stepped on my car.*

14.20 One other semantic peculiarity associated with quantifiers is important enough to mention here. In its simplest form it can be illustrated with the following sentences:

(22)   a. All elephants are big.
         b. All (of) the elephants are big.
         c. Some elephants are big.
         d. Some of the elephants are big.

Examples (22a, c) have patient nouns of the type already discussed, in which the inflection of the noun as either generic plural or as nongeneric has been reinforced by the quantifier *all* or *some*. Sentences (22b, d) have meanings which are different from those of the corresponding (22a, c). The difference is the same in each case; namely, that the universe of elephants which forms a starting point for the inflection is not the universe of all elephants, as it is in (22a, c), but some subset of elephants already known to the hearer—some *definite plural* subset. In (22b) the speaker is not saying that all conceivable elephants are big but that all elephants of this definite subset are. Similarly, in (22d) he is saying that a nongeneric subset of this definite subset has this property. The domain to which the several noun inflections are applied has been reduced from the total domain specified by the noun root to a definite plural subset of that domain. If the surface structures of (22b, d) reflected more closely the semantic structures, they would appear as follows:

for (22b): All elephants of the elephants are big.
for (22d): Some elephants of the elephants are big.

It is evident that a postsemantic deletion process has removed the first occurrence of the repeated noun from the surface structures in (22). (The word *of* may also be deleted in [22b], though not in [22d].) The phrase *of the elephants* in these two surface structures, then, reflects something in the semantic structure whose function is to shrink the domain from the class of all elephants to a definite plural subset of that class. I am inclined to see in this situation the necessity for the introduction of a new semantic relation, which I shall call *partitive*. It is a relation which holds between one noun and another, rather than between a noun and verb, and thus it differs from relations like *agent, patient, experiencer,* and so on. In a general way it can be said that a noun which contains a quantifier may have attached to it another noun, its *partitive*, which contains a noun root identical to that of the first noun and which is inflected as definite and plural:

(S14–14)

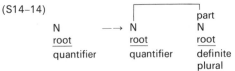

N   ⟶   N   part
                      N
root   root   root
quantifier   quantifier definite
                       plural

The term *quantifier* in this rule is a cover term for any member of the
set of inflectional units to which this label is appropriately given.
The rule is an oversimplification and ignores complexities of various
sorts. In this form, for example, it applies only to count nouns; both
here and above the situation with regard to noncount nouns has
been overlooked. In some such way as this, however, sentences like
(22b, d) can be produced. The crucial device is the introduction of a
partitive noun whose function is to limit in a specified way the
domain of objects specified by the noun root. The semantic structure of (22b) can be diagramed as shown in (23). The partitive

(23)

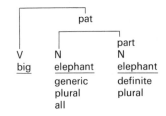

                pat

V   N   part
                      N
big   elephant   elephant
         generic   definite
         plural   plural
         all

relation is reflected in the surface structure by the presence of the
preposition *of*.

14.21   It is interesting to note, in connection with what was just said,
that (24b) is a natural thing to say, though (24a) is not:

(24)   a. *Any of the elephants stepped on my car.
        b. All of the elephants stepped on my car.

The verb here is nongeneric, a fact which must mean that the agent
noun is nongeneric also. The trouble with (24a) is that *any* is a
quantifier which occurs only in a generic noun. Thus, *any elephants
(of the elephants)* is incompatible with the nongeneric verb. One
might expect the same to be true of *all elephants (of the elephants)*
in (24b), but evidently it is not, for there is nothing wrong with this
sentence. What may be significant here is that the meaning of *all*
is such that the focus is on the totality of the class, not on one
member at a time as is the case with *any*. Consequently, *all elephants*
in (24b) has a meaning that coincides with the meaning of the

partitive noun *the elephants.* The class of objects which is in question here is the definite plural class defined by *the elephants,* and *all elephants of the elephants* means that we are dealing with that entire class. Now, *the elephants* is nongeneric, and thus compatible with the nongeneric verb. Thus *all elephants,* in itself generic, in this case happens to have a meaning which coincides with a meaning which is nongeneric; for that reason it is capable of occurring with a nongeneric verb. The genericness of the agent in (24b) extends only over a definite plural domain, not over the domain of all elephants. But when *all elephants* is not limited thus by a partitive element, when its domain is the universal class, then occurrence with a nongeneric verb continues to be ruled out:

(25)   *All elephants stepped on my car.

15

New and Old Information

15.1   The subject matter of this chapter is of unusual importance to our understanding of how language works. Once it is more fully understood, it promises to explain a number of significant facts which are now obscure. It is a subject which has been seriously neglected by the mainstream of linguistics,[1] and it is easy to see that this neglect has stemmed from the very situation which it is the aim of this book to combat: the refusal to admit and come to grips with the basic role played by semantic structure in the structure of language. As a starting point for our tentative discussion here, we can recall that language permits the transfer of information from the mind of the speaker to the mind of the hearer. We have seen that this information can be regarded as organized into sentences, each with a number of semantic units arranged to form a complex configuration. Now, typically it is the case that the speaker assumes that some of the information he is communicating is new; it is information he is introducing into the hearer's mind for the first time. But typically it is also the case that some of the information in the sentence is not new. Some of it is information which the speaker

---

[1] It has not been totally neglected, however. Some members of the "Prague School" have given it considerable attention, beginning with Vilém Mathesius and continuing now with, especially, the work of Czech linguists such as Jan Firbas (see Firbas 1966 and numerous other publications). Other recent discussions of this area have included Halliday (1967–68) and Kirkwood (1969).

and hearer already share at the time the sentence is spoken. This shared information constitutes a kind of starting point based on concepts already "in the air," to which the new information can be related. The old information may be shared from the common environment in which both the speaker and the hearer are interacting. Frequently it is also shared on the basis of sentences already uttered, in which case we might say that the common environment has been created linguistically. Consider, for example, the circumstances under which sentences like the following might be uttered:

(1)   a. The box is empty.
       b. The box was empty.

(Since the pitch assigned to items in the surface structure will be crucial to the examples given here, I shall follow a convention of underlining the word or words in a sentence on whose stressed syllable the strongest stress and highest pitch of the sentence falls. Thus, the strongest stress and highest pitch of the sentences in (1) is intended to fall on the first syllable of the word *empty*.) Sentence (1a) might be uttered, for example, when the speaker and the hearer have both been confronted by a box. This box, or rather the concept of this box, is part of the conceptual framework in the forefront of both the speaker's and the hearer's minds at the time (1a) is spoken. The sentence presupposes this framework and adds the new information that the box is empty—a fact, perhaps, which the speaker has just learned by looking into the box and which he is communicating to the hearer as new information by means of (1a). In (1b) it is most likely, because of the presence of *past*, that the common conceptual framework was created linguistically. That is, the speaker can be imagined to be recounting some past events. He may already have said that he found a box somewhere and looked into it. When first introduced, the concept of the box was new information. Thereafter, however, it became old information, part of the matrix of concepts present in the forefront of the minds of both the speaker and the hearer. By the time the speaker has come to utter (1b), *the box* is old information, and only the verb *was empty* is the new information which is being communicated.

15.2   This distinction between old and new information is the principal phenomenon which underlies discussions of what have been called *topic* and *comment*, or *theme* and *rheme*; other terms have also been used occasionally.[2] In a certain limited way the same distinction is also reflected in the terms *subject* and *predicate*. These last two terms have to do more properly with particular parts of surface structures, not semantic structures, but we shall see that there is a strong correlation between old information in semantic structures and *subject* in surface structure, at least in languages like English. During the discussion in this chapter I shall regard the common conceptual matrix within which the new information is placed — that is, the old information — as unmarked, and the new information as marked. We need, then, a term which will designate the semantic entity whose meaning is describable as "new information." The terms *comment* and *rheme* are both somewhat awkward, and it may present most clearly the meaning involved if I simply use the term *new*. I shall take the position that *new* is a specification which may be added, not to a whole verb or noun, but to a particular semantic unit within a verb or noun. At first we shall consider only cases in which it is a lexical unit that is specified as new; later we shall encounter some cases of other units which are so specified, in particular "quantifiers" and the inflectional unit *affirmative*. The fact that *new* applies only to a single semantic unit — say, to a lexical unit — and not to the entire verb or noun will be indicated in diagrams by indenting it below the unit to which it applies. The relevant aspects of the semantic structure underlying sentence (1a), for example, can be diagramed as in (2). This example can also be used

(2)
```
        ┌──────────┐
        │        pat
 V          N
 empty      box
 new
```

to illustrate in a general way the postsemantic treatment accorded new and old information in English. The distinction is reflected in English surface structure in two ways: through the establishment of surface structure *subjects* and through intonation. In what may be called the "least marked" instances, a surface structure subject carries the old information of a sentence. (The postsemantic identification of a noun as a *subject* has several consequences: in English such a noun will be linearized to precede the verb; if pronominalized it may show up in a special "subjective" case form; and in a limited

---

[2] Halliday (1967–68), however, sees theme and rheme as constituting a separate parameter from old and new information.

way the surface structure verb will show "agreement" with it.)
In addition, those surface structure items which reflect *new* information are (with some exceptions) spoken with a higher pitch (and
greater amplitude) than those which reflect old information, as
might, in fact, be expected from the fact that it is primarily the
new information the speaker wants to convey. Higher pitch and
amplitude quite evidently are related to an increase in the effectiveness of communication. We shall see as we proceed that neither the
establishment of postsemantic subjects nor the assignment of
higher pitch are related in a completely one-to-one fashion to the
new vs. old distinction, but the general correlation just described
can be taken as a basis for the description of exceptions to it.
Meanwhile, we can note that in the two sentences of (1) the noun,
which carries old information, is indeed the subject, while the item
which reflects the new information (*empty*) is indeed given the
highest pitch.

15.3   There is an interesting and understandable way in which the kind
of noun inflection discussed in Chapter 14 is restricted by the prior
inflection of a noun as new or not new. The unnaturalness of the
following surface structures may be cited by way of exemplification:

(3)   a. *A box is <u>empty</u>.
        b. *(Sm) boxes are <u>empty</u>.

(It must be remembered that these sentences are to be pronounced
with low pitch everywhere except on the word *empty*.) It is possible
that (3a) might be uttered in a situation where the speaker had been
looking through a group of boxes and suddenly came on one that
was empty. In that case its meaning would be like that of *One of the
boxes is empty*, where the universe of boxes is restricted to some
known subset. In characterizing (3a) as unnatural I have in mind a
meaning in which the selection of *a box* is made from the universe
of all boxes; the remarks which follow will apply to such a meaning.
In both the sentences of (3) the noun *box* is neither definite nor
generic. Its nondefinite character, of course, is evident from the
absence of the definite article. If *sm* is present in (3b), the surface
structure confirms that *box* is nongeneric as well, since a generic
plural is never represented by *sm*. By itself, the surface phrase *a box*
in (3a) could be either generic or nongeneric; however, *empty* is a
nonrelative state and therefore must be nongeneric (13.4); con-

sequently *a box* must be nongeneric also. If we accept, then, that the nouns in (3) are neither definite nor generic, how can we explain the fact that these sentences are unnatural? To put the question the other way around, why does a noun which conveys old information have to be either definite or generic? Old information means that the concept is already familiar to the hearer (or at least that the speaker assumes this to be the case). This familiarity is consistent with a definite noun, where the speaker assumes that the hearer knows the identity of the box, or with a generic noun (as in *A box is a container*), where the entire class of boxes can justifiably be assumed to be a familiar concept to anyone who is a speaker of the language. (Lack of familiarity with the generic concept would imply a pathological gap in the hearer's linguistic competence.) In the nondefinite nongeneric case, however, as in (3), the speaker assumes that the hearer does not know which box or boxes is being talked about. He is introducing this particular subset of boxes for the first time. The concept therefore must be new information. The trouble with the sentences of (3) is that they treat something which has to be new information as if it were old information by placing it first in the surface structure and giving it low pitch. How can we formalize this semantic restriction? Actually, we can do it quite easily by adding a stipulation to rule (S14-1), the rule that was stated in Chapter 14 in order to introduce the *definite* inflection, to the effect that that rule is obligatory if the noun does not contain *new* and if at the same time the verb to which this noun is attached is not inflected as generic. With a nongeneric verb the noun would have to be nongeneric also, if it were not definite. This stipulation prevents the conjunction of nondefinite, nongeneric, and non-new from occurring. It implies, however, that the status of a noun as new or not new must be determined before rule (S14-1) applies. Let us turn now to the question of how such a determination is made, with the understanding that the rules which follow are to be applied before (S14-1).

15.4   An assumption that will be basic to the remarks which follow is that there is one "least marked" distribution of new and old information in a sentence. It will be assumed that other distributions are also possible but that they are in some way more marked. It is necessary for the reader to be aware of this point now, since he will be able to imagine sentences similar to those about to be cited in which the distribution of new information is not what I say it is. At least some of these other sentences, however, will be accounted for later in the chapter. Let us now consider the following set of sentences, in which (1a) is repeated, along with two others:

(4)   a. It's <u>raining</u>.
        b. The box is <u>empty</u>.
        c. David <u>laughed</u>.

Semantically these sentences consist of nothing but a verb, as in the ambient sentence (4a), or of a verb accompanied by a single noun: either a patient, as in (4b), or an agent, as in (4c). In all three sentences it is the verb root which supplies the new information. When a single noun root is present, its information is not new. These sentences suggest, therefore, the hypothesis that in least marked sentences the verb, and only the verb, contains new information.

15.5   But we need only look at any sentence in which there is more than one noun to see that this is not quite the case. In each of the following sentences there are two nouns:

(5)   a. The box is under the <u>table</u>.
        b. David emptied the <u>box</u>.
        c. Lisa received a <u>present</u>.

It might appear from the surface structures of these sentences that *new* is assigned only to the root of the final noun in each: to the location noun root *table* in (5a), to the patient noun root *box* in (5b), and to the patient noun root *present* in (5c). These are the items whose surface reflections come last in the sentences, and the only items to be given high pitch. I have in mind, however, that these sentences should be understood in the meanings that would be appropriate as answers to questions like:

(6)   a. Where is the <u>box</u>?
        b. What did David do <u>then</u>?
        c. Why is Lisa so <u>excited</u>?

In these meanings it is not only the noun roots *table*, *box*, and *present* which are new, but the verb roots *under*, *empty*, and *receive* as well. It must, then, be true of the postsemantic treatment of new information in English that sentence-final nouns receive high pitch in the surface structure, but that the verbs which precede them do not

receive this high pitch even though they do convey new information. At this point it might appear that high pitch simply falls
automatically on the last word of a surface structure sentence, and
that it does not necessarily have anything to do with the semantic
presence of new information. As we proceed, however, we shall see
that high pitch is indeed a surface reflection of the semantic presence
of *new*, and that the fact about the sentences in (5) which must be
remarked upon is that the surface structure verbs are not given
high pitch even though they *do* reflect new information. What is
more interesting about these sentences is the light they shed on the
distribution of new information within semantic structure. It would
appear that in these least marked cases there is a certain priority
which determines the assignment of *new*. In such sentences, evidently,
the verb root always supplies new information. The same can be said
of a location noun root, as in (5a). We can thus state rules which say
that a verb root and a location noun are obligatorily new:

(S15–1) $\dfrac{\text{V}}{\text{root}} \longrightarrow \dfrac{\text{V}}{\underset{\text{new}}{\text{root}}}$

(S15–2) $\dfrac{\underset{\text{root}}{\overset{\text{loc}}{\text{N}}}}{} \longrightarrow \underset{\text{new}}{\dfrac{\overset{\text{loc}}{\text{N}}}{\text{root}}}$

Sentences (4b) and (5a) make it clear that a patient noun root does
not convey new information if it is the only noun root in the sentence
or if the sentence also contains only a location noun in addition.
Sentences (5b, c), however, suggest that a patient noun root *is*
specified as new if the sentence also contains either an agent noun
or a beneficiary (*David* and *Lisa* respectively). It is only if such other
nouns are absent that a patient noun root conveys old information.
Taking into account also that a complement noun root behaves in
the same manner, we can state this requirement for patient noun
roots as follows:

(S15–3) $\begin{Bmatrix}\text{pat}\\\text{comp}\end{Bmatrix} \atop {\underset{\text{root}}{\text{N}}} \longrightarrow \begin{Bmatrix}\text{pat}\\\text{comp}\end{Bmatrix} \atop {\underset{\text{new}}{\dfrac{\text{N}}{\text{root}}}} \Big/ \begin{Bmatrix}\text{ben}\\\text{agt}\end{Bmatrix}$

15.6 But there remains the question of what happens to the distribution of new information if a sentence contains both a beneficiary and an agent noun, as in:

(7)   David gave Lisa a picture.

In (7) the verb root, the patient noun root *picture*, and the beneficiary noun root *Lisa* are all new information, and the only old information is conveyed by the agent noun root *David*. The continuous underlining in (7) indicates that in the pronunciation of this sentence the pitch is high on the first syllable of *Lisa* and remains high up the stressed syllable of *picture*. This example, like those of (5), illustrates the fact that high pitch regularly reflects new information except that a *verb* root specified as new is not represented in the surface structure with high pitch unless it is final. The main point to be made about (7), however, is that it shows that a beneficiary noun root is new when the sentence also contains an agent, a fact which can be expressed as follows:

(S15–4) ben   ben
        N $\longrightarrow$ N   /agt
        root   root
                    new

15.7   To summarize, in a least marked sentence the verb root and a location noun root (if there is one) will always be new, a patient noun root will be new if the sentence also has a beneficiary or agent noun, and a beneficiary noun root will be new if the sentence also has an agent noun. To look at this situation from the opposite point of view, a sentence of this kind, if it contains a noun at all, will always contain one and only one noun root which is *not* new—which conveys *old* information. This noun root will always be in the agent if there is one, in the beneficiary if there is one without an agent, and in the patient if there is one without either an agent or a beneficiary. A location noun does not occur without a patient present also; if there are only the two nouns, the patient noun root will be old, the location noun root new. It is this hierarchy consisting of location, patient, beneficiary, and agent with respect to the assignment of *new* that was one of the chief reasons for positioning these relations as they have been positioned in diagrams of semantic structure. It can be seen that new information is on the left in these diagrams, while old information is contained only within the one noun which is farthest to the right. In fact, an alternative to rules (S15–1) through

(S15–4) as they are stated above would be to say simply that every lexical unit in a diagram is new except for the last noun root to the right. This distribution of new and old information creates semantic structures like the following, whose surface structures are given in the examples indicated. (The derivational structure of certain verb roots is not shown, and many other details are omitted.)

(4a)   V
      rain
        new
                                                     It's raining.

(4b)
           pat
    V   N
    empty box   The box is empty.
    new

(4c)
           agt
    V   N
    laugh David   David laughed.
    new

(5a)
           loc   pat
    V   N   N
    under table box   The box is under the table.
    new   new

(5b)
           pat   agt
    V   N   N
    empty box David   David emptied the box.
    new   new

(5c)
           pat   ben
    V   N   N
    receive present Lisa   Lisa received a present.
      new   new

(7)
           pat   ben   agt
    V   N   N   N
    give picture Lisa David   David gave Lisa a picture.
    new   new   new

15.8   **Passive.** It is a consequence of the rules set forth in the above
       paragraph that, if the verb of a sentence is an action-process, its
       patient noun root will convey new information and its agent noun
       root old information. It is not surprising that situations sometimes
       arise in which this distribution of new and old information is
       inappropriate; there are sometimes situations in which the patient
       noun root of an action-process verb conveys old information and in
       which the agent noun root conveys new information. One way in
       which situations like these are accommodated in English is through
       the specification of the verb as *passive*. The semantic function of a
       passive verb I think is explained most easily if we regard *passive* as
       an inflectional unit which can be added to an action-process (as
       well as to an experiential-process) verb:

(S15–5) V   ——→ passive
         process
         {action   }
         {experiential}

       The presence of this inflectional unit actually changes the semantic
       functioning of the verb in two major ways. For one thing, it allows
       an action-process or experiential-process verb to exist without
       an accompanying agent or experiencer. Thus, we find sentences
       like:

(8)   a. The box was emptied.
        b. David was seen.

       in which there is only one noun, and that noun is a patient. There
       seems no reason to believe that a sentence like (8a) contains an agent
       in its semantic structure or that (8b) contains an experiencer whose
       absence from the surface structure is only the result of postsemantic
       deletion. It seems more in line with the meanings of these sentences
       to say that there is no agent or experiencer in their semantic struc-
       tures to begin with. It is possible to account for this absence formally
       by modifying rule (S9–5) in Chapter 9, the rule which assigns an
       agent noun to an action verb, and rule (S12–3) in Chapter 12, the
       rule which assigns an experiencer noun to an experiential verb. To
       both rules a statement can be added to the effect that the rule is
       optional if the verb is passive. Rule (S15–5), therefore, the rule which
       introduces the passive inflection, must be ordered to apply before
       (S9–5) and (S12–3). One function of passive, then, is to allow an

action-process or experiential-process verb to occur without an agent or experiencer.

15.9   The other function of the passive inflection is to change the order of priorities for the distribution of new information. Let us begin our consideration of this matter with the following examples:

(9)   a. The box was emptied.
        b. The picture was given to Lisa.
        c. Lisa was given the picture.

As before, there is more than one meaning which can lead to each of these surface structures, but the intended meanings are those which would be appropriate answers to questions like:

(10)   a. What was done with the box?
        b. What became of the picture?
        c. Why is Lisa so excited?

With these meanings, the verb root of each sentence conveys new information, as does the beneficiary noun root in (9b) and the patient noun root in (9c). Old information is conveyed by the patient noun roots in (9a, b), and by the beneficiary noun root in (9c). Our conclusion must be that a passive verb is like other verbs in being subject to rule (S15–1), which causes its lexical unit to be specified as new, but that rules (S15–3) and (S15–4) are inapplicable when the verb is passive. Instead, the following rules apply:

(S15–6)   ben   ben
          N   ⟶   N   /V
          root   root passive
                           new

(S15–7) $\begin{Bmatrix} \text{pat} \\ \text{comp} \end{Bmatrix}$ $\begin{Bmatrix} \text{pat} \\ \text{comp} \end{Bmatrix}$ ben
          N   ⟶   N   /V   N
          root   root   passive   −new
                           new

Rule (S15–6) says that a beneficiary noun root *may* be specified as new if it is attached to a passive verb. If it is so specified, the result is a sentence like (9b); if not, we have a sentence like (9c). Rule (S15–7) says that a patient (or complement) noun root *must* be specified as new if it is attached to a passive verb which is also accompanied by a beneficiary noun root that is not so specified, as in (9c). In other words, when there is both a patient and a beneficiary, one or the other must contain new information, but not both. Under one of these two possibilities, and under any other circumstance, as in (9a), the patient of a passive verb contains old information, in direct contrast to the patient of a nonpassive verb which, except in a locative sentence like (5a), regularly contains new information. It should be noted that rules (S15-6) and (S15-7) must be ordered in such a way that sentences with passive verbs are subject solely to them and not to (S15-3) and (S15-4). The same is true of the rule described in the next paragraph.

15.10   In addition to the fact that the patient noun root of a passive verb normally conveys old information, it is also true that the agent noun root of a passive verb normally conveys new information. We saw earlier that the agent noun root of a nonpassive verb never conveys new information in sentences of this least marked kind. Thus, the passive inflection provides a useful device for assigning *new* to an agent noun root, as in the following:

(11)   a. The box was emptied by David.
         b. The picture was given to Lisa by David.
         c. Lisa was given the picture by David.

The following rule seems called for, then, in addition to (S15-6) and (S15-7):

(S15-8) agt   agt
         N $\longrightarrow$ N   /V
         root   root passive
                       new

That is, an agent noun root must be inflected as new in the environment of a passive verb. In the sentences of (11) it is to be understood that, after the high pitch is reached on the stressed syllable of the first underlined word, the pitch falls. It falls, however, only part way, and not to its lowest level as it does at the end of the sentence (as indicated by the period). The convention is that an underlined word has a falling pitch, beginning as soon as the high pitch is reached on its stressed syllable, if the underline does not continue unbroken into the next word—as in sentence (7) earlier. The fall will be only partial unless the word is followed by a period without the intervention of another underlined word. The pitch will remain at its mid level until it rises again on the stressed syllable of the next underlined word. It can be seen in the sentences of (11) that high pitch is assigned not only to the surface representation of the agent at the end but also to the preceding noun or verb in the manner that it would be assigned if the agent were not there. To summarize the last two paragraphs, a passive verb need not have an agent (or experiencer) noun accompanying it. If it does have one, however, that noun contains new information. The patient (or complement) of a passive verb usually contains old information but does not do so if there is also a beneficiary in the sentence and that beneficiary contains old information. Undoubtedly there are other semantic units besides *passive* which have the effect of changing the distribution of new and old information originally described. On the basis of sentences like (5a), *The box is under the table*, for example, it was hypothesized that when a sentence contains simply a patient and a location noun, it is the root of the location noun which conveys new information while that of the patient noun is old. Precisely the reverse distribution is found in sentences like the following, where we might assume that the presence of some semantic element has brought about a situation in which the location is old and the patient new:

(12)   a. The table has a box under it.
        b. The box has a pencil in it.
        c. The box contains a pencil.

15.11   **More marked distributions of new.** It was seen above that the normal distribution of new and old information, whether in a nonpassive or a passive sentence, results in *new* being assigned to the verb root and also to all of the noun roots except one. That is, in each sentence there is one noun root which conveys old information, while everything else conveys information that is new. Sometimes, however, sentences are found in which *all* the noun roots (as well as the verb root) carry new information. The following are examples:

(13)   a. The box is empty.
        b. David laughed.
        c. David emptied the box.
        d. The box was emptied.
        e. An elephant stepped on my car.

All the noun roots and verb roots in these sentences are specified semantically as new. The last four sentences can be imagined as answers to the questions *What happened then?*, rather than, for example, *What did David do?* Sentence (13a) might be the answer to the question *What's the matter?* Although other meanings, of a type to be discussed below, can be imagined for the sentences in (13), we are concerned now only with the meanings in which the new inflection has been extended to all the noun roots: to the patient noun root in (13a, d), to the agent noun root in (13b, c, e). There are also sentences in which more than one noun root conveys old information:

(14)   David emptied the box.

The meaning intended for (14) is that which might appropriately follow a sentence like *David came upon a box.* As is true of sentences given earlier as well, the non-new elements in this sentence would usually be "pronominalized"—that is, the non-new lexical units would be lost postsemantically (see 16.15)—so that the sentence ultimately would have the surface form *He emptied it.* But with or without pronominalization, the semantic structure of (14) is one in which not only the agent noun root *David* but also the patient noun root *box* conveys old information, contrary to the least marked distribution in which the patient noun root would be specified as new. In producing sentences like (13), in which an otherwise non-new noun root is marked as new, and like (14), in which an otherwise new noun root is non-new, we can first assume that *new* has already been distributed in the least marked manner described earlier. The sentences in (13) and (14) can then be regarded as having arisen from the operation of a rule with a Greek letter variable of the type often employed in phonological rules:

(S15–9) N $\longrightarrow$ N
         root   root
         αnew $-\alpha$new

This rule says that a noun root specified as new may be converted optionally into one that is not so specified, while at the same time a noun root not specified as new may optionally receive this specification.

15.12 **Contrastive sentences.** The following illustrate sentences of a still more specialized kind:

(15)   a. The box is empty.
        b. David laughed.

c. <u>David</u> emptied the box.
d. David <u>emptied</u> the box.
e. David emptied the <u>box</u>.
f. <u>David</u> gave Lisa a picture.
g. David <u>gave</u> Lisa a picture.
h. David gave <u>Lisa</u> a picture.
i. David gave Lisa a <u>picture</u>.
j. The <u>box</u> was emptied by David.
k. The box was <u>emptied</u> by David.
l. The box was emptied by <u>David</u>.

Because there is no other underlined word between the first such word and the sentence-final period, it is understood that the pitch begins falling to its lowest point as soon as it has reached its high point on the stressed syllable of the underlined word. In each of these sentences the lexical unit specified as new (signaled in the surface structure by the high pitch) can be understood as if it were selected from a list of alternatives which might have occurred in its place. The speaker is saying that this lexical unit is the correct one, taken from an implicit set of possible alternatives. I shall say that a sentence whose new information is understood in this way is *contrastive*. More precisely, I shall say that there is an inflectional unit *contrastive* which may be added to a verb. Like other inflections of a verb, its meaning applies to the sentence as a whole, so that we can talk of a contrastive sentence in the same way that we may talk of a past or perfective or negative sentence. To repeat, a contrastive sentence conveys the information that the *new* semantic unit within it has been selected by the speaker from various implied alternatives as the correct one to make the sentence a true sentence. Thus, for example, (15c) implies a context in which there were several people who might have emptied the box; the speaker is saying that the member of this group who actually did so was David. What is new, therefore, is not so much the semantic unit *David* as the fact that the speaker selected *David* rather than some other possibility. In a contrastive sentence, *new* means that the *choice* of the unit to which it is attached (rather than some other possible choice) is being presented by the speaker as new information.[3] Sentence (15d) implies that

---

[3] Perhaps, then, contrastive sentences should not be thought to contain the specification *new* at all, but rather some other specification which might be labeled *focus*. In that case, *new* and *focus* would be in complementary distribution, the former occurring only in noncontrastive sentences, the latter only in contrastive ones. See n. 4 below, and n. 2 in chap. 16.

David might have done several different things with the box, but it says that what he actually did was to empty it. Sentence (15e) implies that there was a set of things which David might have emptied, but that what he did empty was the box. The reader might also take note of the fact that (15e) is homonymous with (5b) above, and that this surface structure is indeed ambiguous. Either both the verb root and the patient noun root are new, as in (5b), or the sentence is contrastive and only the patient noun root is new, as in (15e). In contrastive sentences, as we shall see below, those items which are new are always given high pitch; thus the verb root in (15e), unlike that in (5b), cannot be new. These two sentences would be answers to different questions: (5b) to the question *What did David do?*, (15e) to a question such as *Did David empty the box or the suitcase?*

15.13   It is possible to account formally for sentences like those of (15) by adding a rule to the effect that the verb of any sentence may optionally be inflected as contrastive:

(S15–10)   V —→» contrastive

In the presence of a contrastive verb, the rules cited earlier for the least marked distribution of *new* do not apply. Instead, some such rule as the following can be posited:

(S15–11)   <u>root</u> ——→ <u>root</u> (applied one or more times)
                                 new

That is, any root whatsoever may take on the *new* specification and thereby be established as the item being focused on. There is no priority or hierarchy in which this specification is assigned. Probably the majority of contrastive sentences show only one item that is new, as is the case in all the sentences of (15). The corresponding noncontrastive sentences, on the other hand, in the least marked distribution, will show more than one new item in any sentence containing more than a single noun. Diagrams of the relevant aspects of the semantic structures of (15c, d, e) are provided by way of illustration.

(15c)
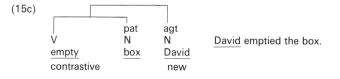

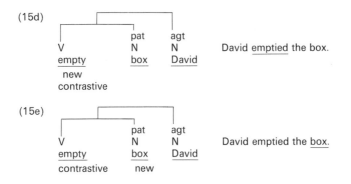

(15d) David emptied the box.

(15e) David emptied the box.

15.14 There are, nevertheless, numerous contrastive sentences in which more than one item is new. In each of the sentences of (16) there are two new items, and contrastive sentences with more than two items are also found:

(16) a. David emptied the box.
      b. David emptied the box.
      c. David emptied the box.

The fact that the underline is broken at the end of *David* in (16a) means that the pitch falls part way during the pronunciation of this word, to rise again on the stressed syllable of the following underlined word *emptied*, where it then begins to fall to its lowest point because no other underlined word intervenes before the period. As mentioned above, every item which conveys new information in a contrastive sentence is represented with high pitch. Thus (16c), which contains the same distribution of *new* as (5b):

(5b) David emptied the box.

exhibits, because of its contrastiveness, a high pitch on the verb which is absent in (5b). Sentence (5b) is instead homonymous with the contrastive sentence (15e), in which only the patient noun root *box* is new. Furthermore, there is a fall in pitch within each of these words which is not present in a noncontrastive sentence. That is, every new item in a contrastive sentence is represented with a high falling pitch.[4] Thus there is a difference in pronunciation between the

[4]If *new* and *focus* were distinguished, as suggested in n. 3, the falling pitch could be considered a reflex of *focus*. Here I am regarding it as triggered by the presence of *contrastive* within the verb.

noncontrastive sentence (13b):

(13b)   David laughed.

where there is no fall during the first word, and the corresponding
contrastive sentence, where there is such a fall, as would be indicated with a break in the underline between the two words:

(17)   David laughed.

The relevant semantic structure of (16a) can be diagramed as shown:

(16a)

```
         ┌─────────────┐
   ┌─────┤             │
   │         pat     agt
   V         N       N
   empty     box     David
    new              new
   contrastive
```

The meanings of these contrastive sentences with more than one
new item call for some comment. In accordance with what was
said earlier regarding the meaning of *contrastive*, (16a) means
that *David* is selected by the speaker from a list of several possibilities
and that the same is true of *empty*. As a result, the new information
provided by the sentence is really the pairing of *David* with *empty*.
The speaker is saying that this pairing is a valid one, within the
given context. Thus, while *George* might have *filled* the box, the
appropriate pairing of *David* is with *empty* and vice versa. Similar
remarks could be made for the other pairings of new elements in
(16). In (16b) *George* might have emptied the *suitcase*, but it was
David who emptied the *box*, and so on.

15.15 **Quantifiers again.** We are now in a better position to understand
one of the main properties of quantifiers, an incomplete discussion
of which was given at the end of Chapter 14. Quantifiers, it seems,
regularly communicate new information. While it is not generally
the case that inflectional units, as I have assumed quantifiers to be,
can be singled out as new information, it is nevertheless the normal
role of quantifiers to be so treated:

(18)   All elephants like peanuts.

Using again the term *quantifier* as a cover term for any inflectional unit of this kind, we can state a rule which regularly makes a quantifier new:

(S15–12) quantifier $\longrightarrow$ quantifier
                                          new

As before, the unit *new* is indented below the quantifier to indicate that it applies only to that unit, and not to the noun as a whole. Sentence (18) can be diagramed as shown in (19). The fact that a

(19)

```
       ┌─────────┐
   ┌───┘          │
   │      pat         exp
   V      N           N
   like   peanut      elephant
                      generic
                      plural
                      all
                        new
```

quantifier can be specified—in fact, regularly *is* specified—as *new* might suggest that quantifiers should not be regarded as inflectional elements within nouns, but that they should be handled as semantic units with independent status, perhaps as verbs of a special kind, perhaps as a third kind of entity parallel to nouns and verbs. A particular quantifier like *all* or *some* would then be a lexical unit within such a verb or other entity. I do not wish to rule out such a possibility. It should be pointed out, however, that quantifiers differ from lexical units such as verb roots in several ways. For one thing, there are relatively few of them, if we ignore the trivial fact that numerals, a type of quantifier, are unlimited. The number of quantifier roots would be quite small, relative to the great number of both verb and noun roots. Second, quantifiers evidently are not subject to inflection. In this way too they are strikingly different from verbs and nouns. Third, their meanings are based essentially on a reinforcement of the meaning of the inflectional units of a noun, even though typically they add some further meaning of their own. They are intimately tied to noun inflection in a way that we might not expect of a more independent kind of unit. One further bit of evidence against interpreting quantifiers as verbs, or as something sui generis, will appear in the following paragraph.

15.16 The assignment of *new* to a quantifier does not hinder its assignment to other elements in the sentence. Thus, we find sentences like:

(20)   a. All elephants like peanuts.
        b. Some elephants are small.

It is easiest to interpret such sentences as if they were contrastive,
and in fact the fall in pitch at the end of *elephants* in (20a) can only
reflect a contrastive meaning. Taking this fact into account, sentence (20a), which has three *new* elements, can be diagramed as
shown. *New* is a feature of the verb, of the experiencer noun, and of

(20a)

```
        ┌─────────────┬──────────────┐
┌───────┤             │              │
│             pat           exp
V             N             N
like          peanut        elephant
    new                         new
    contrastive                 generic
                                plural
                                all
                                    new
```

the quantifier *all* within that noun. The sentence means that *all*,
elephant, and *like* have all three been chosen from three sets of
possibilities as correctly belonging together in this way, with the
implication that there may be at least some members of other
species of animals which do not like peanuts. It is interesting to
observe that we do not find the expected fall in pitch on the word
all in (20a) as we do on the word *elephant*. This fact, it seems to me,
may be explainable on the basis that *all* is a nonlexical unit, as was
hypothesized in the last paragraph and earlier. It can be observed
further that the pitch does not fall *during* the word *some* in (20b)
either, although it begins at a lower point at the beginning of the
following non-new word. We might conclude that the special
intonational feature which is associated with the presence of
contrastive, the fall in pitch during a word reflecting new information, is present only when the word reflects a lexical unit, and
specifically not a quantifier.

15.17 **Negative and affirmative sentences.** If quantifiers are indeed inflectional units they need not be regarded as the only inflectional
units which are subject to the *new* specification. Particularly
noteworthy among the other possibilities are two closely related
inflections of verbs, one of which perhaps may best be regarded as
the antonym of the other. I refer to the inflectional units *negative*
and *affirmative*. The former *may* be new, the latter *must* be so. If

either is new, the sentence containing it apparently must also be contrastive. These possibilities are illustrated in the following sentences:

(21)   a. Elephants don't like peanuts.
       b. Elephants don't like peanuts.
       c. Elephants do like peanuts.

The first two sentences both contain the *negative* inflection. Sentence (21a) has the regular distribution of new information, in which both the verb and the patient are new. Sentence (21b), on the other hand, shows the inflectional unit *negative* specified as new, within a contrastive sentence. The meaning of such a sentence stresses the fact that it is the negative and not the affirmative assertion which is true. Its most likely implication is that something has already been said about elephants *liking* peanuts. Sentence (21c), on the contrary, contains a semantic unit *affirmative* (perhaps, as suggested, an antonymous derivation from *negative*). This sentence is most likely to imply that a negative sentence like (21a) or (21b) has preceded, and that the speaker is asserting the truth of the opposite. There are many sentences in which a so-called verb auxiliary is given high pitch in the surface structure, for example:

(22)   a. David is tall.
       b. David can sing.
       c. David must have sung.

where it is actually the presence of the semantic unit *affirmative*, accompanied necessarily by *new* within a sentence that is contrastive, which is being signaled. In (22c), for example, the meaning is paraphrasable as *I infer that David did sing*. In none of these sentences is *new* attached to whatever semantic element, if any, the high-pitched surface structure item directly reflects. Rather, in all of them it is a contrastive affirmation which is responsible for the high pitch.

15.18 **"Ergative" languages.** One often hears it said that certain languages are of the *ergative* type. Among such languages, for example, is the Onondaga language discussed in Chapter 4 and again to be discussed in Chapter 17. It is customary to say that a language of this kind has two ways of representing subject nouns. A noun which is the subject of a transitive verb is represented in one way (say, by the *ergative case*), while a noun which is either the subject of an intransitive verb or the object of a transitive verb is represented in a different way (say, by a case which I shall refer to here simply as *nonergative*). A language of this type may seem perverse to a speaker of English. Why should not all subjects be represented in the same way, and what do the subjects of intransitive verbs have in common with the objects of transitive ones? In the light of what was said in this chapter together with the earlier discussion of patient and agent nouns, the situation, I think, should be clear. In the first place, it is evident that the features *ergative* and *nonergative case*, as well as the features *subject* and *object*, belong to surface structure, not semantic structure. Nevertheless, they do reflect semantic features in some way. Ergative and nonergative, as they are found in the surface structures of certain languages, evidently reflect the relation which a noun bears to a verb. Although there are exceptions, generally it is true that an agent noun is represented in the surface structure in the ergative case, while a patient noun is represented in the nonergative case. On the other hand, subject and object in the surface structure of English reflect the distinction between old and new information. We have seen that in English, except in the more marked kinds of sentences, the subject of a sentence represents a noun which supplies old information while the object represents a noun which supplies new information. The statement that an ergative noun represents the subject of a transitive verb while a nonergative noun represents the subject of an intransitive verb and the object of a transitive one is thus a confusion of two distinct semantic parameters: the agent-patient distinction on the one hand and the new-old information distinction on the other. (This confusion is only compounded by the fact that in the descriptions of some languages, among them the Iroquois languages, the term *subjective* is used instead of *ergative* and the term *objective* instead of *nonergative*.) How did this confusion arise? Is there any way in which the agent-patient distinction and the new-old information distinction are related? In fact there is. The connection between the various noun relations (including those of agent and patient) and the distribution of new and old information was discussed earlier in this chapter. A patient was seen to supply old information in a sentence where it is the only noun, or where the only other noun is a location. Such a sentence is "intransitive." Because it is old information, such a patient noun is represented in the surface structure of English as a subject. Thus it is true that while it is the patient status of the noun which is marked in the surface structure of the exotic language by the nonergative case, this case happens to coincide with the subject of an intransitive verb in English. In a sentence where there is an agent as well as a patient—in a "transitive" sentence—the patient supplies new information. Therefore such a patient is represented in the surface structure of English as an object. In this kind of sentence, if the patient status of the noun is again marked in the surface structure of the exotic language by its nonergative case, this case happens to coincide with the object of a transitive verb in English. Finally, an agent is typically old information, so that it is represented in the surface structure of English as a subject. If its agent status is marked in the surface structure of the exotic language by the ergative case, this case happens to coincide with the subject of a transitive verb in English. There is one complication, however: the fact that the subject of an intransitive verb in English will sometimes correspond to an agent rather than a patient in the other language. It will do so in those instances where the verb is a simple action, not an action-process (a transitive verb) or a simple process or state (the kinds of intransitive verbs which fit the discussion above). In a sentence like *The dog barked*, for example, *the dog*, being an agent, ought to appear in the ergative case in the surface structure of the exotic language. We would then expect the subject of an intransitive verb in English to correspond to an ergative noun in the other language, contrary to the statement made earlier. That is precisely the situation with respect to the Iroquois languages, at least.[5] In those languages the statement made at the beginning of this paragraph holds for intransitive verbs which are states or processes, but not for intransitive verbs which are actions. Thus the correlation between semantic agent and surface ergative— as well as between semantic patient and surface nonergative—is complete in those languages (although, as we might expect in the assignment of surface structure features, there are some random exceptions). This is not to say that surface structure cases analogous to these may not represent semantic relations like patient and agent in a different way in some other language. The point is that the English surface structure features of subject and object do not represent such semantic relations at all, but rather the distribution

[5]There are other languages of the ergative type for which the following statements do not hold.

of old and new information. Subject and object are connected with patient, agent, and other semantic relations only indirectly, through the fact that these relations do play a role in the distribution of old and new information.

15.19 Every language, it should be remarked in closing, has its own way of representing old and new information in its surface structure. Word order and intonation seem to play the major role in such representation, perhaps in all languages. It is impossible, however, to make general statements of this kind with much assurance, since the matter has been so little studied. Other devices, certainly, are found. In Japanese, for example, we find the surface structure particles *wa*, reflecting old information, and *ga*, reflecting new. Undoubtedly various surface structure features which have seemed problematic in the past will yield to a more satisfactory explanation in the light of this distinction.

16

Some Postsemantic Processes

16.1   Except for a few passing remarks, the preceding chapters have
dealt almost exclusively with the formation of semantic structures.
There is of course, much of language which lies outside the semantic
area proper. In Chapter 7 we saw the remainder of language in
terms of several kinds of processes whose function is to convert
semantic structures into phonetic ones. These processes were seen
as falling into three major types: first, *postsemantic processes*, by
which a semantic structure is converted into a surface structure;
second, *symbolization*, by which the postsemantic items in a surface
structure are converted into underlying phonological configurations;
and third, *phonological processes*, which finally lead to a phonetic
output. I have been most concerned with the nature of semantic
structure because it has been viewed here as constituting the most
important and at the same time the least understood area of language.
As far as phonological processes are concerned, it is fortunate that
the syntacticist view of language assigns them a place which is not
essentially different from that given them here. They have been the
subject of careful investigation for some time, and it is not the
intention of the present work to add anything new in this area. As
it happens, there is also little need to devote much space to the
process of symbolization, since it is essentially a matter of the
one-to-one replacement of surface structure items by configurations
of underlying phonological units. Minor complications arise
from the fact that some surface items are symbolized in different

ways in different environments, and that occasionally two or more items may be given a composite symbolization. A few examples will be given toward the end of this chapter. The third kind of process, to which I have given the label *postsemantic*, is roughly analogous to the transformations of syntactist theory. Because of this analogy, which means that some—perhaps a great deal—of what has been learned about transformations can be translated validly into terms appropriate to the present theory, as well as because a detailed treatment of postsemantic processes would require such an extended discussion that the main thrust of the present work would be diverted, I shall devote only a small amount of space to this area. I shall focus the discussion on one example, in which a particular sentence is carried from semantic structure to surface structure. I hope thereby to illustrate the kinds of processes which a fuller treatment would investigate in detail. In so doing, also, I hope once again to make the point that it is the nature of semantic structure which is the crucial issue in linguistics at the present time. It will be seen, I think, that the kinds of semantic structures which have been described so far are amenable to conversion into surface structures of a kind which, after symbolization, will serve as an appropriate input to phonological processes as they are presently understood. The details of postsemantic processes, both the individual processes and the ordering of their application, are intricate. So far as I can see, however, the resolution of these details presents no unusual problems within the framework here set forth. It goes without saying that the following illustration is meant to be suggestive only.

16.2   The sentence which I shall use as an example is the following:

(1)   John has been lengthening the driveway.

Although my purpose is to use this sentence to illustrate the operation of postsemantic processes, it is necessary first to consider the semantic structure which provides the input to such processes. We can take advantage of this opportunity to illustrate and, in a selective way, recapitulate the formation of semantic structures as well. My assertion has been that the generation of a semantic structure begins with the element *verb*. Given this initial element, the first rule which applies in the generation of sentence (1) is:

(S9-1) V $\longrightarrow$ state

Application of this optional rule produces the structure shown in (2). The next rules which are relevant are those which allow a state

(2)   V
        state

to be *relative*, and which then provide a lexical unit (a verb root) for a relative state:

(S11–1) state ——→ relative

(S11–2b) $\begin{bmatrix} \text{relative} \\ -\text{ambient} \end{bmatrix}$ ——→ long, . . .

These two rules give us the structure of (3). In sentence (1), however,

(3)   V
        state
        relative
        long

two derivational rules have been applied to the verb. The first is that which optionally converts a state into a process by means of the derivational unit *inchoative*:

(S11–3) state ——→ process
         root   root + inchoative

This rule yields the configuration shown in (4). The second derivational rule is that which converts a process into an action-process

385 (4)   V
              process
              relative
              long + inchoative

through the derivational unit *causative*:

(S11–8) process ——→ process
         root   action
                         root + causative

Application of this rule to (4) produces (5). We can take (5) to represent the semantic structure of the verb in sentence (1), so far

(5)   V
        process
        relative
        action
        long + inchoative + causative

as its selectional units and its (derived) root are concerned. We need also to specify the verb in terms of inflectional units. One inflectional rule which should be applied is that which makes the verb *perfective*:

(S13–3) V   —→ perfective

$$\left\{ \begin{array}{l} \text{action} \\ \left[\begin{array}{l} -\text{action} \\ -\text{generic} \end{array} \right] \end{array} \right\}$$

and another is that which makes it *progressive*:

(S13–4) V   —→ progressive

$$\begin{array}{l} -\text{state} \\ \left\{ \begin{array}{l} \text{action} \\ \left[\begin{array}{l} -\text{action} \\ -\text{generic} \end{array} \right] \end{array} \right\} \end{array}$$

The verb root needs also to be specified as *new*, in accordance with (S15–1):

(S15–1) V   —→ V
       root   root
                  new

These three rules lead us to (6), which we can take to be the complete structure of the verb in sentence (1) with respect to the semantic

(6)   V
      process
      relative
      action
      long + inchoative + causative
        new
      perfective
      progressive

units that have been discussed in earlier chapters. Next we can consider the manner in which the accompanying nouns are added. Being a process, this verb must be accompanied by a patient noun:

(S9–4)   ⌐————————¬
                               pat
V   —→   V   N

$$\left\{ \begin{array}{l} \text{state} \\ \text{process} \end{array} \right\} \qquad \left\{ \begin{array}{l} \text{state} \\ \text{process} \end{array} \right\}$$
    −ambient

Being a nonambient action, it must also be accompanied by an agent noun:

(S9–5)

$$
\begin{array}{ccc}
\text{V} & \longrightarrow & \overset{\displaystyle\overline{}^{\text{agt}}}{\text{V} \quad \text{N}} \\
\text{action} & & \text{action} \\
\text{–ambient} & &
\end{array}
$$

The result is the structure shown in (7) with, of course, the verb

(7)

$$
\overset{\displaystyle\overline{}}{\underset{\text{V} \quad \text{N} \quad \text{N}}{\quad \text{pat}\quad \text{agt}}}
$$

filled in as indicated above. Now it is necessary to complete the semantic specifications of the two nouns. Let us begin with the patient. First of all, it is specified selectionally as a *count* noun, in accordance with the possibility offered by rule (S10–2):

(S10–2) $\text{N} \; \longrightarrow\!\!\!\rightarrow \; \left(\begin{array}{c} \text{count} \\ \text{potent} \end{array} \right)$

Second, a lexical unit (noun root) can be added:

(S10–7b) $\left[\begin{array}{c} \text{count} \\ \text{–potent} \end{array} \right] \longrightarrow\!\!\!\rightarrow \; \text{driveway}, \ldots$

The structure resulting from the application of these two rules is that of (8). Prior to the rules which introduce inflections to a

(8)

$$
\overset{\displaystyle\overline{}}{\underset{\begin{array}{ccc} \text{V} & \text{N} & \text{N} \\ & \text{count} & \\ & \text{driveway} & \end{array}}{\quad \text{pat}\quad\quad \text{agt}}}
$$

noun, that which introduces *new* to the noun root must be applied, since the presence or absence of *new* is relevant to the subsequent introduction of *definite* as discussed in 15.3. The rule which is relevant to a patient noun root is:

(S15–3) $\begin{array}{c} \left\{ \begin{array}{c} \text{pat} \\ \text{comp} \end{array} \right\} \\ \text{N} \\ \underline{\text{root}} \end{array} \longrightarrow \begin{array}{c} \left\{ \begin{array}{c} \text{pat} \\ \text{comp} \end{array} \right\} \\ \text{N} \\ \underline{\text{root}} \\ \text{new} \end{array} \quad / \left\{ \begin{array}{c} \text{ben} \\ \text{agt} \end{array} \right\}$

Since there is an agent noun present in this case, the patient noun root must be specified as *new*. The inflection of this noun is then introduced by:

(S14–1) N —→» definite

> These two rules lead to a patient noun specified as shown in (9).
> If we turn finally to the agent noun, we can say again that (S10–2)

(9)

```
         ┌─────────────┐
    ┌─┐  │ pat       agt
    │ │  │ N         N
    V     count
          driveway
            new
            definite
```

> applies to produce a count noun, but that in addition the noun
> must be made potent in accordance with (S10–8):

(S10–8) agt   agt
         N   ——→ N
                    potent

> Additional selectional units are added by the rules:

(S10–3) $\begin{bmatrix} \text{count} \\ \text{potent} \end{bmatrix}$ —→» animate

(S10–4) animate —→» human

(S10–6) human —→» unique

> and a noun root by the rule:

(S10–7h) $\begin{bmatrix} \text{unique} \\ -\text{feminine} \end{bmatrix}$ ——→» John, . . .

> Thus the complete selectional and lexical specification of this noun
> is as shown in (10). As for its inflection, the only relevant rule is

(10)

```
         ┌─────────────┐
    ┌─┐  │ pat       agt
    │ │  │ N         N
    V     count
          potent
          animate
          human
          unique
          John
```

> (S14–9), which introduces obligatorily the inflection *definite* for a
> unique noun:

(S14–9) N
         unique   ——→» definite

Adding this specification to the agent noun, and filling in all the specifications already described for the patient noun and the verb, we arrive at the semantic structure diagramed in (11). In terms of the semantic units which have been discussed in this work, (11) is the semantic structure hypothesized for sentence (1). (Undoubtedly,

(11)

	pat	agt
V	N	N
process	count	count
relative	driveway	potent
action	new	animate
long + inchoative + causative	definite	human
new		unique
perfective		John
progressive		definite

there are many additional semantic features relevant to this sentence of which a fuller treatment would take account.) The problem now before us is the conversion of (11) into a surface structure that will be an appropriate basis for symbolization and the subsequent application of phonological processes.

16.3   **Subjects.** In describing this conversion I shall cite various post-semantic rules, labeling them with a prefixed T (for *transformation*) in place of the S employed in earlier chapters for the labeling of semantic structure rules. Thus, (T16–1) will indicate the first transformation cited in Chapter 16. I shall discuss these rules in an order which is appropriate to the postsemantic conversion of sentence (1) and other sentences of a similar type. The final ordering which must be given to such rules, however, is a complex problem which cannot be settled here. First we might consider the fact that nouns do not appear in the surface structure of English in the role of agents, patients, beneficiaries, and the like, but rather as subjects, direct and indirect objects, objects of prepositions, and so forth. Let us take as our first postsemantic rule the one which turns certain nouns into subjects. It will be recalled from the last chapter that there is a close connection between the semantic specification of a noun root as old information, or more exactly its failure to be specified as new, and the appearance of the noun which contains it as a surface structure subject, at least in English and other languages of a similar type. We might imagine, then, a postsemantic rule which said simply that any noun whose noun root was not specified as new was converted into the subject of the verb, this relation of subject replacing that of agent, beneficiary, patient, or the like which the noun would have exhibited semantically. To see how such a rule would operate, we might look again at certain semantic structures that were used as examples in 15.5–6:

(12)

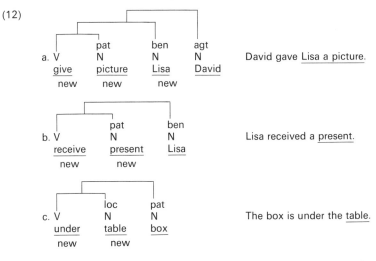

a. David gave Lisa a picture.

b. Lisa received a present.

c. The box is under the table.

If we applied the postsemantic rule just suggested to each of these sentences, it would convert into a subject noun the agent in (12a), the beneficiary in (12b), and the patient in (12c):

(13)

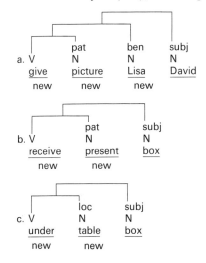

The establishment of a noun as subject would then assign it a position at the beginning of the sentence in the course of linearization. To a small extent in English and to a much greater extent in some other languages, it would also lead the postsemantic verb to "agree" with it in certain ways. At the end of 16.2 we had arrived at a semantic structure for sentence (1) in which the two nouns were related to the verb as shown in (14), and in which the distribution

(14)

```
        ┌──────────┬──────────┐
        │          │          │
        │          pat        agt
   V         N          N
   root      root       root
     new        new
```

of *new* was as indicated. A rule which changed the noun containing old information into a postsemantic subject would operate on this structure to change the agent noun to a subject, with the result shown in (15).

(15)

```
        ┌──────────┬──────────┐
        │          │          │
        │          pat        subj
   V         N          N
   root      root       root
     new        new
```

16.4   As soon as we tried to apply such a rule to certain other sentences created by the semantic processes of Chapter 15, however, we would run into difficulty. The difficulty would stem from the fact that we would find nouns containing *new* which nevertheless ought to be converted into surface structure subjects, while at the same time we would find nouns not containing *new* which nevertheless ought not to be converted into subjects. Such cases would arise through the action of rules like (S15-9), whose purpose and effect is precisely to disturb the distribution of new and old information on which such a rule for the creation of subjects would depend. Thus, given semantic structure (16), in which the agent noun root has been made new through (S15-9), no longer is there any noun conveying

(16)

```
        ┌──────────┬──────────┐
        │          │          │
        │          pat        agt
   V         N          N              David emptied the box.
   empty     box        David
     new        new        new
```

old information on which the suggested postsemantic rule could operate. The implication might be that the surface structure of this sentence had no subject, but of course it does have one. Its subject is precisely the one we would expect if (S15-9) had not made the agent noun root new. Again, given semantic structure (17) in which the

(17)

	pat	agt	
V	N	N	David emptied the box.
empty	box	David	
contrastive		new	

sentence has been made contrastive by (S15-10) and the only instance of *new* is that contained within the agent noun, the suggested rule, wrongly, would convert the patient noun into the subject. Again, what actually happens is that the agent becomes the subject, just as it would if the least marked, noncontrastive distribution of new and old information were present. There is more than one way in which we might cope with this situation. For example, we might think of applying the postsemantic rule which creates subjects before we applied any rule like (S15-9) which disturbs the least marked distribution of new and old information. To make a subject out of the noun which conveys old information in the least marked distribution is just what we want to do. This device, however, would have the somewhat undesirable effect of placing an important postsemantic rule—that which creates subjects—in the midst of those rules by which semantic structures are formed. At the very least, the postsemantic rule which creates subjects would have to be ordered to apply before any semantic rule which disturbs the least marked distribution of *new*. Perhaps it is indeed the case that some aspects of a surface structure are determined before the final formation of a semantic structure has been completed, as was suggested in 7.19. On the other hand, it is worth looking for an alternative way to explain such situations, and perhaps to avoid hypothesizing them when we can. For that reason, and without any overwhelming conviction that it is the right course, I am inclined to prefer an alternative explanation by which postsemantic subjects are established, not directly on the basis of the semantic distribution of new and old information, but instead on the basis of the semantic relations agent, patient, and so on. The rule can be formulated in approximately the manner suggested in (T16-1),

where the several parts of the rule are to be applied disjunctively
in the order given:

(T16–1)   ben   subj
        a. N   ⟶   N   /V
            root   root   passive
              – new   new

        b. pat   ⟶   subj /V
                                passive

        c. $\left\{ \begin{array}{l} \text{agt} \\ \text{exp} \end{array} \right\}$ ⟶   subj

        d. ben   ⟶   subj

        e. pat   ⟶   subj

Part (a) of this rule says that in the environment of a passive verb
a beneficiary noun becomes the subject if its root is not new, as in
Lisa was given the picture. Part (b) says that otherwise, in the
environment of a passive verb, a patient noun becomes the subject,
as in *The picture was given to Lisa.* The remainder of the rule deals
with nouns attached to nonpassive verbs. Part (c) says that an agent
or experiencer noun takes priority in becoming the subject, as in
David emptied the box or *David saw the box.* Part (d) says that a
beneficiary noun has the next priority, as in *David owned the box.*
And finally part (e) says that otherwise a patient noun becomes the
subject, as in *The box is empty.* The application of this rule to our
sample sentence produces the configuration shown in (15) above.[1]

16.5   **Objects.** It appears that a patient noun which is not converted into a
postsemantic subject by (T16–1) will become a postsemantic object.
This fact is very simply stated in the following rule:

(T16–2) pat   ⟶   obj

Ordered to apply after (T16–1), this rule will turn all remaining
patients into objects. As the result of both (T16–1) and (T16–2),

[1]Still another possibility, and perhaps ultimately the best one, would be to state
simply that the noun which is not new becomes the subject, as originally suggested,
but to make this rule dependent on the distribution of newness which is present,
not at the time the rule applies, but at the earlier, least marked stage when such a
statement would be correct. The possibility that postsemantic rules may be
sensitive to structures other than those on which they immediately operate has
recently been discussed in terms of "global derivational constraints" (Lakoff Ms.).

our original semantic structure for sentence (1) has been converted into one with the postsemantic relations of noun to verb that are indicated in (18). Other nouns in other sentences will be converted postsemantically into indirect objects or prepositional phrases. No

(18)

```
         ┌─────────┐
         │         │
    │   obj     subj
    V    N        N
```

unusual problems seem to arise from such conversions, and I shall forego discussion of them here.

16.6   **Agreement.** In some languages a major function of postsemantic processes is the shifting of semantic units from one or more nouns into the verb. We are apt to say that the verb "agrees" with its subject as to person, number, or the like. In some languages of the "polysynthetic" type the verb may swallow up an entire noun, including its root (a process known as *incorporation*), as well as, perhaps, some semantic units from other nouns. In such languages the verb may have a formidably complex structure by the time the surface structure is reached. In the next chapter we shall see an example of this kind. At present, however, we need take note only of a surface structure suffix which is sometimes attached in English to a surface verb. Thus, we find *John drinks*, with a suffix symbolized *s* on the surface verb, but *I drink, you drink, the men drink*, without this suffix. Suppose we arbitrarily label this suffix *present*. When will the surface verb contain this item? Apparently it is when the verb is (a) not inflected as *past* and (b) accompanied by a subject which is neither *first person, second person*, nor *plural*. That a noun can be specified semantically as first or second person has not been discussed, but we shall have occasion to return to this possibility in 17.7. The rule which introduces *present* can be written:

(T16–3) $\begin{array}{l} V \\ -past \end{array} \longrightarrow present/N \begin{array}{l} subj \\ -first \\ -second \\ -plural \end{array}$

That is, to repeat, a verb will acquire this particular postsemantic specification if it is nonpast and accompanied by a subject noun which is neither first, second, nor plural. Our example sentence can now be represented as having an additional item *present* among the inflectional units of its verb as in (19), since this verb fulfills the criteria just mentioned:

(19)   V
         process
         relative
         action
         long + inchoative + causative
         _____
           new
         perfective
         progressive
         present

16.7   **Literalization.** Sentence (1) contains at least three semantic units which are idioms—semantic units, that is, which must be converted into arbitrary configurations of postsemantic units before a surface structure is reached. These units are still present in their original semantic form in the intermediate structure just diagramed, and we must concern ourselves now with their proper literalization. They include two inflections of the verb—*perfective* and *progressive*—plus the noun root *driveway*. Let us look at *driveway* first. Its surface representation appears to be made up of two lexical units, *drive* and *way*. Somehow, then, the unitary semantic element *driveway* must be converted into a configuration of these two postsemantic units. As with every other idiom, the particular postsemantic units which appear in the literalization must be specified uniquely for the particular semantic unit. Ignoring possible complicating factors, I shall suggest for the moment a literalization rule like the following:

(T16–4) $\underline{\text{driveway}} \longrightarrow \dfrac{\text{drive}}{\text{way}}$

A large number of similar rules are necessary to produce the literalizations of the many idiomatic noun roots which English possesses. The structure of the object noun in our sample sentence is now shown in (20).

(20)   N
         drive
         ____
         way
         ____
           new
         definite

16.8   The literalization of *perfective* and *progressive* is of a different sort. Since that of *progressive* seems to require that it be applied prior to the literalization of *perfective*, let us consider it first. The rule which literalizes progressive can be stated as follows:

(T16–5)

```
                    ┌──────────┐
                              aux
V           ⟶     V          V
root               root        be
 (new)              (new)       X
progressive        pres-ptl
X
```

This rule says that a verb which contains the progressive inflection is converted postsemantically into a configuration of two verbs. One of these two will contain as its lexical unit the verb root that was present in the original verb (here *root*). (It may also be regarded as containing whatever selectional units were present in the original verb, although later they will be deleted in any case; see [16.12].) The root will be specified as new if it was so specified in the original verb. This verb will also contain the postsemantic inflectional unit *present participle* (or *pres-ptl*). This last unit will be symbolized eventually as *ing*. The second of the two verbs will be identified as the *auxiliary* (*aux*) of the first. It will contain as its lexical unit the postsemantic verb root *be*. As inflectional units it will contain whatever inflectional units, other than *progressive*, were contained in the original verb; these units are indicated here by X. Consider, for example, the sentence *John is eating*, whose intermediate post-semantic structure prior to the application of (T16–5) can be dia-gramed as in (21). The effect of (T16–5) is to convert this single

(21)

```
       ┌──────────┐
                 subj
V                N
eat              John
 new
progressive
present
```

verb into a configuration of verb with auxiliary. The first verb will contain the original verb root, still specified as new, and the in-flectional unit *pres-ptl*. The auxiliary will contain the verb root *be* and the inflectional unit *present* from the original verb. Thus, the postsemantic structure after the literalization of *progressive* will be as shown in (22). After linearization has applied to produce the final surface structure, symbolization will yield the eventual phonetic output *John is eating*, where *eat* appears with the present

(22)

```
        ┌──────────────┐
   ┌──── │              │
   V      aux           subj
   V      V             N
   eat    be            John
   new    present
   pres-ptl
```

participle suffix and the high pitch resulting from *new*, and where *be* and *present* combine to be symbolized irregularly *is*. The result of applying (T16–5) to the verb structure diagrammed in (19) is given in (23).

(23)

```
   ┌──────────────────────────────┐
   V                              aux
   process                        V
   relative                       be
   action                         perfective
   long + inchoative + causative  present
   new
   pres-ptl
```

16.9   A rule quite similar to (T16–5) can be written for the literalization of *perfective*:

(T16–6)

```
                        ┌──────────┐
   V        ⟶   V       aux
   root          root    V
   (new)         (new)   have
   perfective    past-ptl  X
   X
```

This rule says that a verb which contains the perfective inflection is also converted postsemantically into a configuration of two verbs. One of these two will contain the verb root that was originally present (plus, trivially, the original selectional units), the specification *new* if it was originally present, and the postsemantic inflectional unit *past participle* (or *past-ptl*). This last unit eventually will be symbolized *ed* or *en* (as in *acted* or *eaten*), by an internal modification of the verb root symbolization (as in *brought*), or in other ways. The second of the two verbs again will be related to the first verb as its auxiliary. It will contain as its lexical unit the postsemantic verb root *have*. As inflectional units it will contain whatever inflectional units, other than *perfective*, were contained in the original verb. These units are again indicated by X. We may take as an example the sentence *John has eaten*, whose intermediate postsemantic structure prior to the application of (T16–6) can be diagramed as in (24). The effect of (T16–6) is to convert this configuration into one

(24)

```
        ┌──────────┐
        │       subj
V                N
eat              John
 new
perfective
present
```

with two verbs, as shown in (25). The eventual output is *John has*

(25)

```
        ┌────────┬──────────┐
        │     aux        subj
V             V            N
eat           have         John
 new          present
past-ptl
```

eaten, where *eat* appears with the past participle suffix and the high pitch resulting from *new*, and where *have* and *present* combine to be symbolized irregularly *has*. In the structure which we now have in our sample sentence (1), subsequent to the literalization of *progressive* through (T16–5), the verb which is inflected as perfective is the postsemantic auxiliary verb *be*. Applying (T16–6) to that verb, we arrive at the following result:

```
        ┌──────────────────────┬──────────┐
        │                    aux        aux
V                            V            V
process                      be           have
relative                     past-ptl     present
action
long + inchoative + causative
 new
pres-ptl
```

That is, we now have a sentence with two auxiliaries, one specified lexically as *be* and the other as *have*. The latter has inherited the inflectional unit *present* of the original verb. It is important that (T16–5) and (T16–6) be applied in that order; the opposite order would produce a surface structure *is having lengthened* instead of the proper structure *has been lengthening*. At this point it will be useful for us to look at the total intermediate postsemantic structure which has been produced through the application of rules (T16–1) through (T16–6) to the semantic structure diagramed in (11). What we have now is shown in (26).

(26)

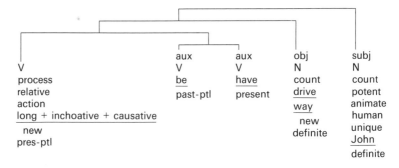

16.10 **Primary linearization.** Before we arrive at a surface structure for this sentence, it is necessary that the various elements in this intermediate postsemantic structure be linearized; they must be spread out along a single dimension which will then be symbolized by the phonetic dimension of time. Linearization seems to fall into two major types, which I shall call *primary* and *secondary*. Primary linearization involves the linearization of nouns and verbs with relation to each other; the V's and N's in the above diagram must be arranged in a certain linear order. Secondary linearization involves the linearization of the elements within each noun and verb—the lexical, derivational, and inflectional units which are present at this stage. Let us consider primary linearization first. There may be some advantage in describing it as if it proceeded from the smallest constituents to the largest. We can begin, then, with the linearization of the two auxiliaries relative to each other. Some rule which states that *have* precedes *be* is necessary:

(T16–7)

```
          ┌──────┐              aux
  aux    aux               ┌──────┐
  V      V      ⟶    V        V
  be     have        have     be
```

The configuration on the left is understood to be nonlinear, that on the right linear. I shall follow a notational convention of diagraming linearity by the absence of any indicator of relation above either of the V's and/or N's in a linearized pair. That is, if we take the following as general models, where X indicates either V or N and so does

Y, and *rel* indicates a relation such as subject, object, auxiliary, and so on, the configuration on the left is understood to be nonlinear, that on the right to be linear:

```
┌──────┐
│    rel           ┌──────┐
X    Y          X     Y
```

This convention depends on the assumption that there is no longer any need to specify such relations once linearization has applied, and that there *is* a need to specify them up to the point of linearization. If these assumptions prove to be wrong, a different convention for indicating linearity can easily be devised. As for rule (T16–7), the linearity of the configuration on the right is shown by the fact that neither V has the notation *aux* directly above it. The raising of *aux* to a higher position in this diagram serves also a second function, as will be seen. The application of (T16–7) to the postsemantic structure of (26) yields (27), where I include only the lexical specifications:

(27)

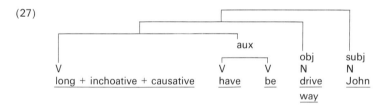

The next rule we should consider is the one which places an auxiliary verb in front of the verb to which it is auxiliary:

(T16–8)
```
┌──────┐
│    aux           ┌──────┐
V₁    V₂   ⟶   V₂     V₁
```

The subscripts in this rule are simply a device to enable us to tell which verb is which. The device is necessary because, in accordance with the convention described above, the designation *aux* is removed in the process of linearization; without the subscripts we would have two indistinguishable V's on the right side of the rule. Frequently this rule places a single auxiliary before the verb to which it is attached. In the present case there are two verbs which are so positioned. The result is as shown in (28).

(28)

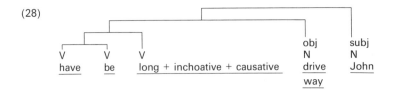

Now we can state that an object noun follows its verb:

(T16–9)

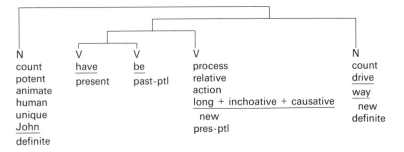

and finally that a subject noun precedes its verb:

(T16–10)

Application of this last rule brings our example to the state shown in (29), where all of the nouns and verbs have been set in linear order. In many—perhaps all—languages it is necessary that a

(29)

surface structure contain a specification of the boundaries of *words*. Such boundaries are often relevant to the operation of subsequent phonological processes. In a rough way, a *word* is equatable with a *noun* or *verb*, including all of its lexical, derivational, and inflectional specifications. More particularly, a word is equatable with one of the postsemantic nouns or verbs that we have arrived at now. The rules which have been stated in this paragraph, therefore, are essentially rules which establish the order of words. The nouns and verbs in the diagram just above can be imagined as separated by word boundaries. There are instances, to be sure, where secondary linearization rules (16.13) separate additional elements as words. Most such secondarily introduced words, however, function in a distinguishable way as enclitics or, at best, as particles. With such exceptions, we have arrived now at a configuration of words in their proper surface structure order.

16.11 **Miscellaneous deletions.** Not all the elements in a semantic structure are retained in its surface structure. We have seen how new elements like *present* and the auxiliary verbs may be added postsemantically, but it is also important to consider how various units present in a semantic structure are lost. In this paragraph and the next I shall mention deletions which apply to our sample sentence. Further investigation might show grounds for ordering some of these deletions at other places among the postsemantic rules. There is good reason to think, however, that some of them should not be applied until after primary linearization has taken place, and we shall see also that the last one to be mentioned in this paragraph must be applied before the kind of deletion to be discussed in (16.12), which in turn must apply ahead of secondary linearization. First of all, we might notice that the semantic unit *new* determines where the high pitch of a sentence will be placed. Now, we noted in 15.4 that verbs sometimes are not given a high pitch phonetically even though semantically they are new. Evidently in English a verb root retains its new specification in the surface structure only when there is no noun root that is new accompanying it. If there is such a noun root, the new specification of the verb is postsemantically dropped. Thus, in (30a), where there is no new noun root accompanying the verb, the verb retains this specification and is eventually symbolized with a high pitch:

(30) a. David <u>laughed</u>.
      b. David emptied the <u>box</u>.

In (30b), however, the verb is accompanied by a patient noun root which is specified as new. The verb then loses its new specification in the surface structure and is not symbolized with a high pitch; only the patient noun (the surface object) is so symbolized. The rule which deletes *new* from the verb under the proper circumstances might be stated:

(T16–11)

$$\begin{array}{cccc} \overline{\text{V}} & \overline{\text{N}} & \longrightarrow & \overline{\text{V}} \quad \overline{\text{N}} \\ \underline{\text{root}} & \underline{\text{root}} & & \underline{\text{root}} \quad \underline{\text{root}} \\ \text{new} & \text{new} & & \text{new} \end{array}$$

It is understood that any item which appears on the left of a post-semantic rule but not on the right (in this case *new* in the verb) has been deleted by the rule. It is also understood in this case that the noun may be related to the verb in any possible way. The result of applying this rule to our sample sentence is that *new* is retained only within the patient noun (now the object), which is then the only element to receive high pitch: *John has been lengthening the drive-way.* The second deletion we might consider is that which erases the semantic unit *causative*. It may be noted that the inchoative *lengthen* and the causative (as well as inchoative) *lengthen* are indistinguishable in their surface structures. The derivational unit which I have been calling causative has no surface reflection of its own and can be deleted through a rule like the following:

(T16–12) V $\longrightarrow$ V
          causative

The third deletion of relevance here is that which removes *definite* as an inflection of the agent noun. This deletion is necessary because proper names like *John* appear without a "definite article" in surface structure. It is possible to make a general statement to the effect that *definite* is deleted from a noun which is *unique*:

(T16–13) N $\longrightarrow$ N
          unique   unique
          definite

Some unique noun roots, however, may have to be marked as inhibiting the operation of this rule. Thus, although there is no definite article with *John*, there is one in *the sun*. We can say, then, that *sun* prevents (T16–13) from applying.

16.12 **Deletion of selectional units.** Undoubtedly it is true that every language exhibits a postsemantic process by which most or all selectional units are deleted. A rationale for this process can be seen in the fact that, as was mentioned in 13.1, selectional units are redundant once the lexical unit is known. It would be superfluous for them to appear in surface structure and to go on to receive a phonetic symbolization. A symbolization of the lexical unit is sufficient to indicate to the hearer what selectional units were present semantically. The rule which deletes selectional units might be stated as follows:

(T16–14)

The X on the left side of the arrow is a cover symbol for whatever units are positioned in a semantic structure diagram between the V or N and the root. As these diagrams are constructed, such units are selectional. Thus X is a symbol for any and all selectional units which may be present in the semantic structure, and the rule says that these units are deleted. At times in other languages certain selectional units of certain nouns are transferred into the verb by agreement, prior to the deletion of these units from the nouns themselves. In general, therefore, it seems that the deletion of selectional units must be ordered to apply after rules of agreement. This fact is not evident from the rather peculiar rule of English, (T16–3), which is more a relic of an agreement rule than a true rule of that sort. We shall see in 17.12 that selectional units from a noun do not enter a verb as selectional units there, but rather as *inflectional* units of the verb. Thus, they are not themselves deleted from the verb by (T16–14). It should be noted also that (T16–14) must be applied after (T16–13), the rule that deletes *definite* from a unique noun, since that rule depends on the presence of *unique*, one of the selectional units which is deleted by (T16–14). If, now, we delete all the units indicated in rules (T16–11) through (T16–14), we arrive at the intermediate postsemantic structure for sentence (1) which is diagramed in (31).

(31)

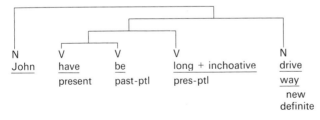

16.13 **Secondary linearization.** It remains only to specify the order of elements within each surface noun and verb—essentially, here, to order the noun roots and verb roots with relation to their inflectional units. Since English has a relatively simple word structure, the problem is not as complex as it would be for some other languages. So far as the verbs in (31) are concerned, it is enough to state a rule like the following, where X indicates the inflectional unit:

(T16–15) V ⟶ V
    root
    X   root   X

That is, each verb is linearized so that the verb root precedes its inflection. Applying this rule to the three verbs in (31), we arrive at (32). The last of these three verbs also contains a combination of root with derivational unit. Using X this time to indicate the

(32)

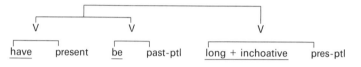

have   present   be   past-ptl   long + inchoative   pres-ptl

derivational unit, we can describe the linearization of this combination as follows:

(T16–16)
root + X ⟶ root   X

Thus we are led to the configuration shown in (33).

(33)   V

long   inchoative   pres-ptl

Turning now to the nouns, we find one whose internal structure consists of nothing but *John*. The other, however, appears in (31) in the configuration repeated in (34). Here we need to state, first

(34) N
    drive
    way
     new
    definite

of all, that *definite* is linearized to precede the noun, to become, at this stage, the item which we would identify traditionally as the definite article:

(T16–17) N   ⟶ definite   N
         definite

In addition, we need to provide for the linearization of *drive* and *way*. Let us do so here in an ad hoc fashion, recognizing that this kind of process ultimately may need to be handled in a more sophisticated way:

(T16–18) N   ⟶   N
root$_1$
root$_2$ root$_1$ root$_2$
new   new

This is simply to say that *drive* precedes *way*, and that it is *drive* which retains the *new* specification of the original noun root. Applied to (34), (T16–17) and (T16–18) together lead to (35). With these

(35)
definite   N

drive   way
new

secondary linearizations completed we have arrived at a configuration which may be regarded as the surface structure of sentence (1), *John has been lengthening the driveway*. It is diagramed in (36). I am assuming that this structure can be accorded a symbolization, and that the result will then be a proper input to the phonological rules of English. That input will coincide roughly with the kind of surface structure that has been posited within the syntacticist theory of language structure. It differs in not exhibiting labels like NP and VP on the various upper nodes. If such labels are indeed relevant to the operation of phonological rules, it seems that (36) contains enough information to enable them to be added. If it does not, some adjustments in the postsemantic rules which have led to (36) may be called for. Perhaps, however, the amount and kind of information which a surface structure must contain is still not fully understood, so that a final evaluation of the adequacy of (36) depends on further investigations of what is necessary as an input to phonological processes. Evidently investigations of postsemantic processes, as sketched above, are dependent in part on what is learned about phonology.

16.14 **Symbolization.** At this point symbolization applies to the surface structure just diagramed in a relatively straightforward fashion. Each item along the bottom of the diagram is conceived of as still a semantically oriented item, even though it may be related only indirectly to semantic structure. Thus, the item *John*, in effect, is still the semantic noun root *John* which has been carried along

(36)

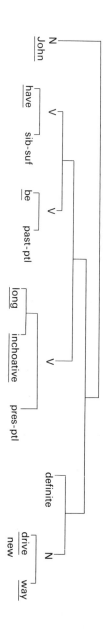

unmodified through the various postsemantic modifications. The item *have* was not present in the semantic structure at all, having been introduced by rule (T16-6). Nevertheless, it is to be regarded as a unit of the same kind as *John* to the extent that it is oriented toward semantic structure, not phonetic structure. It is a "semantoid" unit, if not directly semantic. It is necessary, then, that each of these surface units be replaced by a configuration of phonetically oriented units—again, not directly phonetic in every case, but at least "phonetoid." To a large extent, this conversion can be accomplished through symbolization rules of a very simple type, rules which come closest within language to mirroring the symbolization rules of a primitive communication system as described in 2.10. Thus we can posit many symbolization rules such as the following:

(Sy16–1) a. John $\longrightarrow$ AAA
b. pres-ptl $\longrightarrow$ BBB
c. definite $\longrightarrow$ CCC

where AAA, BBB, and CCC stand for whatever configurations of underlying phonological units are appropriately seen as underlying the phonetic representations of *John*, *ing*, and *the* respectively. In present phonological theory, AAA, BBB, and CCC would be viewed as matrices of distinctive feature specifications. The only complications which arise in the above picture result from the fact that the symbolizations of certain sequences of surface structure items are irregular, in the sense that the final phonetic output cannot be predicted from one-to-one symbolizations like those in (Sy16-1) plus a sequence of phonological rules. That is, it may be necessary to posit also certain symbolization rules of the type:

(Sy16–2) a. have + present $\longrightarrow$ DDD
b. be + past-ptl $\longrightarrow$ EEE

where DDD and EEE stand for whatever configurations of phonological units are appropriately posited as underlying the phonetic representations of *has* and *been* respectively. Other rules of the following type also may be called for:

(Sy16–3) long $\longrightarrow \begin{Bmatrix} \text{FFF/inchoative} \\ \text{GGG} \end{Bmatrix}$

where FFF stands for the arrangement of phonological units underlying the phonetic representation of *length*, while GGG stands for that underlying the phonetic representation of *long*.

That is, the surface structure unit *long* appears as *length* before the inchoative suffix, but as *long* elsewhere.

16.15 **Pronominalization.** Obviously there are many refinements and problems in the area of postsemantic processes which were not touched upon in the preceding discussion, based on only a single sentence. One kind of process is of such importance, however, that it deserves at least a cursory discussion here. I am referring to that special variety of deletion which is commonly known as *pronominalization*. Pronominalization is the deletion of a lexical unit. The term itself is appropriate, of course, only to the deletion of a noun root, but the deletion of a verb root is also possible under certain circumstances. I shall focus only on the deletion of noun roots here. In general (and disregarding contrastive sentences[2]) we can say that a noun root is subject to deletion—sometimes optionally, sometimes obligatorily—if it is not specified as new; that is, if it conveys old information. The rationale is obvious. If a noun conveys old information, there is no need for the speaker to repeat it in its entirety. In some languages, under some circumstances, he may delete the noun altogether. Such total deletion is especially common in those languages where certain nonlexical units of the noun may have been transferred into the verb by agreement processes, leaving some traces in the verb of the noun's original semantic makeup as well as, perhaps, of its relation to the verb. In English, where such agreement rules do not operate except in the relic form captured in rule (T16–3), certain nonlexical units of the noun usually are retained in the surface structure to form a separate word, commonly called a *pronoun*. (A conspicuous case where such retention is not necessary is with the second person agents—later subjects—of imperative verbs, so that we usually say *Eat!* rather than *You eat!*) Suppose we say, in general, that a noun root which is not specified as new may optionally be deleted. For example, in the sample sentence discussed in this chapter the agent noun root carried old information. If it had been deleted we would have arrived at surface structure (37b) instead of (37a):

(37) a. John has been lengthening the driveway.
      b. He's been lengthening the driveway.

[2] The fact that contrastive sentences sometimes allow a *new* item to be pronominalized, as in *He emptied the box*, might be an argument in favor of identifying such an item as *focus* rather than *new*; cf. nn. 3 and 4 in chap. 15.

Here the noun root *John* has been deleted, leaving certain nonlexical units which come to be symbolized as *he*.

16.16 It is necessary to concern ourselves with the nature of these residual nonlexical units which ultimately come to be symbolized as pronouns. Certainly not all the nonlexical units of a pronominalized noun are preserved in the surface structure in this way. Furthermore, it would seem that the units which are preserved are not necessarily units that were present in the original semantic structure; some of them may be units that were introduced postsemantically. Let us consider as examples the English pronouns *he*, *she*, and *it*. Apparently the surface structure configurations which are so symbolized are those shown in (38). These configurations are then subject to

(38)   subjective   subjective   neuter
       masculine   feminine

symbolizations of the following kind:

(Sy16–4)   a. $\begin{bmatrix} \text{subjective} \\ \text{masculine} \end{bmatrix} \longrightarrow$ HHH

           b. $\begin{bmatrix} \text{subjective} \\ \text{feminine} \end{bmatrix} \longrightarrow$ III

           c. neuter $\longrightarrow$ JJJ

where HHH, III, and JJJ stand for whatever arrangements of underlying phonological units are appropriate for *he*, *she*, and *it*. (Actually, English may be moving away from a system in which the specification of a pronoun as *subjective* is important to symbolizations like *he* and *she* as opposed to *him* and *her*, and toward a system in which these distinctions are determined by the position of the pronoun in the linearized surface structure.) The point to be made about the three configurations in (38) is that only one unit contained in them directly reflects a semantic unit, namely *feminine*. This is so, at least, with respect to the system for the semantic specification of nouns that has been presented here. In addition, it is evident that other nonlexical specifications of the relevant nouns are, or may be, present. That is, a noun may be specified not only as *feminine* but also as *count, potent, animate, human*, perhaps *unique*, and so on. It may also be inflected as *definite, generic*, and the like. None of these other semantic units are relevant to the surface structure pronouns or their symbolizations. In short, we must consider how items like *masculine, neuter,* and *subjective* are introduced postsemantically, and also how these (and some others) are retained in the semantic structure while other units are deleted. So far as *masculine* is concerned, it was hypothesized in Chapter 10 that the unmarked condition of nouns specified as *human* is one in which such nouns are not further specified as *feminine.* The absence of *feminine* leaves us with a noun that can be described informally as masculine but that has been treated here as semantically unmarked. Nevertheless, since *masculine* is necessary to posit as a surface structure unit in order to explain certain distinctions among pronouns, it must be introduced at some point in the sequence of postsemantic rules:

(T16–19) human $\longrightarrow$ human
          −feminine   masculine

That is, a noun which is specified as human but not as feminine is converted into one that is specified as both human and masculine. As for the surface unit *neuter,* also necessary to explain distinctions among pronouns, evidently it reflects the absence of the specification *human* in the semantic structure. Either a noun which is not specified as animate or one that is animate but not further specified as human, if pronominalized, will be symbolized *it.* Neuter, then, can be introduced with the following rule:

(T16–20) N $\longrightarrow$ N
          −human   neuter

That is, any noun that is not human semantically will be neuter postsemantically. Thus we have provided for a postsemantic situation in which all nouns are either masculine, feminine, or neuter, although semantically only the feminine specification was present as such. In addition, (Sy16–4) makes it clear that the specification of a noun as *subjective* must also be accounted for. Earlier we saw how semantic relations such as *agent* and *patient* are converted postsemantically into the relation *subject. Subject,* however, has been viewed as a relation of noun to verb, not as a selectional unit analogous to *animate, human,* and so forth. But the surface structure unit *subjective,* the unit that takes part in symbolizations like those in (Sy16–4), is not a noun-verb relation but a selectional unit, a unit of the same kind as *masculine, feminine,* and *neuter.* It can be introduced with a rule like the following:

(T16–21) subj   subj
          N   ⟶   N
                        subjective

That is, at some point after the subject relation has been introduced by (T16-1), but before it has been lost during primary linearization by (T16-10), a subject noun receives the specification *subjective*. In essence, in this paragraph we have seen how surface structure "genders" and, to a limited extent, "cases" (such as subjective or "nominative") can be postsemantically introduced.

16.17 Given, then, postsemantic nouns which contain specifications like *masculine, femine, neuter*, and *subjective*, we can return to the matter of pronominalization. A rule of essentially the following type is called for:

(T16–22) N   ⟶   N
          (subjective)   (subjective)
          $\begin{Bmatrix} \text{masculine} \\ \text{feminine} \\ \text{neuter} \end{Bmatrix}$ $\begin{Bmatrix} \text{masculine} \\ \text{feminine} \\ \text{neuter} \end{Bmatrix}$
          X   (plural)
          root
          −new
          (plural)
          Y

The chief effect of this rule is to delete, optionally, a noun root which is not specified as new. In the course of this noun root deletion, a number of other units within the noun are deleted also: every selectional unit except *masculine, feminine*, or *neuter*, and *subjective* if present (the deleted selectional units being represented by X), and every inflectional unit except *plural* if present (the deleted

(39)   a. masculine
        b. subjective
           masculine
        c. masculine
           plural
        d. subjective
           masculine
           plural
        e. neuter
        f. subjective
           neuter
           etc.

inflectional units being represented by Y). The result is to leave postsemantic configurations like those shown in (39). There are certain "neutralizations," however, which obliterate certain specifications in certain environments. For example, no distinction is made between *masculine, feminine,* and *neuter* when *plural* is present; the pronoun is symbolized simply *they* or *them* regardless of gender. This fact can be accounted for by an additional postsemantic rule as follows:

(T16–23) $\begin{Bmatrix} \text{masculine} \\ \text{feminine} \\ \text{neuter} \end{Bmatrix} \longrightarrow \text{plural}$
           plural

Furthermore, no distinction is made between subjective and nonsubjective when *neuter* is present; the pronoun is *it* in either case. Thus:

(T16–24) subjective $\longrightarrow$ neuter
          neuter

These two rules change the configurations shown in (39) to those in (40), which then go on to be symbolized (a) *him*, (b) *he*, (c) *them*, (d) *they*, and (e, f) *it*. It may be noted as one of the important

(40)   a. masculine
        b. subjective
           masculine
        c. plural
        d. subjective
           plural
        e. neuter
        f. neuter

characteristics of the pronominalization rule (T16–22) that it deletes some but not all of the selectional units from the noun which contains a root. It is clear that (T16–14) must be applied after (T16–22) so that the selectional units which are significant to a pronoun are not deleted. The pronoun resulting from (T16–22) will not have a root and will not, therefore, be subject to (T16–14).

16.18 The pronominalization rule (T16–22) implies that any noun root which has not been specified as new may optionally be deleted. Actually, the application of (T16–22) is not that simple a matter. Of considerable interest and complexity are the postsemantic factors which operate when two or more nouns in the same sentence communicate the same concept or have the same "reference," as is usually said. Pronominalization seems to be obligatory for all but one of such nouns. It is in part (though only in part) correct to say that the obligatorily pronominalized noun is the one that comes later in the linearization of the sentence. Thus, it would appear that pronominalization is a process which must follow linearization. Furthermore, it would appear that conceptual identity, or "coreferentiality," is an additional factor which must be taken into account within semantic structure. Further discussion would carry us far afield and to a considerable extent would repeat work already reported within the syntacticist tradition.

16.19 **Literalization of a lexical idiom.** As a final example of a postsemantic process it might be useful for us to examine in some detail the literalization of another idiom. Earlier, in rules (T16–5, 6), we saw how literalization affects the idiomatic inflectional units *progressive* and *perfective*, and in (T16–4) we encountered the literalization of the noun root *driveway*. That lexical unit, however, did not provide us with a very complex example of a lexical idiom, and one more example will be helpful in throwing more light on processes of this sort. Let us return to a sentence cited in 5.7:

(41)   Helen spilled the beans.

I am concerned with the meaning in which Helen is understood to have disclosed information in an indiscreet way. The semantic structure of this sentence contains a verb root which is an idiom and has the meaning just described. A label is needed for this semantic unit, and I shall arbitrarily label it *disclose*. The semantic structure of (41) can be diagramed as in (42), where the details of

(42)
```
        ┌───────────┐
        |         agt
        V           N
        action    Helen
        disclose  ─────
         new
        past
```

the agent noun have been omitted. The sentence is a simple one, consisting of nothing but an action verb and an agent noun. Since *disclose* is an idiom, it is subject to a postsemantic literalization, which can be formalized as suggested in (T16–25):

(T16–25)

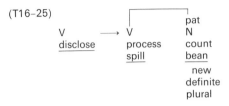

Much as with the inflectional units *progressive* and *perfective*, this literalization converts a simple semantic configuration into a complex postsemantic one. Postsemantically we no longer have the lexical unit *disclose* at all but a configuration in which it has been replaced by *spill* and in which the new verb is, additionally, a process. As a process, it is accompanied by a patient noun, specified lexically as *bean*, with the specification *new* and the inflections *definite* and *plural*. The result of (T16–25) is to convert (42) into the structure shown in (43). As is typically the case with

(43)

	pat	agt
V	N	N
action	count	Helen
process	bean	
spill		
	new	
new	definite	
past	plural	

the literalization of a lexical idiom, (43) is also a possible semantic structure. It might have arisen through the application of semantic structure rules alone rather than through the application of (T16–25) to the idiom *disclose*. Hence the ambiguity of the surface structure in (41). Whatever its origin, (43) is now subject to the usual post-semantic rules which lead to the surface structure given. From (43) on, the fate of the two sentences is identical.

16.20 Recalling the discussion in 7.15, we can now see more precisely why surface structures like the following do not have the idiomatic meaning:

(44)   a. Helen spilled some beans.
        b. Helen spilled the beans.
        c. Helen spilled them.
        d. The beans were spilled by Helen.

There is no way in which these surface structures could have arisen from a semantic structure which contained the idiom *disclose* and which therefore was subject to (T16–25). For example, that rule leads to a postsemantic configuration in which there is a patient noun specified as *bean, new, definite,* and *plural.* In (44a) there is a noun specified as *bean, new,* and *plural,* but not as *definite.* Such a noun can have arisen only within the semantic area and not post-semantically as the result of (T16–25). The surface structure in (44b) reflects a contrastive verb together with a noun root *bean* which is not specified as new. It is not entirely obvious that an idiom of this type can be treated contrastively at all. Typically, idioms seem to convey new but noncontrastive information. If this idiom were able to be made contrastive, however, there is no doubt that *beans* would be assigned a high pitch, not a low pitch as in (44b). Sentence (44c) is like (44b) except that the patient noun has been pronominalized. But (if we ignore certain contrastive possibilities) pronominalization is impossible for a noun whose root has been specified as *new,* and it should be evident that *beans* in (41) cannot refer to objects which are already in the foreground of the conversation—cannot, that is, have an "antecedent." Finally, (44d) exhibits a verb which has been inflected as *passive.* When the passive inflection was introduced in rule (S15–5), it was noted that to be eligible a verb must be specified not only as an action but also as a process. The verb in (42) is an action but not a process, and thus cannot be inflected in this way. Sentence (44d) can result only from a semantic structure in which there is an action-process verb—*spill* qualifies, but the idiom *disclose* does not. These examples may help to show that the so-called transformational deficiencies of idioms, although they are puzzling from the syntacticist point of view, are only what we would expect within the framework that has been elaborated here.

17

A Brief Look at a Polysynthetic Language

17.1   Up to now the discussion has been focused on the semantic and postsemantic structure of English. There have been several reasons for this preoccupation with one language, among them that English is the native language of the author and a language with which the reader can be assumed to have some familiarity. In this chapter I wish to introduce a small degree of breadth to the discussion by turning to another language, one familiar to the author only through a relatively brief period of field work and, it can safely be assumed, one with which the reader is not likely to be familiar at all. The language is Onondaga[1] the Iroquois language used in Chapter 4 to illustrate the general nature of phonological processes. Being a language of the so-called polysynthetic type, Onondaga gives us an excellent opportunity to see how the theoretical framework set forth above can be applied to a language which differs radically from the type represented by English. We shall find, as I think might be expected from the preceding discussion as well as from the general tenor of current linguistic thought, that the *semantic* structure of Onondaga differs from that of English in relatively trivial ways, and that the striking differences between the two languages arise largely as the result of postsemantic processes, which lead to markedly different surface structures.

[1]For further details on this language see Chafe 1970.

17.2   It is futile to attempt to give an adequate synopsis of a language in the compass of a single chapter. Instead, I shall follow here the same method of exposition that I used in Chapter 16; that is, I shall take a single sentence and discuss both the formation of its semantic structure and the postsemantic processes which lead to a surface structure. The sentence on which I shall base the discussion is the following:

(1)   wa ?shagnihwȩhtǫnyḝ ? bíl. We made a snowsnake for Bill.

I have given the sentence in an approximately phonetic representation, followed by a "translation"; that is, an English sentence which reflects approximately the same semantic structure as the Onondaga. Exactly how alike are the semantic structures of the Onondaga and the English sentences is one of the things we shall consider.

17.3   **Semantic structure.** Let us turn first to the question of how the semantic structure of the Onondaga sentence is formed. Taking the notion *verb* as a starting point, we can begin by applying rule (S9–2):

(S9–2) $V_{-\text{state}} \longrightarrow \left(\begin{matrix} \text{process} \\ \text{action} \end{matrix} \right)$

On the basis of the English translation, one might at first suppose that the verb in sentence (1) is both an action and a process, and that semantically the noun *snowsnake* is a patient. There is some question, however, whether the surface structure "direct object" of *make* really does reflect a semantic patient, either in English or in Onondaga. If, for example, we consider questions like:

What happened to the snowsnake?
What did Bill do to the snowsnake?
What did Bill do with the snowsnake?

we do not find that *Bill made it* qualifies as an answer. It is likely that suitability as an answer to one or more questions like these can be used as a rule of thumb for the identification of processes and their patients. Further reflection suggests, I think, that *make* and its surface structure object reflect the same semantic relation as do, for example, *sing* and *play* and their surface structure objects in sentences like *We sang the Marsellaise* or *We played lacrosse*. In other words, it seems probable that *make* should be regarded as a *completable* verb which, as such, must be accompanied by a *complement* and not a patient. If this hypothesis is correct, we do not want to apply (S9–2) in full, but only to introduce *action* (not *process*). Subsequently we can apply rule (S12–11):

(S12–11) V $\longrightarrow$ completable
          −process

and then the rule which introduces verb roots of this type:

(S12–12b) ⌈action   ⌉ $\longrightarrow$ make, . . .
           ⌊completable⌋

to arrive at a verb which is specified as indicated in (2). We can

(2)   V
         action
         completable
         <u>make</u>

assume that the normal distribution of new information is the same as that in English, and that the rule which was posited earlier to assign the specification *new* to a verb root is equally applicable here:

(S15–1) V $\longrightarrow$ V
         <u>root</u>   <u>root</u>
                       new

So far we have been able to use semantic structure rules exactly as they were stated previously, and the structure which has been developed up to this point is a semantic verb structure of both Onondaga and English. In describing another aspect of the inflection of an Onondaga verb, however, it may be necessary to introduce a rule which is different from any stated for English in earlier chapters:

(S17–1)   ⎧ descriptive   ⎫
              ⎪ ⎧ iterative ⎫   ⎪
          V $\longrightarrow$ ⎨ ⎨ punctual ⎬/−state ⎬
              ⎪ ⎩   ⎭   ⎪
              ⎩ purposive/action   ⎭

That is, an Onondaga verb must be inflected as either *descriptive* (with no environmental restriction), *iterative* or *punctual* (only if the verb is not a state), or *purposive* (only if the verb is an action). I need not describe the meaning of each of these semantic units here but will mention only that the one labeled *punctual* has to do with an event which occurs only once. There does seem to be at least a considerable overlap between this meaning and the meaning associated in English with a verb that is *nongeneric*. The relevant part of conceptual space, however, seems to be divided rather differently in the two languages, and it may be valid to say that the semantic unit *punctual* in Onondaga is not precisely matched by any semantic unit in English. Onondaga also has the verb inflection *past*, which can be introduced by the same rule (S13-6) that was stated earlier:

(S13-6) V $\longrightarrow$ past

Adding these inflections, we now have the structure shown in (3).

(3)   V
         action
         completable
         <u>make</u>
           new
         punctual
         past

17.4   With the verb specified in this way, we can turn our attention to the nouns which accompany it. Three nouns are present in sentence (1), and each must be introduced by a separate rule. First, a completable verb requires the accompaniment of a complement noun:

(S12-13)
                              ┌──────────────┐
                              │   comp
         V $\longrightarrow$ V   N
         completable   completable

Second, an action requires an agent:

(S9-5)
                              ┌──────────────┐
                              │   agt
         V $\longrightarrow$ V   N
         action   action
         −ambient

These two obligatory rules lead to the skeletal structure shown in (4). In addition, however, since the verb is an action, it is optionally

(4)   ┌──────────────┐
         ┌───────┤   │
         │   comp   agt
         V   N   N

possible to add a beneficiary noun as allowed by rule (S12-7).

(S12–7)

```
                    ┌──────┐
                    │   ben
  V        ──→   V    N
action
```

Applying all three rules, and taking into account also the hierarchical arrangement which is related especially to the distribution of new information as discussed in 15.7, we arrive at the structure shown in (5), which equally well, except possibly for the presence of *punctual*, could be a semantic structure of English.

(5)

```
                      ┌──────────────────────┐
              ┌───────────────┐           │
      ┌───────┐       │       │           │
      │       V     comp     ben         agt
      V              N        N           N
action
completable
make

 new
punctual
past
```

17.5 Each of the three nouns must now be specified in terms of selectional, lexical, and inflectional units. Let us move from left to right in the diagram. Taking the complement noun first, we find that it is selectionally specified as *count* by (S10–2):

(S10–2) $N \longrightarrow \left(\begin{array}{c} count \\ potent \end{array} \right)$

but that no other selectional unit among those mentioned in Chapter 10 is present. Next a lexical unit can be added:

(S10–7b) $\left[\begin{array}{c} count \\ -potent \end{array} \right] \longrightarrow$ snowsnake, . . .

Here we meet the second way in which the semantic structure of our Onondaga sentence might be thought to differ from that of a normal English semantic structure. The reader may well have wondered, when sentence (1) was introduced, what a snowsnake was. Unless he had some familiarity with games played by American Indians, the term would have been "meaningless" to him. There is a game played by the Iroquois in the wintertime which makes use of a stick, something like a billiard cue but painstakingly made and polished, which is thrown through a long trough in the snow to see how far it will travel. The concept of this stick is a familiar one in the minds of the speakers of Iroquois languages, but the vast majority of English speakers have no such concept in their minds at all. Some do, however—either through direct contact with the Iroquois or through reading about their games. If this semantic unit is present in the mind of an English speaker, it is symbolized *snowsnake*. Thus it was possible to translate sentence (1) into English, but possible only to the extent that the concept *snowsnake* was shared. For English speakers who did not possess the concept, part of the translation was meaningless up to now. I have just introduced the concept to them, however, and the translation has become more meaningful than it was before. But, like snowsnakes themselves, concepts are subject to polishing and refinement, and the reader who has not seen a snowsnake or the way it is used has only an incipient concept which would have to be further elaborated through experience before it came close to converging with the concept held by those to whom the object is a familiar part of life. (One can often observe among young children the beginning and subsequent refinement of a concept, a process like that just described.) Returning to rule (S10–7b), we can see that such a rule exists in both Onondaga and English, but that the particular list of noun roots which it introduces is not identical for the two languages. We can also see that where the two lists differ—where there is an item in one that is not in the other—adjustments which bring the two lists closer are not difficult to achieve in principle. Anyone can acquire a new concept under the appropriate circumstances. It would seem that the vast majority of semantic differences between languages are of this sort. To the structure which includes the selectional unit *count* and the lexical unit *snowsnake* we need now add only the specification *new*, by the rule:

(S15–3) $\left\{\begin{matrix} \text{pat} \\ \text{comp} \end{matrix}\right\}$ $\left\{\begin{matrix} \text{pat} \\ \text{comp} \end{matrix}\right\}$
N   N $/\left\{\begin{matrix} \text{ben} \\ \text{agt} \end{matrix}\right\}$
root   root
             new

(Both a beneficiary and an agent are present in this case.) Thus we have for our complement noun the configuration shown in (6).

(6)
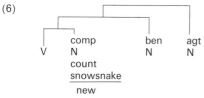

17.6 The beneficiary noun is specified more narrowly but in ways that are already familiar. In addition to the introduction of *count* and *potent* through (S10–2), we find that the following rules also apply:

(S10–3) $\begin{bmatrix} \text{count} \\ \text{potent} \end{bmatrix}$ ——» animate

(S10–4) animate ——» human

(S10–6) human ——» unique

The subsequent addition of a noun root can be accomplished through:

(S10–7h) $\begin{bmatrix} \text{unique} \\ -\text{feminine} \end{bmatrix}$ ——» Bill, . . .

Here we meet an extreme example of how lexical units differ, not just between languages, but also within the same language. *Unique* concepts, as typified by concepts relating to individual people, obviously are shared only by those who know the individuals in question. You do not share with me a particular lexical unit symbolized *Bill* unless we both know this person Bill. The situation is not really different in kind from the snowsnake situation, and serves to illustrate the fact that lexical differences do not exist so much between languages as between people. It is apt to be true, of course, that the speakers of one language share more concepts among themselves than they do with the speakers of some other language. In the case of unique concepts like *Bill*, however, the sharing even within one language is very limited (unless the language has so few speakers that all of them know each other). It may be pointed out also that the concept *Bill* in our example is an imaginary concept which you and I share only to the extent that we have in mind a male human being (as already determined by the selectional units). It is simply a vague concept introduced for the sake of the example, and one that would have to be fleshed out before it could be used to communicate anything significant. It happens also that I have shown this concept to be symbolized in a manner borrowed by Onondaga speakers from English: it is symbolized *bil*. The sounds in this symbolization are borrowed sounds. Native Onondaga phonological configurations contain neither *b* nor *l*, nor do they contain a vowel of precisely this kind. In Onondaga it is usual for the symbolizations of concepts involving unique individuals to be borrowed from English in this way; English personal names are used almost exclusively in normal conversation. It is important to realize, however, that there is nothing borrowed about the concepts themselves. This person Bill is not a foreign individual just because the concept is symbolized with foreign sounds. The specification *new* is now added to this beneficiary noun root through (S15-4), an agent noun being also present:

(S15-4) ben   ben
       N   ⟶ N /agt
       <u>root</u>   <u>root</u>
               new

The total structure which we have for the beneficiary noun is shown in (7).

(7)

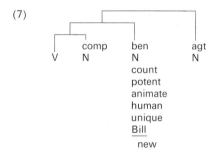

       comp   ben   agt
V   N   N   N
              count
              potent
              animate
              human
              unique
              <u>Bill</u>
                new

17.7   Last of all we need to consider the agent noun. As far as its selectional units are concerned, down through the introduction of *human* the agent noun is no different from the beneficiary. It is further specified, however, in terms of a semantic unit of a rather special kind, one which has properties that set it apart from the usual selectional unit but that do not completely qualify it as a lexical unit either. We can say that this noun is specified as *first person*, or *first*. The meaning of this semantic unit can be paraphrased as "a group of one or more people, including at least the speaker." If the noun is not inflected as *plural* (or as *dual*, as mentioned below), only one person must be involved and that person can only be the speaker. In English, in that case, we have the symbolizations *I* or *me*. If the noun is inflected as plural, the speaker along with one or more others is involved, and we have the symbolizations *we* or *us*. Another unit of similar properties is *second (person)*, whose meaning can be paraphrased as "a group of one or more people, including at least the hearer but excluding the speaker." If the noun is not inflected as plural or dual, only one person must be involved and that person can only be the hearer. In English, no matter what the inflection, *second* is symbolized *you*. There is a real question as to the status of semantic units like *first* and *second*. In some respects they are like lexical units (noun roots); for example, they are in complementary distribution with noun roots of the usual sort so that a particular noun will be specified as *first*, say, or as *carpenter*, but not as both. In other respects, however, they behave differently from lexical units, and I shall treat them here as if they were selectional. A result will be that any noun which contains *first* or *second* will have no noun root. The special behavior of these semantic units arises from the fact that the presence of a speaker and hearer is known automatically from the very nature of the speech act itself. It follows that a noun which is specified as first or second cannot be inflected as new, except in contrastive sentences. The information provided by such a noun is already known to both the speaker and the hearer from the very fact that they *are* the speaker and the hearer. It is for this reason that *first* and *second* show up as pronouns in surface structure, for the nouns containing them behave postsemantically in the same fashion as those nouns whose roots, being old information, are deleted postsemantically through pronominalization. There is another fact which should be mentioned with respect to Onondaga, however. Like a number of other languages, it exhibits a tripartite division of the area of conceptual space we are now concerned with. In Onondaga a paraphrase of the meaning of *first* must be stated somewhat differently: "a group of one or more people, including at least the speaker *but excluding the hearer*." Its meaning thus comes closer to being the mirror image of the meaning of *second* as given above: "a group of one or more people, including at least the hearer but excluding the speaker." There is an additional semantic unit in Onondaga, which can be labeled *inclusive*, whose meaning can be paraphrased as "a group of two or more people, including at least the speaker and the hearer." In English perhaps this meaning is included within that of *first*, although the fact that English has only one surface structure pronoun *we* corresponding to two distinct surface items in Onondaga is not in itself sufficient evidence that English does not make this distinction semantically. Whatever the situation in English may be, for Onondaga we need to incorporate some statement to the effect that a human noun may be further specified as *first*, *second*, or *inclusive*:

(S17–2)

$$\text{human} \longrightarrow \left\{ \begin{array}{l} \text{first} \\ \text{second} \\ \text{inclusive} \end{array} \right\}$$

In some fashion, the disjunctive relation of this rule to those rules which introduce noun roots must be indicated. The agent noun in sentence (1) is, then, specified as *first*. It remains to add an inflectional unit to that noun. As it happens, in sentence (1) the agent noun is inflected as *dual*. Again we seem to have a conceptual area that is more finely divided in Onondaga than it is in English, where *plural* means "two or more." In Onondaga *dual*, of course, means "two" and the semantic unit which can be labeled *plural* means "three or more." Again, as in the case of *inclusive*, it is difficult to say with complete conviction that English lacks this distinction. Just now, however, we are concerned with Onondaga, where the distinction is clearly present, and where the inflections *dual* and *plural* can be introduced in some such way as follows:

(S17–3)

$$\begin{array}{l} \text{N} \\ \text{count} \\ \text{−unique} \end{array} \longrightarrow \left\{ \begin{array}{l} \text{dual} \\ \text{plural} \end{array} \right\}$$

That is, a noun which is specified as count but not as unique may be inflected optionally as dual or plural. Filling in the structure of our agent noun, we can now diagram the entire semantic structure of sentence (1) in the manner shown in (8).

(8)

	comp	ben	agt
V	N	N	N
action	count	count	count
completable	snowsnake	potent	potent
make		animate	animate
	new	human	human
new		unique	first
punctual		Bill	dual
past		new	

17.8 **Postsemantic processes.** Having considered the formation of a semantic structure, we can turn our attention to the postsemantic processes which operate on this structure to convert it into the surface structure which more directly underlies the eventual phonetic output *wa ʔshagnihwęhtǫnyę́ ʔ bíl.* We can no longer make use of very many, if any, of the rules stated earlier for English, for it is in the postsemantic area that the considerable differences between English and Onondaga come to predominate. To be sure, there are some processes which are similar or identical in both languages. Among them, for example, are certain kinds of deletion, including pronominalization. Pronominalization does not take place in our sample sentence, but the deletion of selectional units does, as we shall see below. There are other processes, however, which are not to be found anywhere except in Onondaga or one of its closely related sister languages. For example, our verb contains the inflectional unit *past*, as do many verbs in many languages. In Onondaga it often happens that *past* is retained in the surface structure as a suffix, to be symbolized *hkwa?* or *hna?*, depending on its surface structure environment. In a verb which is also *punctual*, however, as is the verb in our example, *past* does not appear as a surface item at all, with the result that past punctual and "present" punctual verbs are homonymous. Therefore, a rule is called for which deletes *past* in the environment of *punctual*:

(T17–1) V   V
         punctual $\longrightarrow$ punctual
         past

Furthermore, it may be noted that sentence (1) is pronounced with an initial *wa?*. This *wa?* is the symbolization of a surface structure prefix which does not seem to reflect in a direct way any semantic unit at all. As we shall see below, the semantic unit punctual is reflected in surface structure as a suffix. It is a peculiarity of this suffix that it must always be accompanied by one member of a set of three prefixes. Two of these prefixes, which may be labeled *future* and *indefinite*, do reflect semantic units, to whose meanings these labels are more or less appropriate. The third prefix seems only to be a kind of place filler, added in the absence of either *future* or *indefinite* so that some prefix will be present to accompany the punctual suffix, which is unable to exist without one. In Iroquois studies this dummy prefix has been called *aorist*. It can be introduced postsemantically by a rule which adds it to a verb that is neither future nor indefinite:

(T17–2) V   V
         punctual $\longrightarrow$ punctual
         –future   aorist
         –indefinite

The result of (T17–1, 2) together is to replace *past* in (8) with *aorist*.

17.9   It will be recalled that in our English example in Chapter 16 we
        found it necessary to replace noun-verb relations such as *patient*
        and *agent* with other relations such as *subject* and *object*. It is not
        clear that these postsemantic relations are needed in Onondaga. It
        seems that the postsemantic phenomena of verb agreement and
        primary linearization (word order) are kept separate. They do not
        both depend on some notion like *subject*, which postsemantically
        combines the two semantic factors of noun-verb relation and the
        distribution of new information. Instead, agreement and word
        order are determined independently by one of these factors without
        relation to the other. Agreement is dependent on the status of
        nouns as patients or agents; word order is dependent on the
        distribution of new and old information. It is true, however, that in
        Onondaga the postsemantic status of a noun as patient or agent, as
        it is relevant to agreement in the verb, is not always identical to the
        semantic status of that noun. In our example there is, in fact, no
        patient at all semantically. Agreement rules, on the other hand,
        operate as if the sentence contained not only one but two patients,
        one corresponding to the semantic complement and the other to the
        semantic beneficiary. We need, then, a rule which readjusts noun-
        verb relations as follows:

(T17–3) $\begin{pmatrix} \text{comp} \\ \text{ben} \end{pmatrix} \longrightarrow \text{pat}$

        That is, both complements and beneficiaries are converted post-
        semantically into patients. Before (T17–3) applies, however, it is
        necessary to introduce within a beneficiary noun a selectional unit
        which will be moved subsequently into the verb, there to serve as a
        surface reminder of the fact that the sentence originally did contain
        a beneficiary. In much the same manner in which rule (T16–21)
        introduced the "case" *subjective* into an English noun, (T17–4),
        ordered to precede (T17–3), can be used to introduce into an Onon-
        daga beneficiary noun a "case" which can be labeled *dative*. The

(T17–4) ben   ben
         N $\longrightarrow$ N
                      dative

        diagram in (8) now can be revised to contain two patient nouns plus
        the original agent, with the original beneficiary noun now specified
        selectionally as dative, as shown in (9).

(9)

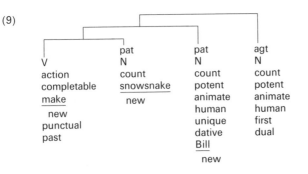

	pat	pat	agt
V	N	N	N
action	count	count	count
completable	snowsnake	potent	potent
make		animate	animate
new	new	human	human
punctual		unique	first
past		dative	dual
		Bill	
		new	

17.10   Next we can consider a postsemantic process which struck early observers of languages like this one as something so noteworthy that they gave it a special name. I refer to *incorporation*. Incorporation is actually a particular kind of agreement, by which a noun *root*, rather than some nonlexical unit, is moved into the verb from elsewhere in a sentence. In Onondaga incorporation is limited to the root of a patient noun, but with the status *patient* established postsemantically through the operation of rules like (T17–3). It is the root of a *postsemantic* patient which is incorporated, not that of a semantic patient, though often the two will be the same. In addition, it is largely the case that only the root of a nonanimate noun will be incorporated. The incorporation rule can be stated as follows:

(T17–5)

	pat	
V	N	$\longrightarrow$ V
root_v	$-$animate	root_v
	root_n	root_n

The subscripts v and n on the verb root and noun root simply provide us with a way of knowing which is which. The rule shows

(10)

	pat	agt
V	N	N
action	count	count
completable	potent	potent
make	animate	animate
snowsnake	human	human
new	unique	first
punctual	dative	dual
aorist	Bill	
	new	

that the root of the noun is added to the verb, and that the entire patient noun is simultaneously lost. The structure we are left with is shown in (10).

17.11 Incorporation has provided us with one example of agreement—the movement of semantic units from a noun into the verb—but other kinds of agreement are operative in Onondaga too. In fact, incorporation is a rather restricted phenomenon, since it involves only the root of a nonanimate patient noun. Less restricted is the kind of agreement that takes place with respect to the selectional and inflectional units of nouns, since in this case both patients and agents are affected and, furthermore, there is no restriction to nonanimate nouns. A different sort of complication arises, however, from the fact that the selectional units of a noun are not moved into the verb in their original, semantic form but are subject to various processes of simplification and replacement. The effect of these processes is, roughly, to leave the noun specified as *masculine, feminine, neuter, first, second,* or *inclusive,* whereas in the semantic structure it may have been specified also as *count, potent, animate, human,* and the like. Moreover, the units *masculine* and *neuter* have not been treated here as semantic units at all. *Masculine* and *neuter* can be introduced through the same rules that served for their introduction in Chapter 16:

(T16–19) human $\longrightarrow$ human
          −feminine   masculine

(T16–20) N $\longrightarrow$ N
          −human   neuter

The first rule says that a noun which is semantically human but not feminine acquires the postsemantic unit *masculine.* The second rule says that a noun which is semantically not human acquires the postsemantic specification *neuter.* In addition, we need a rule which will delete all selectional units except those which must be retained for purposes of agreement. This rule is the Onondaga counterpart of rule (T16–14) which deleted selectional units in English. It can be stated as shown in (T17–6). The notation X stands for any selectional unit of a verb or noun with the exception of the units listed, which are all selectional units of a noun. The rule says simply that X is deleted. All the selectional units of a verb are thereby deleted, and all those of a noun except for *dative* if it is present, the "genders" *masculine, feminine,* and *neuter,* the "persons" *first, second,* and *in-*

(T17–6)

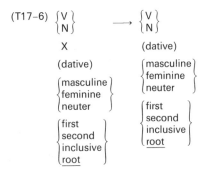

clusive, or the root if one is present. One more rule is necessary to delete *masculine* or *feminine* from a noun which also contains *first*, *second*, or *inclusive*, since a noun which is not "third person" does not have a gender specification reflected in the surface structure of Onondaga:

(T17–7)   N   ⟶   N

{ masculine }   { first }
{ feminine }   { second }
                           { inclusive }
{ first }
{ second }
{ inclusive }

The effect of applying the above-mentioned rules to the structure diagramed in (10) is shown in (11). It can be seen that (T17–6) has

(11)
	pat	agt
V	N	N
make	masculine	first
snowsnake	dative	dual
new	Bill	
punctual	new	
aorist		

applied to the verb to remove all of its selectional units, that (T16–19) has added *masculine* to the patient noun, and that (T17–6) has deleted all the other selectional units of that noun. Rule (T16–19) will have added *masculine* to the agent noun also, only to see it deleted by (T17–7), as the other selectional units of that noun have been deleted by (T17–6).

17.12 With these readjustments accomplished, we are in a position to consider the kind of agreement mentioned at the beginning of the last paragraph. What happens, essentially, is that most of the units which remain within a patient or agent noun at this stage are moved from the noun into the verb. The only units which are not moved are the root of the noun, if there is one, and the specification *new*, if it is present. Before this process takes place, the noun will contain one and only one selectional unit: *masculine, feminine, neuter, first, second,* or *inclusive*, except that *dative* may also be present. The verb, therefore, will be brought to agree with the noun in one of these six ways, and it will also absorb the dative unit when it is there. The noun may or may not contain also one of the inflectional units *dual* or *plural*. If one of them is present, the verb will be be brought to agree with the noun in this respect also. In addition to these units which are moved into the verb, the noun also may contain a root. If it does, the root will remain in the noun. (The noun will not contain a root at this stage if the root has already been moved into the verb by incorporation, or if no root was present semantically, as is the case with a *first, second,* or *inclusive* noun.) Finally, the noun root may be specified as new, in which case this unit also will remain in the noun. The rule which moves the selectional units now present in a patient or agent noun into the verb can be stated as follows:

(T17–8)

$$
\begin{array}{c}
\overline{\left[\begin{array}{cc}
V & N \\
\text{root}_V & X \\
& \left\{\begin{array}{c}\text{pat}\\\text{agt}\end{array}\right\} \\
& (\text{dative}) \\
& (\text{root}_n)
\end{array}\right]}
\longrightarrow
\overline{\left[\begin{array}{cc}
V & N \\
\text{root}_V & (\text{root}_n) \\
X\left\{\begin{array}{c}\text{pat}\\\text{agt}\end{array}\right\} & \left\{\begin{array}{c}\text{pat}\\\text{agt}\end{array}\right\} \\
(\text{dative}) &
\end{array}\right]}
\end{array}
$$

Once more, X stands for whatever selectional unit may be present, aside from *dative*. The rule says that this unit (along with *dative*) is moved from the patient or agent noun into the verb. There is an additional provision, however. After it is in the verb, X is identified as having come from an original patient or agent, so that the specifications added to the verb are not simply *masculine, inclusive,* and so on, but rather *masculine patient, inclusive agent,* and the like. This extra provision is introduced by including *pat* or *agt* in braces to the right of X on the right side of the rule. If the noun from which *masculine* came was a patient noun, the verb now contains the specification *masculine patient,* for example. These new specifications

probably should be regarded as new *inflections* of the verb and not
as new selectional units. I have indicated their status as inflectional
units by placing them below the verb root. It may be noted that a
verb may have both a patient and an agent attached to it, as is in fact
the case in our sample sentence. Rule (T17–8) then moves both the
patient and agent specifications into the verb, so that a verb may
now be inflected simultaneously as *masculine patient* and *inclusive
agent*, or in similar ways. Another rule of this kind can be used to
move the inflection *dual* or *plural* from a patient or agent noun into
the verb, where again it is identified as to its patient or agent origin:

(T17–9)

$$
\begin{array}{llll}
 & \left\{ \begin{matrix} \text{pat} \\ \text{agt} \end{matrix} \right\} & & \left\{ \begin{matrix} \text{pat} \\ \text{agt} \end{matrix} \right\} \\
V & N & \longrightarrow \quad V & N \\
\underline{root}_V & \left\{ \begin{matrix} \text{dual} \\ \text{plural} \end{matrix} \right\} & \underline{root}_V & \\
 & & \left\{ \begin{matrix} \text{dual} \\ \text{plural} \end{matrix} \right\} \left\{ \begin{matrix} \text{pat} \\ \text{agt} \end{matrix} \right\} &
\end{array}
$$

Thus, we now have verbs which are specified inflectionally as
dual patient and/or *plural agent* and the like. The operation of these
two rules, (T17–8, 9), removes all the remaining specifications of
the agent noun in our example. In (11) we saw this noun to consist
of only the units *first* and *dual*. The former is now removed by (T17–8)
and the latter by (T17–9). We might state another rule, or it might
be established by convention, that a noun whose specifications have
been entirely removed by postsemantic processes simply evaporates.
That is, after the operation of these two rules we can consider that
we no longer have an agent noun in the structure at all. The structure
we are left with, then, is that diagramed in (12).

(12)

```
                          pat
V                         N
make                      Bill
snowsnake                 new
 new
punctual
aorist
masculine patient
first agent
dual agent
dative
```

17.13 The next step is primary linearization, by which in our example the
patient noun and the verb are placed in a linear order. Onondaga

seems to be like English in placing the noun which carries new information last in a sentence, with the surface structure verb preceding it. In this case, as often, the agent noun carrying old information has been lost, but if it were present it would occupy initial position. This, at least, is the linearization which results from the unmarked distribution of new and old information; a different distribution might lead to a different ordering. It can be understood that word boundaries have been inserted simultaneously. Let us assume, also, that *new* has been deleted in the process. Now we are left with two words—a postsemantic verb followed by a postsemantic noun—as indicated in (13), where the absence of the relation *pat* shows that

(13)

```
      ┌──────────────────┐
      V                  N
      make               Bill
      snowsnake
      punctual
      aorist
      masculine patient
      first agent
      dual agent
      dative
```

the V and N are in linear order. This structure can now be given secondary linearization, which here is a matter of lining up the items within the verb in their proper order. A useful way to describe this process is by means of a chart as given in (14). We can say that the

(14)

aorist	first		dual	pat	$root_n$	$root_v$	dative	punctual
future	second	pat	plural	agt			inchoative	iterative
indefinite	inclusive	agt					causative	descriptive
								imperative

postsemantic units within an Onondaga verb are ordered in the manner shown (the chart is far from complete). There are a number of positional "slots," each containing one or more units and each occurring in a special linear position with relation to the others. This device recalls ways of describing word structure that were popular during the structuralist period. It departs from the practice of that period, however, in being designed to do nothing more than describe the order of postsemantic elements. The considerations which determine what these elements are, which of them occur with which, and so forth, have already been described before this point is reached. Application of secondary linearization as charted in (14) to the verb structure contained within (13) now leads us to the structure diagramed in (15). This fully ordered configuration may be

(15)

```
                                      ┌────────────────────────┐
                                      V                        │
 ┌──────┬───────────┬────────┬────────┬──────────┬──────┬────────┬─────────┐  N
 aorist masculine pat dual agt         snowsnake  make   dative   punctual   Bill
        first agt
```

regarded as the surface structure toward which we have been aiming. The relevant symbolization rules now will convert *aorist* into an underlying phonological configuration which we can represent as *wa ʔ*, the simultaneous combination of *masculine patient* and *first agent* to *shak*, *dual agent* to *ni*, *snowsnake* to *hwęht*, *make* to *ǫni*, *dative* to *ę*, *punctual* to *ʔ*, and *Bill* to *bil*. Thus we arrive at (16), where spaces

(16)

```
                          ┌──────────────────────┐
                          V                      │
 ┌─────┬──────┬─────┬──────┬──────┬──────┬───────┐  N
 waʔ   shak   ni    hwęht  ǫni    ę      ʔ        bil
```

indicate the boundaries between the symbolizations of the several surface structure units—in traditional terms, "morpheme boundaries." To this structure may be applied whatever phonological rules are relevant; specifically, one which voices a *k* before another voiced segment and another which changes *i* to *y* between a consonant and a vowel, plus rules of accent placement which do nothing more in this case than add an accent, or high pitch, to the final syllable of the verb and to the only syllable of the noun. Thus we arrive at the final phonetic output cited at the beginning of this chapter: *wa ʔshagnihwęhtǫnyę́ ʔ bíl*.

18

Sentences with Two or More Verbs

18.1 Up to this point all of our discussion has dealt with sentences containing only one verb. It is necessary, sooner or later, to recognize that simple sentences of the type we have been considering can be expanded into more complex sentences in which several verbs, each with its accompanying nouns, are present. Undoubtedly, for example, all languages allow two or more simple sentences to be conjoined:

(1)   a. I came, I saw, and I conquered.
      b. Marcia sang and Helen played the piano.

From a semantic point of view conjunction might best be regarded as a relation between two or more verbs (or, in other circumstances, between two or more nouns), by which the meanings of the several verbs (or nouns) are understood to be of equal importance and validity. Evidently the relation of conjunction may be further specified optionally as *sequential*. Sentence (1a), for example, usually would be understood as meaning that the several events followed each other in time. Sentence (1b) is clearly ambiguous in this respect, and may mean either that the events were simultaneous or that the piano playing occurred after the singing. Similar to conjunction is the relation of disjunction, whereby the validity of two or more simple sentences is understood in terms of alternatives:

(2)   Either Marcia will sing or Helen will play the piano.

I will not devote further space here to conjunction and disjunction, although some further attention will be given to the latter in Chapter 19. The present chapter will be devoted to certain devices by which one simple sentence is introduced into another, devices which lately have been referred to by the term "embedding." The embedded sentence may be attached either to the verb or to some particular noun in the "higher" sentence. If it is attached to the verb, the result from the point of view of surface structure is what is usually called an "adverb" or an adverbial phrase or clause. If the embedded sentence is attached to a noun, the surface structure result is commonly referred to as a "(restrictive) relative clause" or, under slightly different circumstances, an "adjective." The first part of this chapter will be devoted to the possibility that an embedded sentence may be attached to a noun.

18.2 **Relative clauses.** We can start with the following example:

(3)   Girls who are beautiful are popular. ˙

The higher sentence in this case is:

(4)   Girls are popular.

It contains a state verb accompanied by a patient noun. The verb is generic, and the noun is therefore generic also. The sentence says that the entire class specified by the noun root *girl* has the quality specified by the verb. The question which concerns us is: what is added to the semantic structure of (4) in order to produce the semantic structure of (3)? Let us consider how the meaning of (3) differs from that of (4). Sentence (3) contains a generic verb identical with that of (4), and again the patient of that verb is generic. That patient, however, does not refer to the entire class of girls. The class specified by the noun root has been narrowed down to a smaller subclass. The patients of (4) and (3) are represented by the shaded areas in (5). The two larger circles represent the set of all girls.

(5)   Patient of (4)   Patient of (3)

What does the smaller circle on the right represent? Obviously, it represents the set of all girls who are beautiful. The generic concept imposed on the noun by the verb is applied, not to girls, but only to girls who are beautiful. But how is this narrower concept arrived at? The situation here should remind us of a similar situation discussed in 14.20, where we were concerned with sentences like *All of the elephants are big*. We saw then that the semantic element which is represented in the surface structure by the phrase *of the elephants* functions to diminish the universe of elephants from the set of all elephants to a particular subset, in that case a subset characterized as definite and plural. The genericness of the patient in that sentence, in consequence, has as its domain not the entire class specified by the noun root *elephant* but the narrower domain specified by *the elephants*. That earlier situation can be pictured equally well as in (5), where the generic meaning of *all elephants* would be as illustrated on the left but the generic meaning of *all of the elephants* would be illustrated on the right. To account for the situation in 14.20 I suggested the existence of a semantic relation which I called *partitive*. I said that the function of this relation was to shrink the domain of a noun root from the entire class of objects which it otherwise specifies to a subset of that class. The structure of the sentence *All of the elephants are big* was diagramed as in (6).

(6)

```
        ┌──────────────────┐
        │          pat     
        │      ┌──────────┐
        │      │       part
 V      N      N
 big    elephant elephant
        generic   definite
        plural    plural
        all
```

Suppose we posit the existence of this same partitive relation in sentence (3), where again the domain of the noun root has been decreased from the entire class of objects otherwise specified by *girl* to a subset of that class. This time, of course, the subset is not characterized as definite and plural as it was in 14.20. Instead, it is characterized by a patient relation to the state *beautiful*. The patient of *beautiful* in sentence (3) is, up to a point, the same noun that is the patient of *popular*; in particular, it is a noun which is specified lexically as *girl*. What is special about the patient of *beautiful*, however, is that it appears to have no inflectional specification. Most obviously, in this example, it is not inflected as *generic*. As the patient of the generic verb *beautiful* we would normally expect it to be so inflected, but the fact that it is not is clear from the smaller circle on the right side of (5). That circle does not represent the entire set of girls but a subset thereof. To be sure, the subset need not be a proper subset; no requirement that it be less inclusive than the set of all girls is imposed by sentence (3). That is, there is nothing intrinsic to sentence (3) that rules out the possibility that all girls are beautiful, in which case the sentence would imply that all girls are popular. But in this, as in most similar examples, we know on the basis of experience that only a proper subset is actually in question; it is part of our knowledge of the world that some girls are not beautiful. What I am saying is that the patient of *beautiful* in sentence (3) simply lacks any inflectional content that would pin it down to a generic or nongeneric specification or, for that matter, to a definite, nondefinite, plural, nonplural, or any other specification of an inflectional nature. Whatever we know about the membership of the set of girls so far as the patient of *beautiful* is concerned, we know on the basis of experience external to the sentence. The inflectional characteristics of the smaller circle on the right side of (5) are left entirely open by sentence (3). All that is specified is that the members of this circle are in the state of being *beautiful*.[1]

18.3   On the basis of the above considerations, the kind of semantic structure I shall suggest for sentence (3) is that diagramed in (7). Without the partitive element on the right, we would simply have sentence (4), *Girls are popular*. The function of the partitive element, as in 14.20, is to narrow the domain of the lexical unit within the noun to which it is attached. In this case the narrowing is accomplished by repeating this lexical unit (the noun root *girl*) within a second, embedded sentence, where it is attached to a different verb. The narrowing of our concept *girl* which is achieved by this device is achieved through whatever semantic specifications are added by

---

[1] It may be profitable to view restrictive relative clauses as functioning semantically in the same manner as inflectional units. Just as *plural*, for example, limits the meaning of a noun root in a certain way, so does *beautiful* in (3). A restrictive relative clause, viewed in this way, is a device by which the speaker can "build his own" inflectional units for a noun. Similarly, it seems likely that a nonrestrictive relative clause can profitably be viewed as a device by which the speaker can create his own *selectional* units for a noun. It would be interesting to explore these possibilities in detail.

(7)

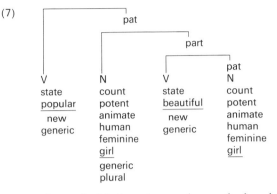

the embedded sentence—in particular, in this case, by the verb
which contains the verb root *beautiful*. This narrowed concept of
girl then constitutes the domain for the inflection of the noun in the
higher sentence; it is the diminished concept *girls who are beautiful*
which is given the generic and plural inflections. A provisional way
of formulating the rule which creates a partitive configuration like
that illustrated in (7) is suggested in (8). We shall go on to see a few
ways in which this rule must be modified. As it is stated in (8),

(8)

the rule says that any noun may optionally be expanded into the
type of configuration shown on the right of the arrow. There the
same noun is repeated, with its full array of selectional units (X),
its lexical unit (*root*), and its inflectional units (Y). This noun has,
however, acquired a partitive appendage, the semantic function of
which, as has been said, is to shrink the domain of the concept
specified by the root of the noun to which it is attached. The appendage consists of a verb accompanied by a noun which is a repetition
of the first noun, except that it lacks any inflection. This noun is
attached to the verb in what may apparently be any relation whatsoever. The notation *rel* thus represents any member from the set
of possible relations which a noun may have to a verb. Examples
of sentences in which this relation is not that of patient are easy to
find:

(9)   a. Girls who dance are popular.
       b. Girls who like boys are popular.
       c. Girls who own convertibles are popular.

In (9a) the relation is that of agent, in (9b) experiencer, in (9c) beneficiary.

18.4   We might now consider modifications which must be added to our provisional rule as stated in (8). In the first place, and I think for quite obvious reasons, the noun on the left side of the rule cannot be specified as *unique*. If there is only one member of the set specified by the noun root to begin with, there is no way in which the set can be narrowed down. The addition of a partitive element therefore would serve no function. There are no semantic structures which would lead to surface structures like those of (10):

(10)   a. *Marcia who is beautiful is popular.
       b. *Marcia who sang played the piano.

There are, of course, sentences of the type *The Marcia who is beautiful is popular*. There the noun root is a different one; it is not unique, but has to do with a set of people named Marcia. We can, then, revise the left side of the rule given in (8) to read as shown in (11). In order to appreciate another modification which must be made

(11)   N
       X
       −unique
       <u>root</u>
       Y

in (8), we need to look carefully at some sentences in which not all the verbs are generic as they were in sentence (3). In (12) the "principal" verb is nongeneric, while the embedded verb remains generic:

(12)   I saw a girl who was beautiful.

This sentence may be contrasted with (13), which is identical to it except that the partitive embedded sentence is lacking:

(13)   I saw a girl.

In both sentences the nongeneric verb *see* dictates that its patient will be nongeneric. In (13) it is understood only that the patient is some particular person within the class of all girls. In (12) something

more specific is understood, namely, that the patient is some
particular person within the subset of girls which is defined by the
placing of *girl* as a patient of *beautiful*. The domain of *girl* has been
narrowed partitively in the same way that it was in sentence (3). It
is also possible for the embedded verb to be nongeneric:

(14)   I saw a girl who had bought a convertible.

Here the patient of *see* is limited to someone who, at a previous time,
was the agent of a particular, nongeneric action of buying some
particular convertible. The domain of *girl* has been narrowed in
what might be considered a much more radical way than was the
case in (12) and (3). We are now led to consider the fourth logical
possibility: that the principal verb may be generic while the embedded verb is nongeneric. Here, however, we run into some
difficulty:

(15)   *Girls who had bought the convertible were beautiful.

As the patient of *beautiful*, the nondefinite noun *girls* must be generic.
There seems to be a problem in attaching to it a partitive element
which contains a nongeneric verb. It would be natural, even if a
little surprising, to say *Girls who had bought convertibles were
beautiful*, with an embedded generic verb, but (15) is not a natural
sentence. The example might suggest the existence of a constraint
to the effect that a nongeneric verb cannot be embedded in this
partitive way within a higher sentence containing a generic verb.
However, there do exist sentences in which the principal verb is
generic, the embedded verb nongeneric, but in which no difficulty
of the sort illustrated in (15) is present; for example:

(16)   The girls who had bought the convertibles were beautiful.

The difference between these sentences and those like (15) is that
the noun in question—the noun to which the partitive element is
attached—is *definite* and therefore nongeneric rather than generic.
A generic verb in the higher sentence is accompanied by a generic
noun only if that noun is nondefinite, as in (15), and it is precisely
in that case that a nongeneric verb cannot be attached partitively
to the noun. It is, then, the status of the noun and not the status of
the principal verb which is important. The constraint can be stated
as follows: if a generic noun is expanded in the manner described
in (8), the verb in the embedded sentence must also be generic.

Let us now restate the rule which was given provisionally in (8) as a full semantic structure rule:

(S18–1)

N	$\longrightarrow$	N	V	N
X		X	(generic)	X
−unique		<u>root</u>		<u>root</u>
root		Y		
Y		(generic)		
(generic)				

part

rel

It is understood that if *generic* is present in the noun on the left, it must be present in both of the positions indicated on the right.

18.5   There is more to be said concerning the application of (S18–1), and especially concerning the subsequent application of other rules. Suppose we consider as an example the manner in which the semantic structure of sentence (9c), *Girls who own convertibles are popular*, is generated. Let us assume that the higher or principal sentence is formed first, in accordance with rules set forth in previous chapters. The semantic structure of this sentence, *Girls are popular*, is diagramed in (17). Suppose we now apply (S18–1) to this structure. As was mentioned above, (S18–1) contains a

(17)

V	pat
state	N
<u>popular</u>	count
new	potent
generic	animate
	human
	feminine
	<u>girl</u>
	generic
	plural

variable, indicated as *rel*, so that each time we apply the rule we must make an arbitrary choice of some noun-verb relation. If we are to arrive at sentence (9c), we must choose to make this relation *beneficiary*. We thereby arrive at the structure diagramed in (18). This structure is not, however, the final semantic structure of any sentence, and further rules must be applied to it in order to fill out the embedded element. What should these rules be? Evidently they are the same rules which are used to generate the semantic structure of

(18)

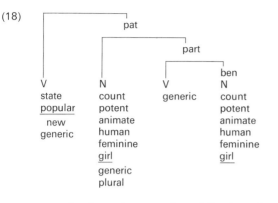

any simple sentence, rules of the type that have been discussed in earlier chapters. In other words, we can start with the new verb which was created by the application of (S18–1) and begin applying to it all the rules which add selectional, lexical, and inflectional specifications to a verb, which add nouns to accompany that verb, and which add selectional, lexical, and inflectional specifications to those nouns. In performing such rule application, however, although we will always arrive at a well-formed semantic structure for the embedded sentence in isolation, we will not necessarily arrive at a well-formed semantic structure for the sentence as a whole. The reason is that the higher sentence has already imposed certain constraints on the embedded sentence. These constraints are included in diagram (18). The verb of the embedded sentence must be *generic*, and it must have a noun attached to it which is specified as *count*, *potent*, *animate*, *human*, *feminine*, and *girl*. The higher sentence, to be sure, does not dictate that this noun must be the beneficiary of the verb, but once we have chosen arbitrarily to make it so, during the application of (S18–1), the beneficiary relation also becomes a constraint which the embedded sentence must fulfil. Suppose, now, for example, that we chose to make the verb a state in accordance with rule (S9–1), but that we did not choose to make it relative in accordance with rule (S11–1), or experiential or bene-factive in accordance with rules (S12–1, 4). Rule (S13–2) says that a relative state is inflected as generic, but we made no provision in the earlier rules for a nonrelative state to be so inflected unless it is experiential or benefactive. But if we do not make this verb generic, it will not conform to the requirements contained in (18). Moving over into the beneficiary noun, suppose we did not choose to make it count, or potent, or animate . . . Suppose we did not choose to specify it lexically as *girl*. Under any or all of these circumstances the result would not conform to the requirements which have been placed on this particular embedded sentence. There may be further requirements of a sort not obvious from a diagram like (18). That is, there may be selectional restrictions limiting the selectional units which may occur within the verb to those which are compatible with the selectional units already present in the noun, given that the noun is in one or another particular relation to the verb. If the noun were a patient, for example, and if it were also animate, the verb would have to include the selectional unit *animate patient*. In summary, an embedded sentence of this kind is not free to be expanded into any well-formed semantic configuration, but must be expanded into a configuration which fits the restrictions already established for it as a result of the application of rule (S18–1).

18.6   So far as the mechanism of sentence generation is concerned, a general way to achieve this dual requirement—conformity to the usual semantic structure rules plus conformity to the restrictions imposed by (S18–1)—might be the following. Let us assume that the new verb established by (S18–1) is, indeed, freely subject to all the semantic structure rules applicable to the verb in a simple sentence, including those rules which add accompanying nouns in various relations. We can assume further that these accompanying nouns are subject to all the rules which add specifications to nouns. Let us assume in addition that the structures which result from the application of these rules are continually (or at specifiable points in the application of these rules) subject to a comparison against the "template" first created by the application of (S18–1). Such comparison will test whatever has been generated for conformity with that template. "Conformity" must be understood in the following terms. Whatever is present in the template created by (S18–1) must be present in the embedded sentence being generated. The embedded sentence, however, may contain anything that is not present in the template. This freedom to add new semantic units and relations beyond what is in the template holds true with one exception: no *inflectional* units can be added to the noun whose root has already been specified (in this example as *girl*). The addition of any such units also results in nonconformity. As soon, then, as a configuration is produced which does not conform to the template in the manner just described, the generative process comes to a halt. In that case the particular options which have been chosen during the application of the rules have turned out to lead to a structure that is not well formed. The creation of ill-formed semantic structures is thus prevented, and it is prevented in a manner that reflects the fact that embedded sentences are limited not only by the usual constraints on semantic structure rules but also by special constraints stemming from their subordinate position within a higher sentence. If we return to (18) as an example, suppose we chose, as suggested above, to make the embedded verb a state, but did not choose to make it relative, experiential, or benefactive, and therefore were unable to make it generic by any later rule. By the time all possible inflectional rules had been applied to this verb, it would be appropriate to test the result against the template provided in (18). It would be found that, while (18) specifies a verb that is inflected as generic, the verb we have arrived at is not so inflected. The sentence is already hopelessly ill-formed, and further attempts to proceed with it would be futile. Suppose, as another example, that we failed to specify the beneficiary noun as *girl*. In that case the ill-formedness of the sentence would show up as soon as we had added some other lexical unit to the beneficiary noun and discovered, through comparison with the template, that it was not the lexical unit required. Among the many configurations which would *not* lead to any lack of conformity when compared against the template, however, would be that diagramed in (19). It is the semantic structure of sentence (9c). It is arrived at by, first, specifying the verb as a state and as benefactive, then adding the

(19)

V	N	V	N	N
state	count	state	count	count
popular	potent	benefactive	convertible	potent
new	animate	own		animate
generic	human		new	human
	feminine	new	generic	feminine
	girl	generic	plural	girl
	generic			
	plural			

lexical unit *own* and the inflectional unit *generic*. Comparing this verb with that in (18), we find conformity. Next we can add a patient noun because the verb is a state, and a beneficiary noun because it is benefactive. Finally, the two nouns are specified as shown. The beneficiary noun cannot be given any inflectional units, as is signaled by the fact that it already contains a noun root in (18). Configuration (19) is, in short, possible as a well-formed semantic structure since its embedded sentence adheres to the constraints which are applicable to any sentence plus the special constraints which are imposed on embedded ones.[2]

18.7   We might now consider briefly what happens to a structure like (19) postsemantically. The transformations which apply to relative clauses have been much discussed in the transformational literature, and there is no need to review them in detail here. For the most part the embedded partitive element on the right of (19) is subject to the same postsemantic processes as a simple sentence in isolation, except that the noun which repeats the noun within the higher sentence is given special treatment. For one thing, it is converted into a surface structure "relative pronoun"—*that, who, which,* and so forth, with the *who-which* distinction reflecting the presence or absence of *human* among the selectional units of the noun. In addition, this item is moved to the beginning of the embedded sentence in the surface structure, regardless of what position it would have occupied if it were not a relative pronoun. Thus we find *who* occurring in initial position with *(girls) who I like,* although if it were not a relative pronoun it would occur following the surface structure verb: *I like girls.* It is also possible for this relative pronoun, because it is a surface *object,* to be deleted: *(girls) I like.* Such deletion is not possible, however, when the pronoun is a surface subject, as in (9c); we cannot say *Girls own convertibles are popular.* There is, however, one very common situation under which the last statement does not hold—under which, that is, the relative pronoun can be deleted even though it is a surface structure subject. I refer to the situation where the following conditions hold: (1) the embedded verb is a state, but neither experiential nor benefactive,

[2] A format which did not attempt to generate well-formed semantic structures through a sequence of ordered rules, but which instead simply laid down constraints on well-formedness, would not encounter the problem raised in the last two paragraphs. This fact seems a strong argument in favor of such an alternative; cf. 20.6.

and (2) the embedded verb is not inflected as perfective, or the like. Under these circumstances the surface structure relative clause would be expected to contain a finite form of the verb *be*:

(20)   a. The box which is on the table is empty.
        b. Girls who are beautiful are popular.

The deletion which is optionally possible under such conditions affects both the surface subject (the semantic patient) of the relative clause and also the verb *be*. Both are redundant, since the relative pronoun carries no more information than its "antecedent," and the verb *be*, sometimes necessary as a carrier of inflectional elements, performs no useful function here. We thus arrive at the following alternative surface structure for (20a):

(21)   The box on the table is empty.

In (20b) English imposes on the nonlocative state an additional process, subsequent to the deletion, which places the embedded verb (or its surface reflection) before the noun:

(22)   Beautiful girls are popular.

A verb which has suffered this fate is, of course, tranditionally called an "adjective" in the surface structures of English and other languages where such deletion takes place. In many languages—particularly many of the polysynthetic type—there is no postsemantic deletion of this kind. Often the nature of other postsemantic processes in such languages would make this kind of deletion awkward or impossible to achieve. Traditionally, languages of this type are said not to have adjectives, or to have adjectives which are verbs, or something of the sort, but such statements of course are based on a comparison of surface structures only. It would be interesting to speculate on the possibility that the seemingly optional deletion processes responsible for the creation of surface structure adjectives in English actually are triggered by certain factors in the semantic structure. For example, one might look for a correlation with the distribution of new and old information. My own cursory investigation of such a possibility has not turned up anything worth reporting. As far as I can see, this kind of deletion, like other kinds, may be simply a way to decrease communicative effort—to save time and breath—but the question whether other factors are involved is not, I think, closed.

18.8 **Adverbs.** Another kind of sentence containing more than one verb
is that in which some semantic element is reflected in surface structure as an adverb or adverbial phrase. The semantic basis of adverbs,
I believe, is more problematic than most other topics that have been
mentioned in this work. The following suggestion is only one of
several that might reasonably be made, but it seems to me to be
among the more promising of the possibilities that come to mind.
At the heart of the matter as I shall present it lies the apparent fact
that many states can be predicated of events as well as of objects—
that is to say, of verbs as well as of nouns:

(23)   a. The fish are in the pond.
        b. The boys are swimming in the pond.

Sentence (23a) contains a locative state, reflected in the surface
structure as *in the pond*, to which is attached a patient noun that is
specified lexically as *fish*. The fish are said to be in the state of being
in the pond. Sentence (23b) contains exactly the same locative
state. This time, however, the patient of the state is not a noun but
the action verb that is specified lexically as *swim*. It is the swimming
which is in the state of being in the pond. An alternative approach
to that which I shall follow could be based on the possible observation that in (23b) it is the boys who are in the pond. I believe, however,
that such an approach does not lead to any theory of general
applicability, and that the observation itself is valid only because,
since the swimming is in the pond, it is a secondary fact that the
boys who are performing the swimming are in the pond also. If,
then, we take this general viewpoint that *in the pond* in sentence
(23b) is a state which has as its patient the verb which is specified
lexically as *swim*, we still need to consider more precisely what kind
of semantic structure this sentence must have. First let us imagine
that the semantic structure of the sentence *The boys are swimming*
is generated in the usual way. The result is diagramed in (24), from

(24)
```
        ┌───────────┐
        │           │  agt
        V           N
        action      boy
        swim        definite
         new        plural
        progressive
```

which the selectional units of the noun have been omitted as irrelevant of the matter at hand. Suppose, now, that there is a rule of the

kind roughly stated as (S18-2). This rule says that a nonstative

(S18–2)

$$V_1 \atop -\text{state} \quad \longrightarrow \quad {V \atop \substack{\text{state} \\ \text{locative}}} \quad {\text{pat} \atop V_1}$$

verb V_1 may optionally be expanded into the configuration shown
on the right of the arrow. In that configuration the original verb
appears as the patient of a state verb which is further specified as
locative. If (S18-2) is applied to the structure given in (24), the
result is as shown in (25). A lexical unit now can be added to the

(25)

	pat	agt
V	V	N
state	action	boy
locative	swim	definite
	new	plural
	progressive	

locative state, for example the verb root *in*, which goes on to be
specified as *new* in the normal way. Is this state verb also subject
to the addition of inflectional units? The answer is evidently no.
The locative state cannot be made past, perfective, or anything of
the sort. In its inflectional possibilities it is defective, for it trades on
the inflections already given to the verb which is now its patient.
How can this deficiency be formalized? Perhaps we can say that
any verb which has another verb directly attached to it, that other
verb being already fully inflected, cannot be given an inflection of
its own. The locative state in our example, however, is like other
locative states in being subject to the addition of a location noun.
One possible structure that will result is diagramed in (26), which

(26)

	loc	pat	agt
V	N	V	N
state	pond	action	boy
locative	new	swim	definite
in	definite	new	plural
new		progressive	

may be taken to represent the relevant semantic structure of sentence (23b). The boys are performing the action specified by the

action verb, but at the same time this verb is the patient of a locative state to which is attached a location noun. It may be of some interest to contrast the structure posited for this sentence with that which could be posited for the superficially similar sentence *The boys fell in the pond* in the light of the earlier discussion in 12.10. The structure of that sentence would be diagramed as in (27). In (27)

(27)

	loc	pat
V	N	N
process	pond	boy
locative	new	definite
fall + in	definite	plural
new		
past		

there is only one verb, the derived locative verb *fall in*. There is no semantic element *in the pond*, of which *fall* is the patient, as, in the other case, *swim* is the patient of *in the pond*. It seems to me that the difference between diagrams (26) and (27) captures the different meanings which we understand these sentences to have.

18.9   The inclusion of a "manner" adverb in a sentence can be assumed to proceed in much the same way as the inclusion of a locative adverb, as just described. There may be a difference, however, in the distribution of new information. By way of illustration we might take the following two sentences, which are roughly parallel to the sentences of (23):

(28)   a. The bus was slow.
        b. Bob spoke slowly.

In (28a) we have a state *slow* which is predicated of the noun *bus*. In (28b), on the other hand, we find the same state predicated of the verb *speak*. Comparing these sentences with those of (23), we can say that (28b) is to (28a) as (23b) is to (23a), with one difference. In (23b) both the action *swim* and the state *in the pond* convey new information (in the least marked, noncontrastive situation). In (28b), however, it seems that only the state *slow* carries new information; the action *speak* does not. We can generate sentences like (28b) with a rule very much like (S18–2), but this rule, (S18–3), must show the deletion of the specification *new* from the original verb:

(S18–3)

The selectional unit *manner* within the state verb introduced by this rule is a unit whose function is to limit the choice of lexical units to *slow, loud, enthusiastic*, and so on—essentially those states which are appropriately predicated of the noun root *manner* in phrases like *in a slow manner*. In other words, the selectional unit *manner* is subject to the introduction of lexical units through a rule like (S18–4):

(S18–4)   manner $\longrightarrow$ slow, loud, enthusiastic, . . .

The semantic structure which can be posited for sentence (28b) is given in (29) It is somewhat simpler than the structure of (26)

(29)

because it lacks the location noun which was required by the presence of a locative state. One statement needs to be added regarding the postsemantic development of a sentence like (29). As was true of the locative state in (23b), the manner state in (28b) becomes the highest pitched and final element in the surface structure. In addition, however, it acquires a surface structure suffix (spelled *ly*). It might be valid to consider this suffix the surface reflection of the selectional unit *manner*. In some colloquial and much of substandard English the suffix fails to materialize: *Bob spoke slow*.

18.10   English also allows the possibility of so-called *sentence* adverbs, as illustrated in (30):

(30)   a. Naturally Bob spoke.
       b. Probably Bob is sick.

Such sentences appear to differ from those like (23b) and (28b) in having as the patient of the adverbial element not simply the verb of the original sentence but the verb plus any nouns that might be attached to it. Thus, for example, the semantic structure of (30a) might be diagramed as in (31). This configuration, where the action

(31)

$$
\begin{array}{lll}
& \text{pat} & \\
& & \text{agt} \\
\text{V} & \text{V} & \text{N} \\
\text{state} & \text{action} & \underline{\text{Bob}} \\
\text{validity} & \underline{\text{speak}} & \\
\underline{\text{natural}} & \text{past} & \\
\text{new} & &
\end{array}
$$

verb together with its agent is the patient of the state verb, can be contrasted with that diagramed in (29), where only the action verb functions as such a patient and the agent is, as it were, "outside" the adverbial construction. How do we arrive at a structure like that illustrated in (31)? Let us suppose that there is a rule, much like rules (S18–2) and (S18–3), which can be stated as (S18–5):

(S18–5)

$$
\begin{array}{lll}
& & \text{pat} \\
V_1 \longrightarrow & V & V_1 \\
& \text{state} & \\
& \text{validity} &
\end{array}
$$

The significantly different property of (S18–5) is that it applies before, rather than after, any nouns are added to V_1. Thus, the semantic structure of sentence (30a) illustrated in (31) is generated in the following three stages. First a verb is specified as *action*, as *speak*, and as *past*. Second, (S18–5) is applied to produce the configuration diagramed in (32). Finally, and only at this point, the

(32)

$$
\begin{array}{ll}
& \text{pat} \\
\text{V} & \text{V} \\
\text{state} & \text{action} \\
\text{validity} & \underline{\text{speak}} \\
& \text{past}
\end{array}
$$

action verb goes on to acquire an agent, thus yielding the configuration shown in (31). Thus, the chief difference between a "sentence adverb" and the kind of adverb illustrated earlier can be formalized in terms of the ordering of the rule which introduces the adverbial element. In the case of a sentence adverb that rule precedes the addition of a noun or nouns to the original verb; in the case of other adverbs it follows. There are still other things which can be said concerning the structure in (31). It must be mentioned that *validity* is another selectional unit which is available to a state, and that it limits the choice of lexical units within such a verb to those like *natural, probable, presumable,* and so forth:

(S18–6)   validity ⟶ natural, probable, presumable, . . .

all of which seem to have something to do with the degree of validity that is attached by the speaker to the sentence as a whole. Post-semantically, it may be noted, the same suffix *ly* is attached—we might say that *validity* coalesces postsemantically with *manner*—and the adverbial element is linearized to precede the surface structure verb. The adverb may be the very first item in the surface structure, as in (30), or it may be positioned between the subject and the verb: *Bob naturally spoke.* The order in (30) seems the more usual one, and perhaps the other order reflects some semantic marking which at the moment I am unable to characterize. It should be noted that the surface structure *Bob spoke naturally,* with the adverb at the end, is entirely different from that whose semantic structure is diagramed in (31), and has a different meaning. It contains a manner adverb attached to the verb alone, and thus results from the application of (S18–5), subsequent to the addition of nouns to the original verb.

18.11   Sentence adverbs are not all of the *validity* type. Particularly common, for example, are *time* adverbs, which differ from those just discussed in at least two ways. For one thing, it is necessary to specify a semantic agreement between the adverbial element and the original verb. For example, while (33a) reflects a well-formed semantic structure, (33b) does not (barring the special possibility of a "historical present," which I have not touched on):

(33)   a. Last Saturday Bob sang.
       b. *Last Saturday Bob sings.

Although it is a considerable oversimplification, we might state a rule like (S18–7) to lead to sentences like (33a):

(S18–7)

$$
V_1 \quad \longrightarrow \quad
\begin{array}{ccc}
 & & \text{pat} \\
V & & V_1 \\
\underline{\text{root}} & \underline{\text{state}} & \underline{\text{root}} \\
\text{new} & \text{time} & \text{(new)} \\
\text{(past)} & \text{(past)} & \text{(past)} \\
 & \underline{\text{root}} & \\
 & \text{new} &
\end{array}
$$

The rule says that if the original verb is inflected as *past*, a *past* specification also must be included (actually as a selectional unit) in the state verb. Thus, in generating sentence (33a), first we would specify a verb in the manner shown in (34). Then (S18-7) would

(34)   V
      action
      <u>sing</u>
       new
      past

apply to yield the configuration shown in (35). A verb that was

(35)
```
    ┌──────┐
    │      pat
V          V
state      action
time       sing
past         new
root       past
  new
```

simultaneously both *time* and *past* would then be specified lexically as *last Saturday, yesterday, in 1967, before the sermon* . . . Evidently these are derived lexical units consisting of a noun of a certain type plus a derivational unit of a temporal nature, the latter typically reflected in the surface structure as *last* or as a preposition. With the state verb filled out and the action verb expanded through the addition of an agent, the structure underlying (33a) could then be diagramed as in (36). Here, it may be noted, both the adverbial

(36)
```
    ┌──────────────┐
    │              pat
    │         ┌─────────┐
    │         │         agt
V             V         N
state         action    Bob
time          sing
past            new
Saturday + last past
  new
```

element and the action verb convey new information. In rule (S18-7), however, *new* was placed in parentheses under V_1 on the right side of the arrow. The intention was to indicate that, even though this verb root is specified as *new* to begin with, it is possible for it to lose this specification during the application of the rule. If, based on this possibility, the action verb in (36) did not contain the specification *new*, only the state verb would convey new information, and in this situation it would be linearized to occur at the end of the surface structure: *Bob sang last Saturday*.

18.12 It would seem that some of the *manner* adverbs described earlier also occur as sentence adverbs, although with a different meaning as a result. Thus, (37a), which repeats (28b), may be compared with (37b) or the possibly more marked (37c). Whereas in (37a) it

(37) a. Bob spoke slowly.
      b. Slowly Bob spoke.
      c. Bob slowly spoke.

is only the verb *speak* which is the patient of *slow*, in (37b, c) it is the entire configuration of verb plus agent, *Bob spoke*, which is its patient. Sentences (37b, c) mean that the total event was slow in unfolding, not just that the speaking was slow. As in (S18-3) this kind of expansion seems available only to a nonstate verb. The rule which produces (37b, c) can be stated as (S18-8):

(S18-8)

$$V_1 \atop {-\text{state}} \quad \longrightarrow \quad {V \atop {\text{state} \atop \text{manner}}} \quad \overset{\displaystyle\ulcorner\!\!\overline{}\!\!\urcorner}{\underset{\text{pat}}{V_1}}$$

This rule is almost identical with (S18-3), differing only in that it does not delete *new* from the original verb and that it is applied before, not after, the original verb acquires its accompanying noun or nouns. The semantic structure which can be posited for (37b, c) is diagramed in (38), which may be compared with (29), the structure posited for (37a).

(38)

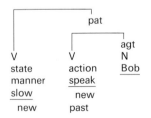

This rule diagram shows:
- V state, manner, slow, new
- V action, speak, new, past (pat)
- N Bob (agt)

18.13 I have tried to explore a few of the consequences of regarding surface structure adverbs as reflecting semantic elements which are state verbs. The items which, in surface structure terms, are regarded traditionally as "modified" by adverbs have been regarded here as the patients of those state verbs. Such patients may be no more than verbs themselves, or they may be verbs to which accompanying nouns are attached. In the latter case we are accustomed to speaking of sentence adverbs. A few idiosyncrasies associated with different types of adverbs were mentioned, but obviously there are many other special restrictions which a more complete discussion would take into account. It remains entirely possible that adverbs must be explained on a different semantic basis. One can easily imagine, for example, a third semantic element comparable to *verb* and *noun* which might be labeled *adverb*. One can also imagine a new semantic relation, perhaps to be labeled *modifier*, which would relate an adverb to its verb. Such devices, however, in addition to burdening semantic structure with extra apparatus that may be dispensable, appear to overlook the parallelism between states whose patients are nouns and states whose patients are verbs. This parallelism is all the more apparent when we consider the results of "nominalization" exhibited in sentences like (39). The meaning

(39)   Bob's speaking was slow.

of this sentence is very similar—though not identical—to that of (28b), *Bob spoke slowly*. In (39) the surface structure can be seen to reflect more directly the patient relation of *speak* to the state *slow*. The close relation of this sentence to (28b) is easily explainable on the basis of the kind of semantic structure I have posited for (28b). It would not be so readily explainable if adverbs were posited to have a different kind of semantic origin.

19

The Nature of Questions

19.1 In English, and undoubtedly in all other languages, there are a number of diverse phenomena which can be brought together under the general heading of "questions."[1] By considering these phenomena in the present chapter we shall be able to tie together various suggestions that have already been made regarding both semantic and postsemantic structures and at the same time to introduce a variety of new observations and hypotheses. We should begin with the understanding that "question" is an informal label that embraces sentences of several distinct types. What such sentences have in common is the fact that "semantically, they are somewhat like imperatives in that questions are requests of a special kind. However, unlike imperatives, which, in general, request some form of non-linguistic behavior or action, questions are concerned primarily with linguistic responses."[2] it is true, of course, that

some imperatives are concerned with eliciting linguistic responses, as are, *say cheese, tell me your name*, etc. However, the linguistic aspect of such imperatives is clearly a function of the nonimperative elements they contain and presents no special problems. Similarly, some answers are nonlinguistic, as are shrugs, gestures, pointing, groans, etc. But the latter may be considered derivative for verbal answers.[3]

[1] This chapter is based on Chafe 1968b.
[2] Katz and Postal 1964:85.
[3] Katz and Postal 1964:151.

Different types of questions, then, have in common the fact that the speaker utters them with the intention of inducing a linguistic response from the hearer, and that he does so without making use of the imperative form of a verb like *say*, *tell*, and so on. We shall be concerned in this chapter with the several different ways of doing this which the English language provides.

19.2 In citing examples in this chapter I shall use the question mark, not as it is normally used to indicate the presence of a question, but rather to indicate the presence of a particular intonation pattern. Specifically, whereas the period was used in Chapter 15 to show a fall in pitch beginning on the high pitched stressed syllable of the nearest preceding underlined word, the question mark will be used to show that the pitch remains high up to the point where the question mark is located. In (1a, c), therefore, the pitch is understood to remain high from the stressed syllable of *Michael* to the end of the sentence:

(1)   a. Did you see <u>Michael</u>?
      b. Did you see <u>Michael</u>.
      c. Did <u>Michael</u> see you?
      d. Did <u>Michael</u> see you.

In (1b, d), on the other hand, the pitch is understood to fall to its lowest point, beginning with the stressed syllable of *Michael*. For convenience I shall refer to the "question mark intonation" (pitch remains high from last preceding underlined word) and the "period intonation" (pitch falls from last preceding underlined word).

19.3 **Disjunctive questions.** As was mentioned at the beginning of Chapter 18, two or more verbs (or nouns) may enter into the semantic relation of *disjunction* (to be abbreviated *disj* in diagrams). A semantic rule such as (S19–1) might serve to introduce this possibility:

(S19–1)
$$X \longrightarrow X \quad \begin{array}{|c|} \hline disj \\ \hline \end{array} \quad X \quad X_n$$

Here X stands for either *verb* or *noun* (V or N), but only one or the other throughout any one application of the rule. Since the relation of disjunction is one in which the two or more terms are of equivalent status, I shall indicate its presence in diagrams by placing it midway between the terms involved, rather than, for example, directly over one of the X's. The dotted line and X_n indicate that there is no theoretical limit to the number of terms in the disjunction. Here, however, we shall be concerned with disjunctions of a restricted kind: those in which X represents a verb, and in which there are only two terms; in other words, with the configuration shown in (2). Furthermore, we shall be concerned with cases in which the disjunction is super-

(2)
$$\overline{\left| \quad \text{disj} \quad \right|}$$
V   V

ordinate to any further expansions which these verbs may undergo. We shall be dealing, that is, with the disjunctive relation as it is found between what would otherwise be two independent sentences. Suppose, for example, that one verb of the disjunction is expanded in a manner which would produce sentence (3a), and the other verb expanded to produce (3b). If these two sentences have been superordinately related by disjunction, the result is (3c):

(3)   a. Michael broke the clock.
        b. The radio fell off the table.
        c. Either Michael broke the clock? or the radio fell off the table.

The basic outline of the semantic structure of (3c) can be sketched as in (4), where only the lexical specifications of the verbs and

(4)

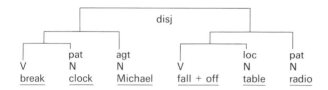

nouns are indicated. It may be noted that the presence of a disjunction has several postsemantic consequences in a sentence like (3c). The element *either* appears before the first of the two disjuncts and the element *or* before the second. In addition, however, the first sentence ends with the question mark intonation; the pitch remains high to the end of *clock*. It resumes a lower position on *or*, as at the beginning of a new sentence, and the intonation of the second part is like that of (3b). Both these factors, then—the addition of *either* . . . *or* and the question mark intonation at the end of the symbolization of the first disjunct—are surface structure consequences of the presence of a disjunction under these circumstances.

19.4   Of interest here is the fact that, under these circumstances, a disjunction may be further specified as interrogative (abbreviated *interrog*):

(S19–2)

$$
\begin{array}{ccc}
\lceil \text{disj} \rceil & & \lceil \text{disj} \rceil \\
& & \text{interrog} \\
\text{V} \quad \text{V} & \longrightarrow & \text{V} \quad \quad \text{V}
\end{array}
$$

If we add this specification to the semantic structure shown in (4), the presence of *interrogative* leads to the following surface structure:

(5)   Did Michael break the <u>clock</u>? or did the radio fall off the <u>table</u>.

The meaning of *interrogative* is that the speaker requests the hearer to provide him with new (and true) information of a sort which is made explicit by the rest of the sentençe. When *interrogative* is attached to a disjunction, as here, the sentence as a whole is a request that the hearer provide information as to which of the disjuncts accords with his knowledge of the facts. In effect, sentence (5) asks the hearer to say whether sentence (3a) or sentence (3b) is true. The hearer is expected to respond by repeating either (3a) or (3b); the question has limited him to a choice of two responses. He might evade the expected answer, of course, by saying *neither* or *both*, but that would not be what the questioner intended.

19.5   We may note the postsemantic consequences of the addition of *interrogative* to the semantic structure in (4). For one thing, the *either* which appears as a reflection of the disjunction in (3c) is not present in (5), so that *interrogative* must either lead to its deletion or inhibit its introduction in the first place. Actually, sentences with "indirect questions" like (6) might suggest that *either* is first converted into *whether* in the presence of *interrogative*, and then subsequently deleted when the question is a "direct" one:

(6)   I wonder whether Michael broke the <u>clock</u>? or the radio fell off the <u>table</u>.

We will not be dealing with indirect questions here, and it will be enough for us to note that the *either* which is one of the postsemantic reflexes of a disjunction does not appear in an interrogative disjunction. More interesting, and more strikingly and consistently a mark of the presence of *interrogative*, is the effect which that unit has on the postsemantic linearization process, an effect which cannot be disassociated from the introduction of the auxiliary *do*. Suppose we posit first a postsemantic process, triggered by the presence of *interrogative*, which is similar to the literalization process associated with the *perfective* and *progressive* inflections as described in (T16–5) and (T16–6). It can be stated as in (T19–1):

(T19–1)

```
                        ┌──────┐
                           aux
V    ────→   V         V    /interrogative
root         root      do
────         ────      ──
X                      X
```

That is, in the environment of *interrogative*, a verb is converted into a configuration of two verbs. One of the two contains the original root (together with, it may be assumed, the selectional units which led to that root). The other verb is related to the first as an auxiliary. It contains the postsemantic root *do*, together with all the inflectional units of the original verb, here designated by X. If we begin in semantic structure with the configuration given on the left of the arrow in (7), and this verb is one term of an interrogative disjunction created by (S19–2), rule (T19–1) operates to produce the configuration shown on the right. In the course of

(7)

```
                     ┌──────┐
                        aux
V      ────→    V      V
break           break  do
─────           ─────  ──
past            past
```

primary linearization, (T16–8) of Chapter 16 places the auxiliary before the other verb and (T16–10) then places the subject of the sentence in initial position, while (T16–9) places the object in final position. At this point the first disjunct of sentence (5) has the structure sketched in (8). Now we can state the characteristic

(8)

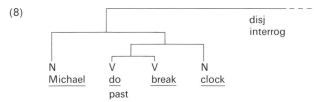

effect which the presence of *interrogative* has on the order of surface structure elements, a matter of transposing the initial noun with its immediately following verb, as the following rule describes: ·

(T19–2)

```
┌──┬──┐          ┌──┬──┐
   │                 │
N    V   X  ────→  V    N   X  /interrogative
```

This rule must be understood to operate in such a way that when it is applied to the structure in (8), the result is as shown in (9). *Do*

(9)

plus *past* is then symbolized *did*, and the final output is *Did Michael break the clock* . . . . In summary, the presence of *interrogative* causes the postsemantic introduction of an auxiliary verb which is specified lexically as *do*; it also causes the transposition of the first noun in the sentence with the verb immediately following it, which in this case turns out to be the auxiliary. It is necessary to prevent the operation of (T19–1), the rule which introduces the auxiliary *do* in the presence of *interrogative*, if some other postsemantic auxiliary is introduced for some other reason. For example, if the original verb is inflected as perfective and/or progressive, (T16–5) and (T16–6) will introduce the auxiliaries *have* and/or *be*. In that case (T19–1) does not apply; no further auxiliary is introduced. *Interrogative* simply causes the transposition of the initial noun with the auxiliary introduced by (T16–5, 6):

(10)   a. Has Michael broken the clock . . .
       b. Is Michael breaking the clock . . .

and not *Does Michael have broken the clock* or *Does Michael be breaking the clock*. The same is true when there is a state verb which is expanded postsemantically with the auxiliary *be* (*Is the road wide* . . .), a verb that is inflected as *obligational* and is thus expanded with the auxiliary *must* (*Must Bob sing* . . .), and so on. In short, it is necessary to order (T19–1) so that it is not eligible for application until the other rules which introduce auxiliaries have applied, and then to prevent it from applying if one of those other rules has applied. In considering the surface structure of sentence (5), it may be noted finally that it exhibits the question mark intonation at the end of the first disjunct. Since that same intonation is present in the noninterrogative disjunction (3c), however, it can be attributed to the presence of a disjunction and not to the presence of *interrogative*.

19.6   Sentences (3a) and (3b) have very little in common. Probably it is
        more often the case that the sentences related in a disjunction
        contain one or more nouns or verbs which are identical:

(11)   a. Michael broke the <u>clock</u>.
        b. David lost the <u>clock</u>.
        c. Either <u>Michael</u> <u>broke</u> the clock? or <u>David</u> <u>lost</u> it.
        d. Did <u>Michael</u> <u>break</u> the clock? or did <u>David</u> <u>lose</u> it.

Normally when a noun is repeated, as is the noun specified as *clock*
in (11c, d), its second occurrence undergoes pronominalization,
leaving us here with the surface structure pronoun *it* in the second
disjunct. The parts of (11a) and (11b) which are not identical are the
verb and the agent noun. In (11c, d) these parts evidently are specified semantically as *new* and the sentence as a whole is *contrastive*.
There seems to be good reason why this should be the case. The
presence of *contrastive* means that the new verbs and nouns are
thought of in terms of alternative choices. Either the speaker simply
states these alternatives, as in (11c), or he asks the hearer to choose
between them, as in (11d). In (11d) the issue to be resolved by the
hearer is Michael's breaking vs. David's losing, whereas the speaker
says that he knows the clock to have been the patient in either case.
This introduction of *contrastive* into the semantic structure is obligatory, as is this particular distribution of *new*; the sentences of (12)
are impossible:

(12)   a. *Either Michael broke the <u>clock</u>? or David <u>lost</u> it.
        b. *Did Michael break the <u>clock</u>? or did David <u>lose</u> it.

Perhaps we can formalize this obligatory occurrence of *new* and
contrastive in roughly the following way. Given a configuration like
that of (13), where two sentences are related by disjunction and A
represents the lexical (or possibly inflectional) units of the sentences

(13)

which are identical (A not being null), while B and C represent the
lexical (or inflectional) units which differ, then rule (S19–3) is
obligatory:

(S19–3) a. B, C ——» new
        b. V ——» contrastive

That is, both B and C must be specified as *new*, while at the same time any verb within the sentence (and thereby the whole sentence) is inflected as *contrastive*. In (11c, d) A consists only of the patient noun root *clock*. If we add the verb to A—that is, if we make the verb root identical in the two disjuncts—we arrive at a situation like that illustrated in (14):

(14)   a. Michael broke the clock.
        b. David broke the clock.
        c. Either Michael broke the clock? or David did.
        d. Did Michael break the clock? or did David.

The relevant semantic structure which underlies (14d) is sketched in (15), where *new* and *contrastive* have been added in accordance with (S19–3). Pronominalization in this case applies not only to the

(15)

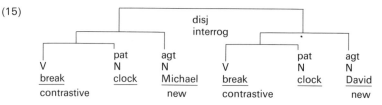

patient noun, as in (11d), but to the entire configuration of verb plus patient noun, since it is this configuration which is repeated in the two disjuncts. The "proverb" which is left in the surface structure is *do it*:

(16)   Did Michael break the clock? or did David do it.

Since, however, this proverb is unnecessary as a carrier of the tense because of the presence of the auxiliary *do* as well, it may be deleted completely, as it was in (14d).

19.7   There is something else that can happen to a semantic structure in which the disjuncts are identical except for one of the nouns, as was the case in (14). There is an alternative postsemantic route which leads to surface structures like the following:

(17)   a. Either Michael? or David broke the clock.
        b. Did Michael? or David break the clock.

The difference between (14c) and (17a), or between (14d) and (17b), seems to involve nothing more than a choice between two possibilities for deletion. Surface structures like those of (17) are probably the more frequently chosen, and need not have the difference between the two disjuncts located in the agents:

(18)   a. Did Michael break the clock? or the radio.
         b. Did Michael break? or dent the clock.

In (18a) it is the patient which is different in the two disjuncts, while in (18b) it is the verb. A possible way to describe the deletion process responsible for the surface structures of (17) and (18) is to posit their application subsequent to the linearization process. At that point, everything positioned between the first *new* word and the terminus of the question mark intonation is deleted, as is everything between the word *or* and the last *new* word. Thus, everything before the first *new* word and after the last *new* word remains undeleted, as does the word *or*. The deleted portions in (19) may be noted:

(19)   a. Did Michael (break the clock?) or (did) David break the clock.
         b. Did Michael break the clock? or (did Michael break) the radio.
         c. Did Michael break (the clock?) or (did Michael) dent the clock.

It must be realized that these questions are entirely different from the "yes-no" questions of (20), for which an explanation will be given shortly:

(20)   a. Did Michael or David break the clock?
         b. Did Michael break the clock or the radio?
         c. Did Michael break or dent the clock?

The difference can be brought out, for example, through the observation that the answer expected for (17b) is either *Michael (broke the clock)* or *David (broke the clock)*. For any of the sentences of (20) it is *yes* or *no*.

19.8   The disjuncts just discussed differed by only one lexical unit. Actually, it is possible for the sentences related by disjunction to be completely identical as far as their lexical units are concerned; they may differ only with respect to some inflection. For example, (21a, b) differ only in the fact that (21a) has a verb which is inflected as progressive while the verb in (21b) is inflected as perfective:

(21)   a. Michael is eating.
         b. Michael has eaten.
         c. Either Michael is eating? or he has eaten.
         d. Is Michael eating? or has he eaten.

Of particular interest to us now, however, are disjunctions in which the verb in one of the disjuncts is *negative*. The following two disjuncts differ only by the presence of *affirmative* in one and *negative* in the other (see 15.17):

(22)   a. Michael did break the clock.
        b. Michael didn't break the clock.
        c. Either Michael did break the clock? or he didn't.
        d. Did Michael break the clock? or didn't he.

Negative and *affirmative* (which, it was suggested in 15.17, might best be regarded as the antonym of negative) have a variety of semantic and postsemantic ramifications, not all of which need to be mentioned here. It is important to note, however, that their presence triggers a postsemantic process which may be stated as follows:

(T19–3)

			aux
V	⟶	V	V
root		root	do
{negative / affirmative}			{negative / affirmative}
X			X

That is, a verb which contains the negative or affirmative inflections, together with other inflectional units indicated by X (possibly null), is converted postsemantically into a configuration of two verbs, one of which contains the original root and the other of which is an auxiliary, specified lexically as *do* and inflected with all the inflectional units of the original verb including *negative* or *affirmative*. If, for example, we began with the configuration shown on the left of the arrow in (23), rule (T19–3) would convert it into the configuration on the right. Subsequently the auxiliary is linearized to precede

(23)

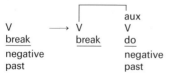

V	⟶	V	aux
break		break	V
negative			do
past			negative
			past

the other verb, *negative* is given secondary linearization as the suffix spelled *n't*, or as the participle *not*, and *do* plus *past* is symbolized as *did*, leading to the symbolization *didn't break*, as in (22b).

Rule (T19–3) bears an obvious similarity to rules (T16–5) and (T16–6), which literalize *perfective* and *progressive* through the introduction of the auxiliaries *have* and *be*, as well as to (T19–1), which introduces the auxiliary *do* on the basis of the presence of *interrogative*. In the ordering of postsemantic rules it appears that (T19–3) must be applied after (T16–5, 6) but before (T19–1). Actually, as suggested in (19.7), (T16–5, 6) are only samples of the many rules that introduce auxiliaries. Others are, for example, the rule that postsemantically expands a state verb with the auxiliary *be* as in *The road is wide*, the rule that expands an inferential or obligational verb with the auxiliary *must*, as in *Bob must sing*, and so forth. All such rules must apply before (T19–3). When one or more of them has applied, (T19–3) will not apply, as may be indicated by adding the specification "-aux" above the V on the left of the arrow; in other words, (T19–3) will not apply to a verb that is an auxiliary. Instead, *negative* or *affirmative* will already have been attached to the auxiliary already there. Thus we arrive at surface structures like *wasn't breaking* rather than *didn't be breaking*. Rule (T19–1), however, which introduces the auxiliary *do* in the presence of *interrogative*, applies still later in the sequence of rules and does not apply if any prior rule, including (T19–3), has already introduced an auxiliary.

19.9 To return to the sentences of (22), where the two disjuncts differ only by the *affirmative* vs. *negative* distinction, the presence of *new* must be noted. It was mentioned in 15.17 that *affirmative* is always further specified as new, a fact which shows up in the presence of a high pitch on *did* in (22a). *Negative*, on the other hand, is normally only optionally new. In (22b) it is, as appears from the high pitch on the word *didn't*. (If the particle *not* were present, it would be the item given this high pitch: *Michael did not break the clock*.) The same sentence could appear, however, without *new* added to *negative*: *Michael didn't break the clock*. But in the disjunction, where *affirmative* and *negative* alone constitute the B and C of (13), it is obligatory that both be made new because of the requirement that was set forth in (S19–3). That is, the disjuncts can only be the sentences given in (22a, b), and the high pitches on the words *did* and *didn't* in (22c) and (22d) are unavoidable.

19.10 It is possible, however, for *affirmative* to be absent from the first disjunct. The two disjuncts, that is, may differ only in having the second specified as negative while the first is not. The sentences of (24) illustrate this possibility:

(24)   a. Michael broke the clock.
        b. Michael didn't break the clock.
        c. Either Michael broke the clock? or he didn't.
        d. Did Michael break the clock? or didn't he.

Sentence (24b) has a semantic structure exactly like that of (24a) except that the verb has been inflected as *negative*. When these two sentences enter into the disjunction illustrated in (24c, d), rule (S19–3) must again apply to add *new*. This time, however, the B of (13) is null; there is nothing in the first disjunct corresponding to *negative* in the second. Hence it is only C, *negative*, which becomes new. The result is the high pitched *didn't* in (24c, d), with no high pitched *did* corresponding to it in the first disjunct. The *did* at the beginning of (24d) results from the application of (T19–1) because of the presence of *interrogative*, not from the application of (T19–3) as in (22d). It may be noted that the interrogative disjunctions (22d) and (24d) are subject to further optional deletion in which all the surface structure elements following the word *or* are reduced to nothing except the surface reflection of *negative* (and *new*), a high pitched *not*:

(25)   a. Did Michael break the clock? or not.
        b. Did Michael break the clock? or not.

19.11 The sentences we have just been considering appear to contain a semantic unit to which we have not yet given recognition. In (22c, d) as well as in (24c, d) the speaker is communicating a certain amount of impatience regarding the information he has so far received. It would seem that he has been given reason to believe that (22a) is true, but that he has also been given reason to believe that (22b) is true. Since they cannot both be true, he is confronted with a contradiction. In those sentences which contain *interrogative*—(22d) and (24d)—he is simultaneously expressing impatience over the contradiction and at the same time asking the hearer to resolve it by saying once and for all whether it is (22a) or (22b), for example, which is correct. We can state a rule which says that the disjunction must be further specified as *impatient* when the verb in one of the two disjuncts is negative (while in the other it is not):

(S19–4)

This rule implies that such a disjunction is always impatient, but in fact that is not the case. An ordinary "yes-no" question appears to be precisely the kind of configuration shown on the left of (S19–4), to which (S19–2) has applied to add *interrogative*, but to which (S19–4) has not applied to add *impatient*. Thus it is that we arrive at questions like:

(26)   Did Michael break the clock?

The suggested semantic structure of this sentence is diagramed in (27). It contains a disjunction in which the second disjunct differs from the first only by the presence of *negative*, and in which the

(27)

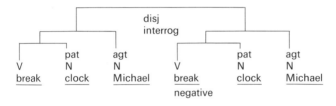

disjunction is specified as interrogative but not as impatient. In order to allow for a possibility of this kind, a stipulation must be added to rule (S19–4) to the effect that that rule is not obligatory if the disjunction is interrogative. The difference between (25b) and (26) is thus a matter of whether (S19–4) has or has not been applied. There is, however, another difference between (25b) and (26), in addition to the fact that the first is impatient and the second not. In (26) *negative* is not further specified as new and the sentence is not contrastive. The reason that it is so specified in (25b) and in all the other disjunctions cited earlier is that rule (S19–3) added *new* to the element in respect to which the two disjuncts differ, here *negative*, at the same time that it added *contrastive* to the sentence as a whole. It now appears that, given the configuration shown in (28), *new* and

(28)

disj
interrog
V   V
−negative   negative

contrastive are added only in those cases where the disjunction is impatient, and not in those cases, created by the optionality of (S19–4) in an interrogative disjunction, where the disjunction is not impatient. In other words, (S19–3) needs to apply after (S19–4), and it needs to be modified so that, when the situation is as shown in (28), it adds *new* and *contrastive* only in the presence of *impatient*.

19.12 The postsemantic effect of an interrogative disjunction like that shown in (27), one which is not impatient and in which the two disjuncts differ only by the presence of *negative* in one of them, is the complete deletion of the second or negative disjunct. It is as if the absence of *new* and *contrastive*, resulting from the absence of *impatient* as just described, results in the postsemantic evaporation not only of the sentence surrounding *negative*, but of *negative* as well. Sentence (26) exhibits the usual symbolization of the first part of a sentential disjunction by the question mark intonation, as well as the usual postsemantic consequences of the presence of *interrogative* as described in (T19–1) and (T19–2).

19.13 A subtype of the kind of question illustrated in (26) is exemplified by the following:

(29)   Didn't Michael break the <u>clock</u>?

This sentence appears to carry an additional meaning over and above that of (26). The speaker seems to be communicating the fact that recent evidence (often, though not necessarily, something the other person just said) suggests that the question will elicit a negative answer, although previously the speaker would have expected an affirmative answer. This meaning has been described elsewhere in the following terms: "Something in the context has indicated that the activity being 'questioned' did not occur, while the questioner up till then had reason to believe it did."[4] I shall say that (29) contains an additional semantic unit which can be labeled *surprised*. This unit can be introduced through the following rule:

(S19–5)

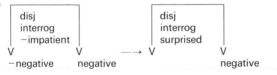

[4] Katz and Postal 1964:97.

That is, an interrogative disjunction which is not impatient, and in which the second disjunct is negative while the first is not, may acquire optionally the further specification *surprised*. The surface structure of (29) differs from that of (26) only in showing the negative suffix *n't* attached to the initial *did*. One conceivable way to arrive at this surface structure would be to delete the first part of the disjunction rather than the second, as was the case in (26). This device, however, would still leave unexplained the intonation of (29). It seems preferable, therefore, to say that (29) is arrived at in the same way as (26), but that the semantic unit *surprised* takes on the same postsemantic representation as *negative*.

19.14 Although (S19-3), as modified, does not add *new* and *contrastive* to *negative* in (28) in the absence of *impatient*, there is no reason why other elements in such sentences cannot be new, or the sentences contrastive. In (30a) the agent noun has been specified as new, in (30b) the verb, in (30c) the patient noun, and all three sentences would normally be contrastive:

(30) a. Did <u>Michael</u> break the clock?
      b. Did Michael <u>break</u> the clock?
      c. Did Michael break the <u>clock</u>?

Of course (30c) is ambiguous, since it is impossible to tell from the phonetic output whether the sentence is contrastive or not. The presence of *contrastive* in questions like these means that the speaker knows the answer to be affirmative with *some* lexical unit in the position of the unit specified as new; he is asking the hearer to say whether it is affirmative or negative with this one. For example, in (30a) the speaker indicates that he knows that someone broke the clock but he wants to know whether it was *Michael* who did it.

19.15 The same kind of meaning is present in the contrastive sentences of (31), where *new* is specified for the same items:

(31) a. Did <u>Michael</u> break the clock.
      b. Did Michael <u>break</u> the clock.
      c. Did Michael break the <u>clock</u>.

This time there is no ambiguity in (31c); the sentence can only be contrastive. Phonetically, the difference between these sentences and those of (30) is that the pitch falls immediately after it is reached in the underlined word (as indicated by the following period). This difference signals the presence of a semantic unit in (31) which is absent from (30). The meaning of this new unit appears to be that the speaker is suggesting that this particular lexical unit might (or might not) be included in a list of several lexical units in this position for which the sentence is true. In (31a) Michael is suggested for inclusion in the list of people who broke the clock. In (31b) the speaker knows that Michael did several things to the clock, and wants to know whether breaking it was one of them. Both (31a) and (31b) are somewhat unlikely sentences. In (31c), however, the speaker indicates quite reasonably that he knows Michael broke several things, and that he wants to know whether the clock was one of them. On the other hand, in (30c) Michael may have broken only one thing, and the speaker wants to know whether that thing was the clock. The other meaning—that he broke several things— is not ruled out in (30c), which is less specific, but it is the only meaning possible for (31c). I shall give this new unit in (31) the label *inclusion*. It can be introduced with the following rule:

(S19–6) contrastive $\longrightarrow$ inclusion/disj
                                   interrog
                                  −impatient
                                  −surprised

That is, the semantic unit *contrastive* may be further specified as *inclusion* in an interrogative disjunction that is neither impatient nor surprised.

19.16   In (32) there is a summary of the principal types of disjunction which have been discussed, with an example of each. In the first row of the matrix, a + indicates that the disjunction is *interrogative*. In the second row, a + indicates that the sentence is *contrastive*; moreover the + in the third and fourth columns indicates that the units which differ in the two disjuncts (B and C in [13]) are *new*; the + in the fifth and sixth columns indicates that *negative* in the second disjunct is *new*; and the + in the last two columns indicates that some unit held in common by the two disjuncts (in this case *Michael*) is *new*. The number of columns could be extended by adding *new* elsewhere. In the third row, a + indicates that the principal or only difference between the two disjuncts is the presence of *negative* in one but not the other. In the fourth and fifth rows a + indicates the presence of *impatient* and *surprised* respectively. In the sixth row a + indicates that *contrastive* has been further specified as *inclusion*.

(32)

	Either Michael broke the clock? or the radio fell off the table. (3c)	Did Michael break the clock? or did the radio fall off the table. (5)	{Either Michael broke the clock? or David did. (14c)} / {Either Michael? or David broke the clock. (17a)}	{Did Michael break the clock? or did David. (14d)} / {Did Michael? or David break the clock. (17b)}	Either Michael broke the clock? or he didn't. (24c)	Did Michael break the clock? or didn't he. (24d)	Did Michael break the clock? (26)	Didn't Michael break the clock? (29)	Did Michael break the clock? (30a)	Did Michael break the clock. (31a)
1. interrogative	+		+		+	+	+	+	+	
2. contrastive		+	+	+	+				+	+
3. negative					+	+	+	+	+	+
4. impatient					+	+				
5. surprised								+		
6. inclusion										+

19.17 **Questions with lexical gaps.** We noted above that the presence of *interrogative* in a semantic structure means the speaker is requesting the hearer to provide him with new information as specified by the element to which *interrogative* is attached. When it is attached to a disjunction, as in all the questions we have considered so far, the speaker is saying that he wants the hearer to tell him which disjunct is factually correct. Evidently, however, *interrogative* can occur in other places in a semantic structure, and particularly within either a verb or noun in lieu of a lexical unit. In this position it indicates that the speaker wants the hearer to supply the missing lexical unit—to fill in the lexical gap:

(33)   a. Who broke the <u>clock</u>.
         b. What did Michael <u>break</u>.

In (33a) there is a lexical gap in the agent noun. The hearer is expected to answer as in (34a), or with whatever lexical unit he knows to

(34)   a. <u>Michael</u> broke the clock.
         b. Michael broke the <u>clock</u>.

be correct. In (33b) the gap is in the patient noun, and the hearer might answer as in (34b). In both the sentences of (34) the information provided is new. It is possible for everything within them except the new elements to be deleted:

(35)   a. <u>Michael</u>.
         b. The <u>clock</u>.

Neither of the questions in (33) contains *contrastive*. *Contrastive* can be added, however, sometimes yielding sentences homophonous with those in (33) and sometimes yielding sentences which are different phonologically:

(36)   What did <u>Michael</u> break.

Sentence (36) indicates that the speaker is focusing his request to have the patient noun lexically completed on the situation where *Michael* did the breaking. He does not care at the moment what other people broke (perhaps he already knows). In all these sentences, however—those of (33) as well as (36)—it is impossible for the lexically impoverished noun or verb to be new, presumably just because it contains no lexical unit. Sentence (37), which might seem to be a case where the noun represented by *what* is new, in fact exhibits a different kind of semantic structure, one that will be discussed in the last section of this chapter:

(37)   <u>What</u> did Michael break.

19.18   The relevant semantic structure of sentence (33b), *What did Michael break*, can be sketched as in (38).

(38)
```
        ┌─────────────┐
     ┌──┤      pat      agt
     V        N         N
     break    interrog  Michael
     past
```

We might consider the postsemantic fate of this structure. First, we might note that neither in (33b) nor in any other of these lexical gap questions is there a question mark intonation. According to the earlier discussion in this chapter, that is just what we should expect. The question mark intonation was said to result from the presence of a *disjunction*, not from the presence of *interrogative*. Since the lexical gap questions do not arise from disjunctions, there is nothing in them which would lead to that intonation. Second, since *interrogative* is present in (38), rule (T19-1), which adds the auxiliary *do* in the presence of interrogative, is applicable. Third, there is an additional process which, late in the establishment of primary linearization, moves an interrogative noun to the beginning of the sentence. Ignoring certain complications, we might state the rule as follows:

(T19-4)

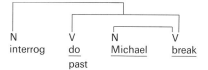

$$X \quad V \quad \underset{\text{interrog}}{N} \quad \longrightarrow \quad \underset{\text{interrog}}{N} \quad X \quad V$$

This rule can be assumed to apply after the linearization of the auxiliary to precede the other verb, and also after the transposing of the subject with its immediately following verb, also triggered by the presence of *interrogative*, as stated in (T19-2). After all three linearization processes have taken place, (38) will have been converted into the structure shown in (39). Subsequently the interrogative noun is symbolized as *who* if it contains *human*, as *what* if it

(39)

$$\underset{\text{interrog}}{N} \quad \underset{\substack{\underline{do} \\ \text{past}}}{V} \quad \underset{\text{Michael}}{N} \quad \underset{\text{break}}{V}$$

does not. To repeat, the surface structure of (33b), based on the semantic structure shown in (38), is arrived at through the introduction of the auxiliary *do* because of the presence of *interrogative*, through linearization which includes the transposition of the initial or subject noun with the verb immediately following it, and finally through a moving of the interrogative noun to the front of the sentence, where it is symbolized as an "interrogative pronoun." But there is something additional which must be said regarding the postsemantic treatment of a sentence like (33a) in which the interrogative noun becomes the postsemantic *subject*. The rules so far stated would lead to the incorrect surface structure (40):

(40)   *Who did break the clock.

That is, the presence of interrogative would lead to the introduction of the auxiliary *do* by (T19-1), the subject noun first would be positioned at the beginning of the sentence, then would be transposed with the *do* by (T19-1), and finally would be repositioned at the beginning because of (T19-4). This last stage of linearization leaves the *do* directly adjacent to the verb *break*. A sequence of this kind is not found in the surface structure of English, except when the *do* is new and therefore receives high pitch, a result which would stem from the presence of *affirmative* in the semantic structure:

(41)   Who did break the clock.

The low pitched *did* in (40) must be ruled out. One way to eliminate it would be through an additional rule like (T19-5):

(T19-5)
$$\begin{array}{ccc} \text{V} & \text{V} & \longrightarrow \quad \text{V} \\ \underline{\text{do}} & \underline{\text{root}} & \underline{\text{root}} \\ \text{X} & & \text{X} \end{array}$$

That is, subsequent to the application of (T19-4), if a verb specified as *do* directly precedes another verb, the configuration is collapsed into a single verb containing the root of the second verb and the inflection of the first. Thus we would arrive at (33a) rather than the unacceptable (40). Rule (T19-5) is more or less the reverse of (T19-1), and simply undoes the effect of that earlier rule in case the moving of nouns leaves the auxiliary positioned directly adjacent to the other verb. There is some duplication of postsemantic effort in these processes, as well as in the processes which first transpose the initial noun with the auxiliary and then move it back to initial position again. It would be possible to arrive at the same results in a more direct way. Certain other complications arise, however, with respect to alternative hypotheses, and I shall not spend more time on the question here.

19.19   It is interesting to note that in complex sentences like (42) the interrogative noun moves to the front of the entire sentence, not just to the front of its own clause:

(42)   What does David think Michael broke.

Furthermore, in this sentence it is the verb of the principal sentence which acquires the auxiliary *do*, even though *interrogative* is located semantically in the embedded sentence. In other words, the type of embedding illustrated in (42) permits an interrogative lexical gap to occur in the embedded sentence. When such is the case, however, the postsemantic processes associated with the presence of *interrogative* exert their effect on the principal verb, not on the embedded one.

19.20 Although we have looked at the postsemantic effects of questions with lexical gaps, we have not considered how such semantic structures are created in the first place—how structures like that illustrated in (38) come into being. The problem is one of substituting *interrogative* for a noun root or verb root, something which evidently can be accomplished by a blanket statement which says that any rule introducing lexical units can alternatively introduce *interrogative* instead. Or the nonlexical unit *interrogative* can be added to the list of lexical units which may be introduced by any such rule. It may be recalled from 10.11 that some lexical units, which I termed *classificatory*, may function alternatively as selectional units. Thus, for example, *color* might be a lexical unit but it might also serve as a selectional unit and go on to be specified lexically as *red* or *blue*. It is interesting to note what happens when this narrower lexical specification of a classificatory unit is replaced by *interrogative*:

(43)   a. What <u>color</u> is it.
        b. What <u>street</u> does Michael live on.
        c. What <u>doctor</u> did you see.

The relevant nouns in (43) can be imagined as having the structures listed in (44). Configurations like these evidently lead post-

(44)   N   N   N
        count   count   count
        color   street   potent
        interrog   interrog   animate
                                  human
                                  doctor
                                  interrog

semantically to surface structures in which the representation of the classificatory noun root is preceded by the word *what*. In (43) these noun roots are also specified as new, and there is a resulting high pitch assigned to the reflection of the classificatory noun root in the surface structure. That need not be the case, however:

(45)   a. What color <u>is</u> it.
        b. What street does Michael <u>live</u> on.
        c. What doctor did you <u>see</u>.

But in either case it would seem that the noun in the answer which fills in the lexical gap will be new:

(46)   a. (It's) <u>red</u>.
        b. (Michael lives on) <u>Telegraph Avenue</u>.
        c. (I saw) <u>Dr. Jones</u>.

19.21 The sentences of (47) illustrate still another possibility:

(47)   a. Which <u>color</u> is it.
        b. Which <u>street</u> does Michael live on.
        c. Which <u>doctor</u> did you see.

In these sentences the classificatory unit has been modified partitively in the manner described in 14.20, so that its meaning encompasses only a definite plural subset of the entire class that it would otherwise encompass. It is as if the speaker were saying:

(48)   a. What color of the colors . . .
        b. What street of the streets . . .
        c. What doctor of the doctors . . .

where the phrases *of the colors, of the streets,* and so on reflect more directly the partitive element which limits the class under consideration to one whose members are already known to the hearer from the context. In such cases, however, we find the semantic partitive element deleted from the surface structure, its original presence signaled by the surface appearance of *which* rather than *what*.

19.22 The examples of lexical gaps so far given have all involved the substitution of the semantic unit *interrogative* for noun roots. It may also occur in place of a verb root, although evidently only under limited conditions. In particular, it might seem that only an *action* verb can be treated in this way:

(49)   What did Michael <u>do</u>.

Sentence (49) can be hypothesized to have the semantic structure shown in (50). The speaker is requesting that the hearer supply the

(50)

```
          ┌──────────┐
          │       agt
    V          N
    action     Michael
    interrog
```

correct root for the action verb, although the hearer is also free to
to add a patient noun or whatever else may be appropriate:

(51)   a. He sang.
       b. He broke the clock.
       c. He threw a rock at the window.

No equally straightforward device is available to question the lexical
unit within a state verb. That is, there is no question comparable to
(49) which would lead to an answer like *He's tall*. Simple processes
may often be questioned in a similar manner by asking, for example,
What happened to Michael (*He died*), but there are some complications in the process area that I shall avoid discussing here. Returning
to the semantic structure shown in (50), we may note that its postsemantic development is like that which leads to the "proverb"
configuration *do it*, except that in this case the noun which would
otherwise be represented as *it* acquires the interrogative specification and hence appears in the surface structure as *what*. Thus we
arrive at the kind of surface structure illustrated by sentence (49).

19.23   Lexical units and various kinds of lexical configurations are also
present within "adverbs," as discussed in Chapter 18. When such
items are replaced by *interrogative*, the surface result is one or another
of the various "proadverbs," as in, for example:

(52)   a. When did Michael break the clock.
       b. Where did Michael break the clock.

Evidently because it is possible to distinguish between various kinds
of adverbial alternatives—between time, location, manner, and so
on—it is possible for such elements to be *new*. That is, we can say
things like:

(53)   a. When did Michael break the clock.
       b. Where did Michael break the clock.

in which we are still using the lexical gap device, and not the device
illustrated in (37) and yet to be discussed.

19.24   In all the examples we have considered to this point, *interrogative* has occurred only once in each sentence. The sentences of (54) show that this is not a necessary restriction:

(54)   a. Who broke <u>what</u>.
       b. Who did <u>what</u>.
       c. Who broke what <u>where</u>.

If these sentences are understood as requests that all the lexical gaps be filled in, they are just like the sentences we have already considered except that they contain several lexical gaps. In (54a) both the agent and the patient nouns are lexically impoverished. In (54b) it is the agent noun and the verb which lack a lexical unit. In (54c) it is the agent noun, the patient noun, and an adverbial element. If there are several interrogative elements, only one of them is moved postsemantically to the front of the sentence by (T19–4). Evidently the postsemantic *subject* noun has priority so far as this moving is concerned, a fact which suggests that the identity of a noun as subject should be retained until (T19–4) has applied. Sentence (55a), which corresponds to (54a) except that the object rather than the subject has been moved to the front, is impossible:

(55)   a. *What did who <u>break</u>.
       b. What did <u>who</u> break.

Sentence (55b), in which the interrogative agent noun is also new, again belongs to a type of sentence that we have not yet considered.

19.25 A final word might be said regarding the occurrence of *negative* in questions with lexical gaps. Questions like the following are possible:

(56)   Who didn't see the <u>gorilla</u>.

a sentence which might be uttered in connection with the visit of a group of children to the zoo. Usually, when the questioner is concentrating on having a lexical unit supplied to him by the hearer, he makes the request in a non-negative form. There seems to be no hard and fast requirement that he do so, however, as (56) indicates. This issue is slightly confused by the existence of another kind of sentence:

(57)   Who <u>didn't</u> see the gorilla.

A "rhetorical question," this sentence is not a true question at all, since it is not designed to produce a linguistic response from the hearer. Rather, it is an exclamation intended to convey the meaning that virtually everyone saw the gorilla. A different kind of semantic structure needs to be hypothesized, but one which nevertheless happens to lead to a surface structure almost identical to that of (56).

19.26 **Confirmative questions.** Although questions like (58a, b) or (58c, d) sometimes might be characterized as "different ways of saying the same thing," there is in fact a subtle difference of meaning between them:

(58)   a. Did Michael break the clock?
        b. Michael broke the clock?
        c. Did you go to Chicago?
        d. You went to Chicago?

In (58a), a disjunctive question, the speaker is giving the hearer two alternatives to choose from: "Either Michael broke the clock or he didn't. Tell me which." In (58b) the speaker is saying, in effect, that he understands or has reason to believe that Michael broke the clock, and he wants the hearer to confirm the truth of it. Similarly, in (58d) the speaker is requesting confirmation of his belief that the hearer went to Chicago. In the disjunctive question (58c), on the other hand, he is asking whether or not this is the case. I shall say that the verb in (58b, d) contains semantically the inflectional unit *confirmative*, with the meaning "confirm that the rest of this sentence is true." The speaker is expected to answer (58b) with something like (59a). He may, of course, disconfirm the speaker's belief, as in (59b), but that is not what the speaker anticipates when he utters (58b):

(59)   a. Yes. (He broke the clock.)
        b. No. (He didn't break the clock.)

Confirmative questions are in complementary distribution with questions that contain *interrogative*. We might introduce this unit into a semantic structure with a rule like the following:

(S19-7) V ——» confirmative/–interrogative

where the environmental notation is meant to indicate that *confirmative* cannot be added to the verb if *interrogative* is present anywhere in the sentence. (Other restrictions would have to be mentioned in a more complete description.) It should be evident from (58b, d) that the presence of *confirmative* is reflected phonetically in the question mark intonation. We have, then, at this point two sources for that intonation—*disjunction* and *confirmative*.

19.27 It seems that there are three ways in which *confirmative* can be further specified. They are illustrated in the sentences of (60):

(60) a. Michael didn't break the <u>clock</u>?
      b. Michael broke the <u>clock</u>. didn't he?
      c. Michael didn't break the <u>clock</u>. did he?
      d. Michael broke the <u>clock</u>. didn't he.
      e. Michael didn't break the <u>clock</u>. <u>did</u> he.

In (60a) the speaker has just been surprised by evidence (very likely something the hearer just said) that Michael didn't break the clock. Previously the speaker thought that Michael did break it. I shall say that this sentence contains the semantic unit *surprised*. The speaker anticipates that (60a) will be confirmed with the answer *no*. Sentences (60b, c) are essentially alike. In both the speaker is requesting confirmation of his knowledge, but he has some doubt that he will receive it. We can call the semantic unit in these two sentences *doubtful*. To confirm (60b) the hearer would answer *yes*; to confirm (60c) he would answer *no*. Sentences (60d, e) are also essentially alike. In both the speaker is confident that his knowledge will be confirmed. He is sure he is right but wants to have the satisfaction of being told that he is. These sentences can be said to contain the semantic unit *confident*. It is, then, possible for *confirmative* to be further specified in one of three different ways:

(S19–8) confirmative $\longrightarrow$ $\begin{cases} \text{surprised/negative} \\ \text{doubtful} \\ \text{confident} \end{cases}$

It may be noted that confirmative questions which are not negative—(60b, d) as well as (58b, d)—anticipate the answer *yes*. Confirmative questions which *are* negative—(60a, c, e)—anticipate the answer *no*.

19.28 We have already met the semantic unit *surprised,* and the two illustrative sentences containing it may be compared:

(29)   Didn't Michael break the <u>clock</u>?
(60a) Michael didn't break the <u>clock</u>?

In (29) *surprised* was added to an interrogative disjunction. The speaker is requesting affirmation or negation, but is saying he would have expected affirmation except that recent evidence makes him expect negation. Unlike (29), which contains both a negative and a non-negative sentence, (60a) contains only a negative one. The speaker is requesting the hearer to confirm this negative sentence by saying *no*. At the same time, however, he is indicating through the use of *surprised* that it is only recent evidence which has led him to this negative conclusion and that earlier he thought the opposite. The question mark at the end of sentences (60b, c) calls for clarification. Up to now both the question mark and the period have been used only at the end of a sequence of words one of which has been underlined. The question mark has meant that the pitch has remained high from the strongest stressed syllable of the underlined word to the point where the question mark is located. In (60b, c), where there is no underlined word preceding it, the question mark indicates that the pitch before it rises from a low level at the beginning of the word sequence to an intermediate level at the end. Thus, *he* at the end of (60b, c) is lower than *clock* but higher in pitch than *didn't* or *did*. In both of these two sentences the presence of the semantic unit *doubtful* is reflected in the surface structure by the presence of a so-called *tag*. That is, (60b, c) differ from (58b) and (60a) by the postsemantic addition, at the end of the sentence, of what looks like the beginning of a disjunctive question: the postsemantic auxiliary *do* with the appropriate tense, followed by the subject, which is necessarily pronominalized. A tag is negative if the preceding verb is not negative, and vice versa. This last statement seems to be violated in a sentence like the following:

(61)   Michael broke the <u>clock</u>. did he?

This sentence is not a question, however, but a way of expressing either disbelief or disapproval (the sentence is actually ambiguous as between these two possibilities). A tag is preceded by the period intonation at the end of the preceding portion of the sentence. The *doubtful* tags of (60b, c) themselves end in the question mark intonation. Nothing in the doubtful tag is *new*. The semantic unit *confident* which is present in (60d, e) also is represented postsemantically by a tag. In this case, however, the *do* of the tag is *new* and thus high pitched, and the tag itself ends in the period intonation. The high pitch on the *do* and the period intonation at the end of the tag are what distinguish *confident* from *doubtful* postsemantically. A summary of the several types of confirmative questions is given in (62).

(62)

	Michael broke the clock? (58b)	Michael didn't break the clock? (60a)	Michael broke the clock. didn't he? (60b)	Michael didn't break the clock. did he? (60c)	Michael broke the clock. didn't he. (60d)	Michael didn't break the clock. did he. (60e)
negative		+		+		+
surprised		+				
doubtful			+	+		
confident					+	+

19.29 It is possible for a confirmative question to be made contrastive. If the agent noun root in such a sentence is new, for example, we find cases like the following:

(63) a. Michael broke the clock?
      b. Michael didn't break the clock?
      c. Michael broke the clock. didn't he?
      d. Michael broke the clock. didn't he.

The following rather odd sentence:

(64) Didn't Michael break the clock.

appears from its surface structure to be a disjunctive question which is also *surprised*, in which *Michael* is *new*, and in which the sentence is both *contrastive* and *inclusion*. Semantically, however, it is no such thing, and perhaps such a semantic combination should be ruled out. If it is anything at all, sentence (64) appears to be an optional postsemantic variant of (63d).

19.30 A word should be said concerning the occurrence in confirmative questions of sentence adverbs which convey the speaker's certainty regarding the truth of the remainder of the sentence, adverbs like *certainly, of course,* or *surely.* Such adverbs are not found in disjunctive questions:[5]

(65) a. *Surely did Michael break the <u>clock</u>?
      b. *Did Michael surely break the <u>clock</u>?

Presumably the speaker cannot express certainty about something whose truth he is trying to determine. In a lexical gap question, too, the speaker is seeking information and cannot be certain about something he does not yet know. Hence, anything like the sentences in (66) is also ruled out:

(66) a. *Surely what did Michael <u>break</u>.
      b. *What did Michael surely <u>break</u>.

With a special intonational result, however, these adverbs of certainty can occur with a confirmative question, in which case the speaker is expressing a certainty about the information he already has, even though he may be either doubtful or confident that it will be confirmed:

(67) a. Surely Michael broke the <u>clock</u>;?
      b. Surely Michael broke the <u>clock</u>; didn't he?
      c. Surely Michael broke the <u>clock</u>; <u>didn't</u> he.

The semicolon is used here as an ad hoc device to indicate another intonation pattern, a fall to an intermediate pitch immediately after the preceding highest pitch has been reached. This "semicolon intonation" appears to be the phonetic result of the encounter between an adverb of certainty and the unit *confirmative.* When it is itself followed by the question mark intonation symbolizing *confirmative,* as in (67a), there is a subsequent small rise in pitch. This rise seems to be absent in (67b, c), where the question mark intonation has been obliterated, as usual, by the following tag.

[5] Cf. Katz and Postal 1964:87–88.

19.31 **Echo questions.** The last type of question we shall consider can be illustrated in its simplest form by the following sentences:

(68)   a. Michael broke the <u>clock</u>?
        b. Did Michael break the <u>clock</u>?
        c. What did Michael <u>break</u>?

Each of these sentences is to be understood as something which is said immediately after the person questioned has said one of the following, respectively:

(69)   a. Michael broke the <u>clock</u>.
        b. Did Michael break the <u>clock</u>?
        c. What did Michael <u>break</u>.

In each case the speaker of one of the sentences in (68) is repeating what the other person said in order to make sure that he received it correctly. I shall say that the sentences of (68) contain the semantic unit *echo*, whose meaning is that the speaker seeks confirmation the remainder of the sentence is a correct rendition of what was just said. This unit can be introduced as an inflection of the verb with a rule like the following:

(S19–9) V ——↠ echo

When this option is chosen, the sentence which contains *echo* is understood to be, in all other respects, an exact repetition of a sentence just uttered by the person questioned (with one important kind of exception to be noted shortly). The earlier sentence may be called the *model*. It is possible for the model itself to be a question. For example, (69b), which is the model for the echo question (68b), is a disjunctive question. Sentence (69c), the model for (68c), is a question with a lexical gap.

19.32 As is true of *confirmative* also, the phonological realization of *echo* is the question mark intonation. This fact is obscured in (68b), since the model sentence also ends with that intonation, but it is clear from (68a) and (68c). There is, however, a real difference in meaning between an echo question and a confirmative one. While both types request confirmation of some sort from the hearer, a confirmative question asks confirmation of some tentative part of the speaker's knowledge, a piece of knowledge which he may have arrived at in a variety of ways. An echo question merely seeks confirmation of the proper reception of an immediately preceding linguistic utterance. Thus (68a) is homophonous with the confirmative question (58b). The two questions, however, are not identical. While (58b) asks confirmation of something the speaker believes to be the case, (68a) asks confirmation that the speaker heard sentence (69a) correctly. Actually, the confirmation which is then provided for the echo question may be quite minimal. At one extreme the other person could respond to (68a) by repeating all of (69a), but he could also say *yes* or simply grunt or nod his head. The speaker who utters the echo question (68a) might even accept no answer at all as confirmation and simply go on to say something else. An echo question, in fact, is often a way by which the speaker can stall for time while he thinks of what to say next:

(70)   a. Michael broke the clock? That's too bad.
        b. Did Michael break the clock? Well, I'm not sure.
        c. What did Michael break? I think it was the clock.

Both sentences in each pair are spoken by the same person. After the first sentence in each pair, the hearer may or may not provide some overt confirmation. Of course, particularly if there has been some noise in the communication channel, the hearer might respond by disconfirming what the questioner thought he heard:

(71)   No. I said Michael woke the cock.

19.33   It was suggested above that an echo question need not always repeat the model exactly. Of particular interest is the possibility that an echo question may differ from the model by virtue of its own introduction of a lexical gap. That is, a noun or verb in the echo question may contain *interrogative* in place of its lexical unit, even though the same noun or verb in the model sentence was lexically specified. This possibility clearly separates echo questions from confirmative ones, for the latter cannot contain *interrogative* at all, as was stated in (S19–7). The following are examples of echo questions which contain a lexical gap not present in the model:

(72)   a. Michael broke what?
        b. Who broke the clock?
        c. Michael did what?
        d. Did Michael break what?
        e. Who broke what?

The meaning ascribed to *echo* above must be reworded slightly to accommodate sentences like these. When the speaker repeats what the other person said in its entirety, as in the sentences of (68), he is merely seeking confirmation that he received the sentence correctly. When, as in (72), he repeats what the other person said but modifies it by introducing a lexical gap through the use of *interrogative,* he is indicating that the lexical unit in the position of the gap was not received at all, was blurred in its reception, or was so incredible that the questioner wants to have it supplied again to overcome his disbelief. We might say, then, that the meaning of *echo* is: "I'm repeating what you just said. Confirm the correctness of my reception or, if so specified through *interrogative,* supply the information which I did not receive properly." In the earlier discussion of lexical gap questions it was suggested that such gaps might be created in semantic structures by allowing every rule that introduces lexical units to introduce, as an alternative, *interrogative* instead. We have now seen that the same option is available within an echo question. It seems, however, that while other sentences allow more than one lexical gap to be introduced, as was mentioned in 19.24, echo questions allow the introduction of only one lexical gap. To be sure, there are echo questions in which more than one such gap is present; that is true of sentence (72e), for example. The *who* in that sentence, however, was already present in the model; it was not newly created in the echo, as was the *what.* It is the additional gap which is allowed by the presence of *echo* that is restricted to a single instance in any one sentence. It was mentioned in 19.17 that in the usual lexical gap question the noun or verb which has the gap cannot be specified as new. In echo questions, however, as shown by the examples in (72), the situation is exactly the reverse: the noun or verb which contains a lexical gap newly introduced within the echo sentence *must* be specified as new. This fact is unambiguously evident from the phonology in sentence (72b) only, but it is evident in the meanings of the other sentences too. The *what* at the end of each of these other sentences clearly represents a new element. The reason why these gaps are obligatorily new appears to be that some lexical unit already uttered is at issue, and the speaker is focusing his attention on this already (but inadequately) communicated item.

19.34   It is fruitful to compare the following, which are also echo questions, with those listed in (72):

(73)   a. Michael broke <u>what</u>.
         b. <u>Who</u> broke the clock.
         c. Michael did <u>what</u>.
         d. Did Michael break <u>what</u>.
         e. Who broke <u>what</u>.

Phonetically these sentences differ from those of (72) only in containing the period rather than the question mark intonation. In (73)
the pitch is low at the end of the sentence, and begins falling immediately after its high point is reached within the underlined word.
I shall suggest that the difference in meaning between (72) and (73)
is as follows. In (72) the speaker has not heard clearly, or been able
to accept, the lexical unit provided by the other person in the model.
That lexical unit, however, was transmitted; there was simply some
failure in the transmission process. In (73), on the other hand, the
lexical unit was not transmitted in the model. The other person
assumed that the speaker would know what it was, but the speaker
did not. The sentences of (73), for example, might be uttered
immediately after such model sentences as the following:

(74)   a. Michael <u>broke</u> it.
         b. He broke the <u>clock</u>.
         c. Michael <u>did</u> it.
         d. Did Michael <u>break</u> it.
         e. Who <u>broke</u> it.

In each of these sentences there has been a pronominalization, based
on the assumption by the speaker that the lexical unit involved
was already known to his hearer. If, however, the hearer responds
with one of the sentences in (73), it is clear that that assumption was
wrong, the relevant lexical unit was not known. He is saying, then,
that the other person made a mistake in pronominalizing, and that
he wants the lexical unit specified. The semantic unit which has this
meaning I shall label *specify*. It might be introduced into a semantic
structure by means of the following rule:

(S19–10) $\begin{bmatrix} \text{new} \\ \text{interrogative} \end{bmatrix}$ ——» specify

As mentioned in the last paragraph, it is only within an echo
question that the combination of new and interrogative within a
noun or verb can be found. Hence, rule (S19–10) can apply only
within such a sentence. The symbolization of *specify* is through a

drop in pitch, as indicated by the period at the end of the sentences in (73). This intonation overrides the question mark intonation otherwise associated with an echo sentence. It is worth noting that *specify* is symbolized in precisely the same way as a unit which may be present in a disjunctive question and which I labeled *inclusion,* as in (31a), *Did __Michael__ break the clock.* One might consider the possibility that the two units are identical, but it does not seem likely.

19.35 I have postponed until this point a discussion of the postsemantic consequences of a lexical gap within an echo question. In the earlier discussion of ordinary lexical gap questions we noted that the presence of *interrogative* within a noun or verb has several post-semantic consequences. One is the creation of an "interrogative pronoun" like *what, who, when,* and so on, to represent the lexically deficient word in the surface structure. This effect is present in echo questions also. Another effect is the moving of an interrogative noun to the beginning of its sentence, as stated in (T19–4). This shift in word order is not evident in (72) or (73), where the word order of the model sentence has been preserved. Nor has the presence of *interro-gative* triggered the introduction of the auxiliary *do,* as dictated by (T19–1). The presence of this auxiliary in (72d) and (73d) is a consequence of its presence in the model and is not something occasioned by the introduction of a lexical gap into the echo. Thus it seems that the presence of the semantic unit *echo* inhibits the operation of both (T19–1) and (T19–4). But how then do we account for the sentences of (75):

(75) a. __What__ did Michael break?
      b. __What__ did Michael break.

I would suggest that these sentences have the same semantic struc-tures as (72a) and (73a) respectively. They show, I think, that the application of (T19–1), adding the auxiliary *do,* and of (T19–4), moving the interrogative noun to the beginning of the sentence, is only *optionally* suspended in the presence of *echo.* The presence of *echo* leads the speaker to repeat the word order of the model. The presence of *interrogative* leads him to disturb that order. Apparently he is free to choose whether he will follow the dictate of *echo* or that of *interrogative.* In the first case he will arrive at sentences like those of (72) and (73). In the second case he will arrive at sentences like those of (75).

19.36 One last point is worth mentioning with regard to echo questions with lexical gaps. In the sentences below, (76b, c) are the two alternative surface structures available in an echo question based on the model sentence (76a), where the echo has introduced a lexical gap into the patient noun:

(76)   a. I said Michael broke the <u>clock</u>.
       b. You said Michael broke <u>what</u>?
       c. <u>What</u> did you say Michael broke?

It may be noted in (76c) that, as already seen in 19.19, the interrogative noun moves to the front of the entire sentence, not just to the front of its own clause, and that it is the verb *say* of the principal sentence which acquires the auxiliary *do*. These sentences were cited, however, in order to make another point. It can be observed that both versions of the echo question—(76b, c)—are ambiguous. They are not necessarily echos of (76a), but may also be echos of the simpler model (77):

(77)   Michael broke the <u>clock</u>.

That is, all four of the following are possible as echos of (77), with a lexical gap introduced into the patient noun:

(78)   a. Michael broke <u>what</u>?
       b. <u>What</u> did Michael break?
       c. You said Michael broke <u>what</u>?
       d. <u>What</u> did you say Michael broke?

Sentences (78c, d) are identical in surface structure with (76b, c). In (78c, d) there is a higher sentence containing the verb *say* which does not repeat anything in (77), but which is added by the speaker of the echo. It seems plausible to hypothesize that the echo sentence represented in (78a, b) is here embedded in the higher sentence, and that this device serves only to make it a little more explicit that the speaker is repeating something the other person just *said*. We might account for this device in terms of *say* being a verb (and probably the only verb) which allows an echo as its complement. It is interesting and significant to observe that *say* will not allow as its complement an echo sentence containing *specify*. Sentences (79b, c) are not possible as sequels to (79a):

(79)   a. Michael <u>broke</u> it.
       b. *You said Michael broke <u>what</u>.
       c. *<u>What</u> did you say Michael broke.

Evidently (79b, c) are ruled out as echo questions based on the model (79a) because the presence of *specify*, signaled by the period intonation in (79b, c), means that the other person did *not* say what it was Michael broke. The embedding of the echo into the higher clause with *say* implies that he did say what it was, and hence there is a contradiction. It may be noted that (79b, c) would be quite possible in the situation where all of them, and not just the embedded part, are echoes of the model:

(80)   a. I said Michael broke it.
       b. You said Michael broke what.
       c. What did you say Michael broke.

19.37   In brief summary of this chapter, consideration has been given to several types of English sentences which are uttered for the purpose of eliciting a linguistic response from the hearer and which, on that basis, can be classed as questions. A semantic unit *interrogative,* whose meaning is that the speaker requests information from the hearer, was seen to play a role in more than one type of question. It may be attached to a sentential disjunction, in which case the speaker is requesting the hearer to tell him which of the disjuncts is factually correct. A variety of this type of question is one in which the disjuncts differ only by the presence of *negative* in one of them, and the ordinary "yes–no" question was seen as a subvariety here. A similar view has been expressed by others who have studied the nature of questions: "These facts suggest that yes-no questions involve the request for a specification of one or two alternatives that are in fact disjunctions of sentences."[6] It is interesting also to compare the "V-not-V" questions of Chinese.[7] The same *interrogative* unit, however, also can be added to a noun or verb in place of a lexical unit. In that case the request is that the hearer supply the correct lexical unit. What is often called a "WH" question is formed in this way; I have spoken of questions with "lexical gaps." Rather than *interrogative*, a question may contain the unit *confirmative*. It is not then a request for information but for confirmation of some more or less tentative knowledge that the speaker already has. Although I am not entirely certain of this, I suspect that some languages, Onondaga among them, do not have disjunctive questions; such languages use confirmative questions in many situations

[6] Katz and Postal 1964:100.
[7] See Chao 1968:269 *et passim*; Wang 1965.

where English would employ the disjunctive type. Last to be discussed were questions containing the semantic unit *echo*. Sentences of this kind were seen as repetitions of immediately preceding sentences uttered by the other person, repetitions intended primarily as checks on the correctness of reception. It is possible, however, for the repetition to introduce its own lexical gap, with the unit *interrogative* present in some noun or verb to indicate that the speaker wishes the gap filled, either because he failed to receive properly the lexical unit that was transmitted or because through pronominalization that unit was improperly deleted by the other person.

20

Some Final Remarks

20.1   Characteristically, theories of language are presented in a dogmatic manner, much as if they were religious pronouncements. If I were to issue any ex cathedra statement here, it would involve what seems to me the high degree of likelihood that the general picture of language summarized in Chapter 7 is essentially correct. As for the rest, I see it as a set of interrelated suggestions, at least some of which may offer more productive leads to further investigation than we find available in linguistics at the present time.

20.2   I have stressed the view that a workable theory of semantic structure is indispensable to the theory of language as a whole. The major portion of this book has been directed toward the development of a semantic theory along lines which can be summarized briefly as follows. The creation of a well-formed semantic structure—conceived of in terms of the structure of a *sentence*—was held to begin with a central semantic element which I called a verb. A verb may be specified in terms of various selectional units, one of whose functions is to narrow the conceptual field until finally a lexical unit, or verb root, is chosen as the narrowest concept of all. There may then be further specification of the verb in terms of inflectional units. Once the verb is specified in these several ways, its selectional units determine the introduction of, usually, one or more accompanying nouns, each bearing one of a limited number of possible relations to the verb. Each noun is then subject to its own specification in terms of selectional units, a lexical unit (noun root), and inflectional units. It was suggested that there is another kind of semantic unit, called derivational, whose function is to convert a particular verb or noun root, having certain intrinsic properties, into a derived lexical unit with different properties. Beyond sentences of this simple kind, containing only a single verb, it was seen that there exist various possibilities for the addition of other verbs, some of which were outlined in Chapter 18. Such added verbs may in turn have their own accompanying nouns, allowing still more possibilities for the addition of verbs; in this way (and others) the well-known recursive properties of language are achieved.

20.3   If further work is undertaken along these lines, it might be expected to produce results of several kinds. For one thing, it would add to and modify the store of selectional, lexical, derivational, and inflectional units already posited as well as the list of possible noun-verb relations. In the latter area it might clarify the apparent priority of the patient and agent relations, and such facts as that the experiencer relation, for example, quite generally falls together postsemantically with the agent relation, having the same surface structure representation in most if not all languages. Work of this kind, of course, also would need to explore the various interdependences which tie together the hypothesized semantic units and relations. With respect to the inventory of selectional and lexical units the task is an enormous one, if not completely open-ended. Inflectional units and the limited number of noun-verb relations, on the other hand, belong within the category of things that linguistics, with a reasonable expenditure of effort, may sooner or later account for exhaustively. The indications are that much of what is discovered within the semantic area will be of universal validity, although it can be expected that different languages will exhibit many differences of detail, above all in the lexical area.

20.4   Such work would be directed toward the refinement of the proposed model through the accumulation and adjustment of specific semantic units and relations. At the same time, it is inevitable that further work will suggest the need for changes in the model itself. For example, it is clear that many semantic constraints exert their influence across the boundaries of sentences. No adequate theory of semantic structure can ignore such constraints, and it is certain that the structure of "paragraphs" or "discourses" is of basic importance.

The theory offered here has not provided a coherent system for the incorporation of such factors, and it remains to be seen whether and to what extent their incorporation will necessitate a significant reformulation. Another possibility might be the introduction of a binary rather than singulary formalism, whereby, for example, a verb would have to be specified as either +perfective or −perfective, whereas here perfective has been treated as a semantic unit which is either present in or absent from a particular verb. When necessary, its absence has been indicated with the notation −perfective in the statement of rules, but not in diagrams of semantic structures. All of the examples which have been given could easily be restated in a binary notation, which would succeed only in making them more cumbersome. There is a basic issue here, however, one that has been touched on within the area of phonology in terms of "markedness."[1] The factors which are relevant, and the formalism most appropriate to their representation, are by no means clearly understood at the present time, even within phonology. The situation within semantics is still more problematic. One may hope, however, that some cross-fertilization will take place, and that an eventual theory which is effective in either of these two areas will have some bearing on the other.

20.5   Still another possibility for change in the semantic model presented here might lie in the need to introduce more structure into the specifications of a verb or noun. For example, the verb in the sample sentence *John has been lengthening the driveway*, used as an illustration of postsemantic processes in Chapter 16, was diagramed as shown in (1). This simple vertical listing of selectional, lexical,

(1)   V
        process
        relative
        action
        long + inchoative + causative
        ----
        perfective
        progressive

derivational, and inflectional specifications overlooks a number of interdependences among the items involved, while a diagram something like that shown in (2) comes closer to representing them (cf. 10.2, 10.8). It is not clear, however, that the additional information present in (2) is needed either for the application of subsequent

[1] See, for example, Chomsky and Halle 1968: chap. 9.

(2)

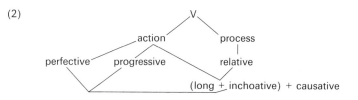

rules of semantic formation or for the later application of post-semantic processes. That is, work undertaken so far suggests that it is enough to know that the verb is an action, that it is perfective, and so on, without having to refer to whatever relations of inclusion and intersection between these units could be extracted from the rules which first introduced them. If that is the case, then the vertical listing in (1) is sufficient, and semantic diagrams need not be complicated in the manner suggested in (2). In any case, two-dimensional diagrams like (2) would not be adequate to the purpose, and some multidimensional representation would have to be devised if it were found necessary to preserve this kind of information. There is another kind of change that might be called for in semantic structure diagrams, however, a change that works in the direction of simplification rather than complication. I have consistently indicated a hierarchy among the several noun-verb relations in the manner illustrated in (3):

(3)

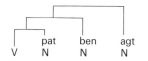

One of the principal justifications for this hierarchy is the manner in which new information is distributed, as described in Chapter 15. It would seem, however, that it is sufficient to say that the inflection *new* is assigned to every element except the rightmost one in these diagrams, in which case (4) would be an adequate substitute for (3).

(4)

```
┌───────┬───────┬───────┐
│      pat     ben     agt
V       N       N       N
```

In such a diagram the positioning of elements from left to right assumes the function which, in (3) and throughout this work, was exercised by the hierarchical notation, where the left to right ordering was assumed to have no significance. Whether anything is gained by the notation used in (3)—whether, for example, it aids in the statement of the rules which add other verbs to the structure or in the statement of postsemantic rules—is another subject for further investigation.

20.6   The model developed here makes use of two types of processes, stated in terms of rules, whose functions are wholly distinct. First, I have posited certain processes of *formation* (stated in semantic structure rules), whose role is the initial generation of a semantic structure. The major portion of this book has concerned itself with such processes. Second, I have suggested certain processes of *transformation* (stated in postsemantic rules), whose role is the conversion of semantic into surface structures. Chapter 16 was especially concerned with processes of this kind, and a few of them were illustrated in later chapters. Now, this process model seems clearly appropriate in the second case. In many instances, postsemantic processes recapitulate (in the reverse direction; see 5.4) the historical changes which brought them into the language in the first place. Since historical changes are by definition processes, it is understandable that their results should be described most appropriately in terms of processes also. Other postsemantic rules account for such phenomena as deletion, which are again obviously processual in nature. It is not nearly as obvious, however, that the initial formation of a semantic structure is described most appropriately in the same terms—in terms, that is, of ordered rules. Such rules of formation bear no evident relation to historical processes, unless they reflect some unknown aspects of language evolution. (It might be, for example, that nouns represent an earlier evolutionary stage than verbs, and that the recency of verbs is reflected in their position of priority in the formation of semantic structures.) Putting aside speculation of this kind, it seems evident that another conceivable alternative, that the processes by which a semantic structure is formed bear some relation to linguistic "performance," cannot be taken seriously. That is, when a person wants to say something he does not first put together the selectional, lexical, and inflectional units of a verb (in that order), and then proceed to add nouns as called for, to fill in their specifications in a parallel way, and so on. The best that can be said is that he starts with certain new information he wishes to communicate and that he places this new information in a matrix of old information in a way not necessarily reflected at all in the abstract processes of semantic structure formation described in earlier chapters. There is, then, no obvious extrinsic justification for handling the formation of semantic structures within the framework of ordered rules, and it is not unlikely that a different model might ultimately be preferred. I do not wish to speculate here on the details of that model, except to note that it would involve statements of unilateral and bilateral dependences among semantic units.[2] Such statements would then constitute a set of conditions on the well-formedness of semantic structures.

20.7   In closing I would like to stress once again the view that the data of meaning are both accessible to linguistic explanation and crucial to the investigation of language structure—in certain ways more crucial than the data of sound to which linguistic studies have given such unbalanced attention. The recognition that a large proportion of primary linguistic data come from the area of meaning leads us to view semantic structure as a first level abstraction which bears a direct relation to the world of observable thoughts and ideas. I make this point because there has recently been a tendency to regard semantic structure, in the guise of a "deeper" kind of "deep structure" than that proposed by Chomsky, as a "highly abstract" construct akin to the constructs of symbolic logic. Such a view, it seems to me, loses sight of the direct tie which must exist between semantic structure and the observable facts of meaning, by virtue of which the abstractness of semantic structure is, on the contrary, minimal. Semantics and phonetics, I would say, constitute the two least abstract components of language, each being most closely related to its own variety of data. While it has been suggested that the deepest deep structure consists of nothing but logical predications, one embedded within another, I cannot see that this approach provides the kind of model that can be related directly to the messages which language conveys. The notion of a *predicate* in the logical sense, for example, is not rich enough to account for the various meaningful relations between semantic nouns and verbs for which I have tried to provide a framework. I do not wish to demean the value of multiple approaches to semantic structure, however, and it will surely be of interest to see what adequacies and inadequacies arise from a variety of hypotheses. If I have done no more

[2]Cf. Hjelmslev (1961:24ff.), who, despite his proliferation of terminology, may have been on the right track.

than add weight to the assertion that linguistics will stagnate unless it thoroughly explores this territory, I have accomplished my principal aim.

References Cited

Allen, Robert Livingston. 1966. *The Verb System of Present-Day American English.* The Hague: Mouton.

Alston, William P. 1964. *Philosophy of Language.* Englewood Cliffs, N.J.: Prentice-Hall.

Baker, C. LeRoy. Ms. Definiteness and Indefiniteness in English.

Bastian, Jarvis. 1965. Primate Signalling Systems and Human Language. *Primate Behavior: Field Studies of Monkeys and Apes,* ed. by Irven DeVore, 585–606. New York: Holt, Rinehart and Winston.

Berlin, Brent, and Paul Kay. 1969. *Basic Color Terms: Their Universality and Evolution.* Berkeley and Los Angeles: University of California.

Bloch, Bernard. 1953. Linguistic Structure and Linguistic Analysis. *Report on the Fourth Annual Round Table Meeting on Linguistics and Language Teaching,* ed. by Archibald A. Hill, 40–44. Washington, D.C.: Georgetown University.

———, and George L. Trager. 1942. *Outline of Linguistic Analysis.* Baltimore: Linguistic Society of America.

Bloomfield, Leonard. 1933. *Language.* New York: Holt.

Brown, Roger. 1958. *Words and Things.* Glencoe, Ill.: Free Press.

Carpenter, C. R. 1940. *A Field Study in Siam of the Behavior and Social Relations of the Gibbon (Hylobates lar).* Comparative Psychology Monographs 16, No. 5.

Chafe, Wallace L. 1959. Internal Reconstruction in Seneca. *Language* 35: 477–95.

———. 1962. Phonetics, Semantics, and Language. *Language* 38: 335–44.

———. 1965. Meaning in Language. *Formal Semantic Analysis,* ed. by E. A. Hammel, 23–36. *American Anthropologist* 67, No. 5, Pt. 2.

———. 1967. Language as Symbolization. *Language* 43: 57–91.

———. 1968a. English Noun Inflection and Related Matters from a Generative Semantic Point of View. *Project on Linguistic Analysis Reports,* 2d Series, No. 6, C1–C51. Berkeley: Dept. of Linguistics, Phonology Lab.

———. 1968b. English Questions. *Project on Linguistic Analysis Reports,* 2d Series, No. 6, 1–60. Berkeley: Dept. of Linguistics, Phonology Lab.

———. 1968c. Idiomaticity as an Anomaly in the Chomskyan Paradigm. *Foundations of Language* 4:109–27.

———. 1968d. The Ordering of Phonological Rules. *International Journal of American Linguistics* 34: 115–36.

———. 1970. *A Semantically Based Sketch of Onondaga.* Indiana University Publications in Anthropology and Linguistics, Memoir 25.

Chao, Yuen Ren. 1968. *A Grammar of Spoken Chinese.* Berkeley and Los Angeles: University of California.

Chomsky, Noam. 1957. *Syntactic Structures.* The Hague: Mouton.

———. 1965. *Aspects of the Theory of Syntax.* Cambridge, Mass.: MIT.

———. 1966a. *Cartesian Linguistics: A Chapter in the History of Rationalist Thought.* New York: Harper and Row.

———. 1966b. Topics in the Theory of Generative Grammar. *Current Trends in Linguistics,* ed. by Thomas A. Sebeok, 3:1–60. The Hague: Mouton.

————. Ms. Deep Structure, Surface Structure, and Semantic Interpretation.

————, and Morris Halle. 1968. *The Sound Pattern of English*. New York: Harper and Row.

Diver, William. 1963. The Chronological System of the English Verb. *Word* 19: 141–81.

Ehrman, Madeline. 1966. *The Meanings of the Modals in Present-Day American English*. The Hague: Mouton.

Fillmore, Charles J. 1968. The Case for Case. *Universals in Linguistic Theory*, ed. by Emmon Bach and Robert T. Harms, 1–88. New York: Holt, Rinehart and Winston.

Firbas, Jan. 1966. Non-Thematic Subjects in Contemporary English. *Travaux Linguistiques de Prague* 2:239–56.

Frisch, Karl von. 1955. *The Dancing Bees*, translated by Dora Ilse. New York: Harcourt, Brace.

Gleason, H. A., Jr. 1961. *An Introduction to Descriptive Linguistics*. Rev. ed. New York: Holt, Rinehart and Winston.

Haas, William. 1954. On Defining Linguistic Units. *Transactions of the Philological Society* 54–84.

Halliday, M. A. K. 1967–68. Notes on Transitivity and Theme in English. *Journal of Linguistics* 3: 37–81, 199–244; 4:179–216.

Hjelmslev, Louis. 1961. *Prolegomena to a Theory of Language*. Madison: University of Wisconsin.

Hockett, Charles F. 1958. *A Course in Modern Linguistics*. New York: Macmillan.

————. 1960. The Origin of Speech. *Scientific American* 203, No. 3, 89–96.

————. 1961. Linguistic Elements and their Relations. *Language* 37:29–53.

————, and Robert Ascher. 1964. The Human Revolution. *Current Anthropology* 5:135–47.

Joos, Martin. 1964. *The English Verb: Form and Meanings*. Madison and Milwaukee: University of Wisconsin.

————, ed. 1966. *Readings in Linguistics I*. 4th ed. Chicago: University of Chicago.

Juilland, Alphonse, and James Macris. 1962. *The English Verb System*. The Hague: Mouton.

Katz, Jerrold J. 1966. *The Philosophy of Language*. New York: Harper and Row.

————. 1967. Recent Issues in Semantic Theory. *Foundations of Language* 3:124–94.

————, and Jerry A. Fodor. 1963. The Structure of a Semantic Theory. *Language* 39:170–210.

————, and Paul M. Postal. 1963. Semantic Interpretation of Idioms and Sentences Containing Them. MIT Research Laboratory of Electronics, *Quarterly Progress Report* 70:275–82.

————. 1964. *An Integrated Theory of Linguistic Descriptions*. Cambridge, Mass.: MIT.

Kiparsky, Paul. 1968. Linguistic Universals and Linguistic Change. *Universals in Linguistic Theory*, ed. by Emmon Bach and Robert T. Harms, 170–202. New York: Holt, Rinehart and Winston.

Kirkwood, Henry W. 1969. Aspects of Word Order and Its Communicative Function in English and German. *Journal of Linguistics* 5:85–107.

Lakoff, George. 1966. Stative Adjectives and Verbs in English. The Computation Laboratory of Harvard University, Report No. NSF-17, I1–I16.

————. 1968. Instrumental Adverbs and the Concept of Deep Structure. *Foundations of Language* 4:4–29.

————. Ms. Global Grammar, or the Inherent Limitations of Transformational Grammars.

Lenneberg, Eric H. 1967. *Biological Foundations of Language*. New York: John Wiley.

————, and John M. Roberts. 1956. The Language of Experience: A Study in Methodology. *International Journal of American Linguistics*, Memoir 13.

Locke, John. 1894. *An Essay Concerning Human Understanding*, ed. by Alexander C. Frazer, Vol. 2. Oxford: Clarendon.

Lounsbury, Floyd G. 1953. *Oneida Verb Morphology*. Yale University Publications in Anthropology, No. 48. New Haven: Yale University.

————. 1956. A Semantic Analysis of the Pawnee Kinship Usage. *Language* 32:158–94.

Marler, Peter. 1965. Communication in Monkeys and Apes. *Primate Behavior: Field Studies of Monkeys and Apes*, ed. by Irven DeVore, 544–84. New York: Holt, Rinehart and Winston.

Martinet, André. 1962. *A Functional View of Language*. Oxford: Oxford University.

McIntosh, Angus. 1961. Patterns and Ranges. *Language* 37:325–37.

Palmer, F. R. 1965. *A Linguistic Study of the English Verb*. London: Longmans.

Perlmutter, David M. 1968. Deep and Surface Structure Constraints in Syntax. Ph.D. dissertation, MIT.

Postal, Paul. 1964. *Constituent Structure: A Study of Contemporary Models of Syntactic Description*. Indiana University Research Center in Anthropology, Folklore, and Linguistics, Publication 30.

Sapir, Edward. 1921. *Language: An Introduction to the Study of Speech*. New York: Harcourt, Brace.

————. 1951. The Psychological Reality of Phonemes. *Selected Writings of Edward Sapir in Language, Culture, and Personality*, ed. by David G. Mandelbaum, 46–60. Berkeley and Los Angeles: University of California.

Saussure, Ferdinand de. 1959. *Course in General Linguistics*, translated by Wade Baskin. New York: Philosophical Library.

Struhsaker, Thomas T. 1967. Auditory Communication Among Vervet Monkeys. *Social Communication Among Primates*, ed. by Stuart A. Altmann, 281–324. Chicago: University of Chicago.

Sturtevant, William C. 1964. Studies in Ethnoscience. *Transcultural Studies in Cognition*, ed. by A. Kimball Romney and Roy Goodwin D'Andrade, 99–131. *American Anthropologist* 66, No. 3, Pt. 2.

Twaddell, W. Freeman. 1935. On Defining the Phoneme. In Joos 1966:55–79. Originally published as *Language* Monograph No. 16.

————. 1960. *The English Verb Auxiliaries*. Providence: Brown University.

Wang, William S-Y. 1965. Two Aspect Markers in Mandarin. *Language* 41:457–70.

Weinreich, Uriel. 1969. Problems in the Analysis of Idioms. *Substance and Structure of Language*, ed. by Jaan Puhvel, 23–81. Berkeley and Los Angeles: University of California.

Wells, Rulon. 1947. Immediate Constituents. *Language* 23:81–117. *Also in* Joos 1966:186–207.

Index